T0369569

Blood Entanglements

Blood Entanglements

Evangelicals and Gangs in El Salvador

STEPHEN OFFUTT

OXFORD
UNIVERSITY PRESS

OXFORD
UNIVERSITY PRESS

Oxford University Press is a department of the University of Oxford. It furthers
the University's objective of excellence in research, scholarship, and education
by publishing worldwide. Oxford is a registered trade mark of Oxford University
Press in the UK and certain other countries.

Published in the United States of America by Oxford University Press
198 Madison Avenue, New York, NY 10016, United States of America.

© Oxford University Press 2023

All rights reserved. No part of this publication may be reproduced, stored in
a retrieval system, or transmitted, in any form or by any means, without the
prior permission in writing of Oxford University Press, or as expressly permitted
by law, by license, or under terms agreed with the appropriate reproduction
rights organization. Inquiries concerning reproduction outside the scope of the
above should be sent to the Rights Department, Oxford University Press, at the
address above.

You must not circulate this work in any other form
and you must impose this same condition on any acquirer.

CIP data is on file at the Library of Congress

ISBN 978-0-19-758731-7 (pbk.)
ISBN 978-0-19-758730-0 (hbk.)

DOI: 10.1093/oso/9780197587300.001.0001

Paperback printed by Marquis, Canada
Hardback printed by Bridgeport National Bindery, Inc., United States of America

This book is dedicated to Raúl A. Bojórquez and Elías García

Contents

Illustrations

Figures

Photos

Tables

Acknowledgments

I am most grateful to the communities and individuals in El Salvador who let me be part of the fabric of their lives during this research. As we built relationships across the many lines that divide us (nationality, ethnicity, educational and socioeconomic status, etc.), we also found basic commonalities that unite us as humans. We became friends, and I heard about difficult and poignant moments in their lives. I shared in their grief when sickness, violence, and death overcame loved ones, and I celebrated with them when graduations, marriages, and newborns came their way. There were some limits to our friendships: we all knew that I would never be able to return the generous hospitality they extended to me in kind. I hope that this book pays, at least in some small way, the debts that I have accrued over the years. This book is also likely not the final chapter in the relationships that we have formed.

Raúl Bojórquez and Elías García are co-workers, research partners, and cultural interlocutors of many years. I knew them before the idea of this book emerged. As we worked in lower-class communities together for reasons unrelated to gangs, Raúl and Elías helped me see, in different ways, the insecurities and vulnerabilities that often escape the eye of the outside observer. Without their assistance and friendship, not only would this book look very different, but likely it would not exist. These are some of the reasons I have dedicated this book to them.

Others who shaped my thinking also deserve mention. Hilda Romero gave me insights into how to think about the changes El Salvador was going through during my project. David Bueno helped me make sense of trends I was seeing within evangelical and Pentecostal circles. Kenton Moody brought me into his work in prisons and communities in El Salvador. Doug Bassett opened doors for me and provided my project with recent historical and contextual depth. Robbie Danielson gave sage advice for my portrayal of early evangelical history. Bob Brenneman provided friendship and wisdom, and sometimes served as a sounding board. David and Lisa Swartz were helpful throughout the (long) life of this project at different points and in different ways. Tim Wank provided helpful feedback on chapters near the end of the writing process. I am grateful for the investments each has made in this project.

Thomas Hampton helped to move this project from a collection of data to a book. Thomas exceeded his role as a graduate assistant as he introduced different theories that might be relevant, helped to organize and process large amounts of data, and provided feedback on chapter drafts. Thomas also designed most of the figures and tables that appear in this book. The project would have wound its way to publication much more slowly, and with lower quality, were it not for Thomas' involvement.

I brought this project home with me in many ways. Amy Reynolds, my wife and closest intellectual confidant, shared my fears and burdens as I undertook the more difficult elements of this project. Our oldest daughter, Addy, was old enough to understand the challenges I was writing about as I typed next to her at the breakfast table. A tech savvy teenager, Addy crafted the second two figures that appear in this book. She also helped me create graphics for presentations and she did a presentation on the topic in school herself. Our next two daughters, Emily and Gabi, were too young to seriously engage this book's content during its composition. But the project affected them nonetheless: we took a family trip to El Salvador during the research, and they missed me (and I missed them) when I took precious family time to traipse off to El Salvador on my own.

I thank two presses for providing necessary copyright permissions. First, this book significantly expands concepts that first appeared in an article I published in *Social Forces*, owned by Oxford University Press. Different parts of that article appear in several chapters of this work. Second, a brief passage in Chapter 2 about the history of El Salvador first appeared in a work I authored that was published by Springer Nature. I appreciated the opportunity to republish this material.

The entire team at Oxford University Press deserves special mention. Theo Calderara expressed an openness to the book when it was merely an idea. His guidance through the various stages of publication was seamless. The members of the production and editing teams were congenial, creative, efficient, and timely. A special thanks to all of you.

Last but not least, I wish to think the organizations that funded this research. The project was generously supported by grants from the Louisville Institute (Project Grant for Researchers Award), the Society for the Scientific Study of Religion (Jack Shand Research Award), and the Religious Research Association (Constant H. Jacquet Research Award). I hope the resulting book pushes the study of religion in new and fruitful directions.

Introduction

El Salvador's lower-class communities are embedded in multiple dimensions of global society. At the macro level, the United States and China's growing rivalry in Latin America helps to shape Salvadoran politics. Such international dynamics merge with local political histories and proclivities, which create push and pull effects toward both global superpowers. Transnational economic chains run through Salvadoran ports, highways, and financial institutions. A wide range of legal and illicit products are thus available in local neighborhoods, while Salvadorans help to get both types of products to larger markets in North America and Europe. Global entertainment outlets bring social media sensations, sports icons, and the most recent Hollywood releases into lower class Salvadoran communities. Emigration out of such neighborhoods (6.5 million people live in El Salvador; more than three million Salvadorans live abroad (World Population Review 2022; World Bank Data 2022c) simultaneously allows churches from Barcelona, Spain to Los Angeles, California to be invigorated by recent arrivals from El Salvador, and *pupusarias*, or Salvadoran restaurants featuring the national dish, can be found from Chattanooga, Tennessee to Sydney, Australia. Such developments are not always welcomed by host communities, and regional politics can be shaped by the immigration question. The ability of lower-class Salvadoran communities to influence people, places, and powers in other parts of the world means that understanding what is happening in such communities, how they are happening, and who the actors are matters not just in El Salvador, but in many parts of global society.

Two groups—evangelicals and gangs—have proliferated in lower-class Salvadoran neighborhoods. Evangelicals constitute 35–40 percent of El Salvador's national population (Pew 2014). The percentages are even higher in poor neighborhoods. Gangs, for their part, have grown to roughly 60,000–70,000 members (Verza 2018). The number of people connected to gangs is far higher: roughly half a million people are, for example, economically dependent on gang members (Bargent 2013). Like evangelicals, gang members are most often found in impoverished areas. The sheer size of the evangelical

Blood Entanglements. Stephen Offutt, Oxford University Press. © Oxford University Press 2023.
DOI: 10.1093/oso/9780197587300.003.0001

and gang populations makes both groups important in shaping neighbor-hood culture.

Evangelical and gang reputations contrast sharply. Community members view evangelical churches as doing God's work and providing light and hope in difficult contexts. Community members, even gang members themselves, perceive gangs' interests to be much darker: these include violence, extor-tion, and for some, an explicit connection to Satan. Their perceived roles ap-pear to put the two groups at opposite ends of the community spectrum.

Sharp as these contrasts might be, it is impossible for evangelicals and gangs to live separate existences in their shared environments. They are, rather, drawn into daily interaction. This straightforward empirical reality has far-reaching implications for the identities of each group, as well as for how events play out in the neighborhoods they populate.

The primary questions that motivate this book are: How do evangelicals and gangs interact? And what does this tell us about how evangelicals in-teract with society and social problems generally?

Gang experts and religion experts, two different tribes, have made some inroads in answering the first question. Gang experts who do not usually spill much ink on religion have noticed the evangelical factor in gang-controlled communities and in gang life. Steven Dudley, cofounder of a leading inves-tigative journalism outlet called *InSight Crime*, calls the evangelical church a "competing community" or an "alternative space" in gang-controlled neighborhoods. Why, Dudley wonders, do gangs find such communities acceptable? Dudley suggests that answers to this question might lead to new solutions to gang violence and control (Williamson 2021). Jose Cruz and colleagues, in a study partially funded by the U.S. Department of State, surveyed 1,196 current and former gang members to learn if and how gang members can leave the gang and start a new life. They found that "the most common and seemingly accepted mechanism to . . . leave the gang in El Salvador occurs through a religious experience," and that "religious awakenings were a common theme among former gang members" (2017, 56). Like Dudley, Cruz and colleagues found that evangelicalism, more than other religious groups, holds sway among gangs.

Such studies confirm earlier research done by religion experts. Brenneman (2012) and Wolseth (2011) published pathbreaking work on the "morgue rule exception"—a gang proviso that allows their members to leave the gang if, and usually only if, they have a conversion experience and join an evan-gelical church. Gangs do this in part because, Brenneman argues, local gang leaders respect God and those who live a disciplined religious life. They expect converts to submit to God through active church attendance, an ascetic lifestyle, and a cessation from violence. Gang leaders monitor but also respect these behavior changes.

I count myself among the tribe of religion experts. I arrived at the evangelical/gang topic by way of my broader research initiative, the Religion, Global Poverty, and International Development Project (RPD). As I sought to measure poverty in Salvadoran communities, I quickly learned that the elements of poverty that mattered most to residents were violence and human insecurity. Gangs were the greatest propagators of both (followed by high incidences of intra-family violence). My study also confirmed the religion statistics cited above: evangelicals were the majority in all of the neighborhoods I surveyed. In two of the communities they accounted for 70 percent or more of the population. I thus turned my attention to the events and actors that, in many respects, seemed to matter most to community members.

The ensuing research has lasted the better part of a decade (see Appendix for my research methods). My close study of gangs, including direct interaction with numerous gang members, allows me to provide insights into gang culture. But I am most interested in contributing to our understanding of how religious actors, and particularly evangelicals, interact with gangs and social problems more generally.

I am not, though, simply retreading ground covered by Brenneman and Wolseth. Both of those authors conducted their research more than fifteen years ago. Identities and roles in society of evangelicals and gangs have evolved in the intervening years. Additionally, Brenneman, Wolseth, and others primarily focused on the morgue rule exception.[1] Other interactions between evangelicals and gangs have long existed and have grown with time. They have remained largely unresearched, yet they constitute a much larger share of the evangelical/gang relationship than the morgue rule exception. They also help to shape the transnational identities and activities of both groups.

My central argument is that within El Salvador's tightly woven lower-class communities, evangelicals and gangs are entangled with one another. Such intimate connections are often glossed over by neighborhood social imaginaries and scholars alike.

I explore how and why such entanglements exist, and in which spheres of community life. In different chapters I ask: do evangelicals and gangs share basic religious beliefs? How do underlying social structures, including family relations, inform their interactions? How do evangelicals and gangs both express local authority within the same geographic areas? What happens when they both participate, as they must, in local economies? Are gang members inside local congregations? Are evangelicals inside local gang cliques? By providing insights into such largely unanswered questions, I begin to reshape our understanding of evangelicals in Latin America and, to a lesser extent, of gangs.

But to address such questions, some historical and theoretical context is necessary. Below I sketch the rise of evangelicals and gangs in lower class El Salvador (see Figure I.1). I then introduce a new theoretical lens, the entanglement thesis, to frame the relationship between evangelicals and gangs.

Historical Backgrounds of Evangelicals and Gangs

Evangelicals

Origins of El Salvador's Evangelicals

The story of El Salvadoran evangelicalism begins in the Italian Alps in 1851. That's when Francisco Penzotti was born in the town of Chiavenna to a devout Catholic family. When Francisco lost his father at the age of six, the parish priest took charge of his education. Francisco was soon serving as an altar boy. When he was thirteen, Francisco's sister-in-law invited him to immigrate to Uruguay. There he learned carpentry and opened his own shop while still a teenager (Espinoza 1997). In 1870, at the age of nineteen, Francisco married Josefa Sagastibelza, who had immigrated from Spain as a child. They were married in the Cathedral of Montevideo (Bravo 2015).

The Penzottis were enjoying a typically Catholic religious life in Uruguay when, at the age of twenty-four, Francisco received a copy of the gospel of John. One of the Penzottis' friends then took them to hear a Methodist missionary who was visiting Montevideo from Argentina in 1875. Josefa soon had a conversion experience. The next year Francisco also converted. He quickly became active in missionary work himself. Not everyone in Uruguay appreciated this turn of events, however, and some who hoped to keep Protestantism out of Uruguay burned his carpentry shop to the ground (Bravo 2015; Espinoza 1997).

Undeterred, Penzotti became a full-time pastor and evangelist. In 1883 he began traveling throughout South America, preaching and distributing

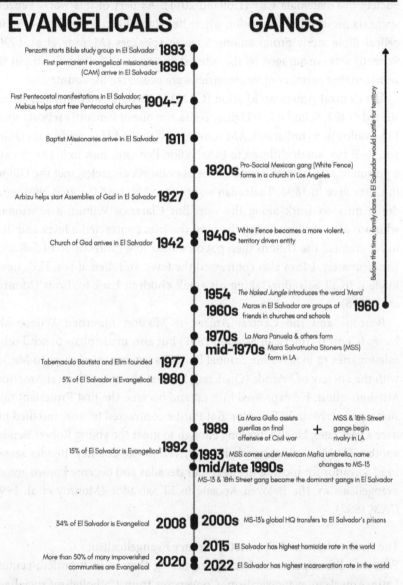

Timeline of Major Events

EVANGELICALS

Penzotti starts Bible study group in El Salvador **1893**
First permanent evangelical missionaries **1896**
(CAM) arrive in El Salvador
First Pentecostal manifestations in El Salvador; **1904-7**
Mebius helps start free Pentecostal churches
Baptist Missionaries arrive in El Salvador **1911**

Arbizu helps start Assemblies of God in El Salvador **1927**

Church of God arrives in El Salvador **1942**

Tabernaculo Bautista and Elim founded **1977**
5% of El Salvador is Evangelical **1980**

15% of El Salvador is Evangelical **1992**

34% of El Salvador is Evangelical **2008**

More than 50% of many impoverished **2020**
communities are Evangelical

GANGS

1920s Pro-Social Mexican gang (White Fence) forms in a church in Los Angeles

1940s White Fence becomes a more violent, territory driven entity

1954 *The Naked Jungle* introduces the word 'Mara'
1960s Maras in El Salvador are groups of friends in churches and schools **1960**

1970s La Mara Panuela & others form
mid-1970s Mara Salvatrucha Stoners (MSS) form in LA

1989 La Mara Gallo assists guerillas on final offensive of Civil war **+** MSS & 18th Street gangs begin rivalry in LA
1993 MSS comes under Mexican Mafia umbrella, name changes to MS-13
mid/late 1990s changes to MS-13
MS-13 & 18th Street gang become the dominant gangs in El Salvador

2000s MS-13's global HQ transfers to El Salvador's prisons

2015 El Salvador has highest homicide rate in the world
2022 El Salvador has highest incarceration rate in the world

Before this time, family clans in El Salvador would battle for territory

Dates in this figure may be approximations

Figure I.1 Timeline: growth of evangelicals and gangs in El Salvador (created by Thomas Hampton).

Bibles with the Waldensian Church[2] and the American Bible Society (House 2019).[3] In 1893, he opened a Central American office for the American Bible Society in Guatemala City (Holland 2011). As part of this work, Penzotti spent six months in El Salvador, where he established the first known evangelical Bible study group among Spanish speakers (Monroy et al. 1996). Penzotti was encouraged by the interest shown in El Salvador and put the word out that permanent missionaries were needed in the country.

The Central American Mission (CAM), a newly formed mission agency started by C.I. Schofield, in Dallas, Texas, ran one of Penzotti's reports about El Salvador in its bulletin. CAM soon agreed to send H.C. and Laura Dillon and their two small children to El Salvador. Penzotti, now in his forties and a person of stature within international evangelical circles, met the Dillons in Costa Rica in 1894. Their plan was to travel by land through Nicaragua, doing mission work along the way. But Clarence Wilbur, a missionary who was also accompanying them on the trip, contracted a fever and died in Nicaragua. The Dillons then got on a boat to go directly to El Salvador. Unfortunately, Laura also contracted the fever and died at sea. H.C. never made it to El Salvador, taking his small children back to Texas (Monroy et al. 1996).

Penzotti and the Central American Mission mourned Wilbur and Laura (Central American Mission 1897) but also made plans to send other missionaries to El Salvador. Samuel Purdie, a veteran missionary to Mexico with the Society of Friends (Quakers), learned about the Central American Mission's quest. He expressed interest and became the first Protestant missionary to arrive in El Salvador. But Purdie contracted tetanus and died just over a year later. He did live long enough to greet the young Robert Bender, another CAM missionary, when he arrived in the country. Bender served in El Salvador for most of the next four decades and became known among evangelicals as The Beloved Apostle to El Salvador (Monroy et al. 1996; CAM 1997).

The Haven Thesis and Twentieth-Century Evangelicalism
Penzotti's life experiences became recurring themes in twentieth-century Latin American evangelicalism. Conversion from Catholicism, social and religious persecution, the fact that Francisco's wife converted before he did, the desire to share the *evangel* or "good news," and participation in a different set of transnational religious networks all reverberated through the coming decades.

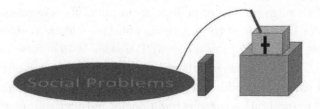

Figure I.2 Haven thesis (created by Adrianna Offutt).

Grinding poverty was also a common denominator for twentieth-century evangelicals. Rural evangelicals often engaged in subsistence agriculture or worked essentially as peasants on coffee or sugar plantations; urban evangelicals scratched out livings in the informal economy. This was true even into the late 1980s, when Coleman and colleagues (1993) found that when compared with practicing Catholics, non-practicing Catholics, and re-ligiously non-affiliated Salvadorans, Protestants ranked last in mean income and median income, displayed the lowest percentage of respondents in the high-end income category, and were the least educated. As one evangelical statesman recollected, twentieth-century evangelicals were considered to be "yahoos" by more educated and affluent Salvadorans.

Such dynamics were what caused Lalive d'Epinay, one of the earliest scholars of Latin American Pentecostalism, to argue that in the midst of so-cial and economic upheaval, Pentecostal churches were providing a haven for the poor. He wrote that this growing religious movement was built "around its condemnation of a world which will not be renewed until the coming of the Lord . . . and around the mission it has assumed of saving souls from this world and offering them temporary refuge in the congrega-tion" (1969, 128).

Lalive d'Epinay's analysis marked the beginning of a robust tradition within the Latin American evangelical and Pentecostal literature. Those who built on it explored the multiple dimensions of evangelical social separa-tion and highlighted the empowering effects of haven life (see Figure I.2). Evangelicals, for example, socially relocate by cutting existing relational ties, sometimes even with family members (Martin 1990, 2002; Smilde 2007). They refrain from common cultural behavior and vacate common gathering spaces through bans on alcohol, tobacco, and extramarital relationships (Brusco 1986; Smilde 1998; Willems 1967). Evangelicals reject key Catholic beliefs and replace them with beliefs that reinforce their practices of exclu-sion and separation (Lindhart 2014; Williams & Peterson 1996). Finally, evangelicals often opt out of politics, socio-political movements, and the more colorful aspects of Latin America's business culture (Lindhart 2014; Stoll 1990; Williams & Peterson 1996). Decisions in all of these venues are sometimes made for evangelicals: society has cast them out as often as they have left society. This adds to evangelicals' sense of marginalization: those who seek evangelical havens were traditionally, and often still are, among the poorest and least educated in society (Brenneman 2012).[4]

Life in the haven can be rewarding. As evangelicals typically attend church five to six times a week (Williams 1997), they improve their organizational and civic skills and gain new characteristics like frugality and increased personal motivation (Berger 1991; Freston 2001). Evangelicals have, in some contexts, hoped these safe spaces would shield them from state violence and persecution (Freston 2001). Transnational connections and opportunities also sometimes open up for evangelicals within congregational contexts (Offutt 2015). In short, as one Venezuelan told David Smilde, the "economic and spiritual fruits [of evangelicalism] were better" (2007, 7) than staying in mainstream society.

Evangelical Growth in El Salvador

The haven thesis captured the experience of most twentieth-century evangelicals regardless of denomination. But denominations are the primary axes around which collective evangelical actions are organized. They are also the strongest expression of difference within the broader evangelical community. A brief introduction to the country's primary denominations can help to explain the growing need for multiple understandings of how evangelicals interface with society. To be sure, differences can be found within as well as across denominations. But denominational life is one of several windows into the growing diversity of evangelical social dynamics.

CAM played the dominant role in establishing traditional Protestant roots in El Salvador. North American CAM missionaries and Salvadoran colporteurs and pastors worked together to establish a small but sustained presence. They were joined by Baptist missionaries in 1911 (Danielson & Danielson 2021), who employed similar organizational strategies. But other traditional Protestant denominations, such as the Presbyterians (who were active in Guatemala) and the Methodists did not have active mission agencies in El Salvador. Such groups developed a small presence in the country much later. CAM and the original Baptist churches remain important parts of the evangelical community today (Monroy et al. 1996).

The global Pentecostal movement exploded onto the scene in the early 1900s. The "starburst" (Martin 2002) that radiated out from the 1906 Azusa Street Revival arrived in El Salvador by 1911. But Pentecostal events were happening in El Salvador before that. Bender, who would not have called himself a Pentecostal (R. Bueno 2019), wrote in 1905 that: "We together waited upon God for the infilling of the spirit and all of a sudden, the power came upon us, and we were all filled with the Holy Ghost to which all testified" (Bender 1905 in Robeck 2016). Others have provided similar accounts: Teresa, a member of one El Salvador's earliest congregations, reported that "the first missionary that arrived to share the Gospel in her village did not come to talk about the Holy Spirit. However, she recalled how during one the meetings 'the promise' (the Holy Spirit) descended surprisingly upon the missionary and those present. She said that the missionary asked those present not discuss with others what had occurred" (R. Bueno 2019, 80). Through such events, independent Pentecostal churches formed in El Salvador before 1910.

Under the encouragement and direction of Fredrick Mebius, a Canadian holiness missionary, these independent groups began to form indigenous denominational networks. Mebius helped to form the Free Pentecostal Churches in the first decades of the twentieth century. In the 1930s, small groups of congregations splintered off of this denomination, creating the Apostolic Church of the Apostles and Prophets (which is now among the largest in rural communities), the Apostolic Church of the Upper Room, and others (Holland 2008). In 1930 such groups were still tiny: several hundred congregants were spread across the nascent Pentecostal denominations (Robeck 2016 in R. Bueno 2019).

The Assemblies of God (AG) and the Church of God (Cleveland, TN) also established an early presence in El Salvador. Francisco Arbizu, a cobbler and Pentecostal lay leader in El Salvador, sold a piece of land to finance a trip to meet with AG leaders in Texas in 1927. The trip generated a visit by an AG missionary to El Salvador, and the AG formally started its work in El Salvador in 1929 (Monroy et al. 1996; Bueno 2019). Mebius, now advanced in years, helped the Church of God become established in El Salvador in the early 1940s (Mebius died in 1944) (Holland 2008). But by mid-century the evangelical movement was still a numerically and socially insignificant part of El Salvador's total population.

The tectonic plates of El Salvador's cultural, political, and economic systems began to shift in the 1960s, opening fissures in the existing sacred canopy and moral order (Offutt 2015). New evangelical groups began to emerge. In 1977, Dr Edgar Lopez Beltran, known as Hermano Toby, founded the Tabernaculo Biblico Bautista "Amigos de Israel," known as Tabernaculo Bautista, in the capital city of San Salvador. The independent church had no formal ties to any international denomination, and it grew quickly. Also in 1977, Sergio Solórzano founded a church called Centro Misionero Elim, known as Elim. Solarzano started the church at the behest of an independent Pentecostal church in Guatemala, but Elim El Salvador soon broke ties with its Guatemalan counterpart and became completely independent (R. Bueno 2019; Wadkins 2017). Other groups also emerged in this era, but Tabernaculo Bautista and Elim rose to national prominence. They helped evangelicalism move from five to fifteen per cent of the population during El Salvador's civil war (1980–1992) (Coleman et al. 1993).

Evangelicalism continued its fast growth in El Salvador's postwar environment. Some of this new growth was driven by evangelicalism's ascension into the country's middle and upper classes. The AG and Tabernaculo Bautista have made inroads in these sectors. Newer groups such as the Camp of God and the International Center of Praise have also flourished (Offutt 2015). These kinds of evangelicals, no longer "yahoos," move fluidly in what remains a predominantly Catholic upper class.

But evangelical gains have been much more significant in the lower classes, which are the focus of this book. Denominations founded before 1980 account for much of this growth. Most of the evangelical subjects interviewed for this book are part of one of the denominations already listed. The few who are not belong to independent congregations or networks of churches that are highly localized. There has thus been continuity in the history and many of the doctrines of lower-class Salvadoran evangelicals, even as their position in, and interactions with, society has dramatically expanded and diversified.

Gangs

Origins of El Salvador's Gangs

The origins of Salvadoran gangs is a tricky subject. I interviewed knowledgeable Salvadorans to get a sense of where they felt Salvadoran gang culture began. Many saw the roots of gangs in El Salvador's earlier historical eras. "There have always been groups of kids that get together, share an identity, and then enter into conflict with other groups. This is often for territory," said one NGO leader. A national media correspondent I talked to picked up the story in a different way: "to understand the gang you have to go back and understand the family clans in El Salvador." He argued that such clans often came to dominate rural and sometimes even urban neighborhoods. Themes of family and territory ran through many conversations I had about gang origins and remain important to gang identity and activity today.

While issues of family and territory date back much further, I pick up the story in the 1970s, when gangs, or maras,[5] which is a distinctly Salvadoran name for gangs, had a free-wheeling but relatively innocuous reputation. Castillo (2014) interviewed former members of several 1970s-era maras, one of which was la Mara del Panuelo, a group that congregated at a student recreation center in San Salvador. Group members listened to heavy metal rock music, hung out with their girlfriends, smoked pot, drank alcohol, or just passed "the day in idle conversation" (Castillo 2014, 47). Alcohol-infused fist fights occasionally occurred with another mara, but la Mara del Paneulo was mostly peaceful, and even had some strains of hippy culture.

Maras evolved as national political and social unrest grew. Full scale civil war broke out in 1980. The fraught environment was one reason that the increasing numbers of maras were becoming harder and more violent. A founding member of La Jade, a mara founded in working class Soyapongo in 1983, stated that "what started as a game was transformed little by little into something more serious" (Castillo 2014, 57). Salvadoran media outlets seldom reported complaints from residents about the 1970s-era maras. But in the 1980s, maras with names like Magia Negra, Morazon, No se Dice, Los Cadenas, La Mara Guacha, and Escorpion increasingly made the news, being accused of rapes, robberies, assaults, drug taking, and glue sniffing (Castillo 2014).

By the late 1980s, even in the midst of a civil war, gangs had worked themselves toward the top of the national agenda. The police reportedly had case files for more than 40,000 " 'burglars, thieves, car thieves, and drug addicts' that operated just within the San Salvadoran region" (El Diario de Hoy 1988 in Castillo 2014, 64). La Mara Gallo was widely believed to have assisted the guerillas in the 1989 Final Offensive (El Diario de Hoy 1990 in Castillo 2014); La Mara Gruesa exchanged fire with a brigade from the 2nd Infantry (La Prensa Grafica 1988 in Castillo 2014). Such engagements implied more heavily armed and trained groups than are typically associated with maras of this era. But it may not have been that uncommon: youths had been forcefully recruited into national armed forces and into guerrilla movements throughout the 1980s. When they escaped or their time of service concluded, it is likely that some of these battle-hardened youths found their way into local maras.

Gangs in Los Angeles

Things were also happening in Los Angeles in the 1980s that would change El Salvador's gang landscape. The flow of Salvadorans out of El Salvador began as a trickle in the 1970s and became a flood in the 1980s. Over a million people fled the country's civil war (Menjívar & Gómez Cervantes 2018). Tens of thousands came to Los Angeles. Some of those who arrived were in maras when they lived in El Salvador. Others innately understood the idea of a local neighborhood group that formed to protect themselves and their barrio. Especially in Los Angeles' inhospitable and often hostile environs, such youths gravitated toward gangs when they arrived.

Los Angeles' Latino gangs have a rich history. Prominent Mexican gangs like White Fence were formed as early as the 1920s. White Fence was formed in a church; members mostly played organized sports and helped with festivals (Dudley 2020). But in the 1940s White Fence became "protective of their own people and predatory toward others . . . [They established the] rules and traditions that are still prevalent in Latino gangs today: establishing cliques, attending meetings, creating bloody initiation rituals and disciplining members who broke these rules," (Dudley 2020, 39).

When Salvadorans arrived, some youths created a distinctly Salvadoran gang while others joined existing gangs. In the late 1970s or early 1980s, Salvadorans started the Mara Salvatrucha Stoners (MSS) (Dudley 2020; Ward 2013).[6] Like La Mara Panuelo back in El Salvador, the MSS was primarily dedicated to listening to heavy metal rock and taking recreational drugs. Members also dabbled in Satanic rituals (Martínez & Martínez 2019; Miller 2017). But not all Salvadorans joined MSS. The 18th Street gang also drew high numbers of Salvadorans. The 18th Street gang had emerged from Clanton 14, one of the oldest Mexican gangs in Los Angeles (Ramsey 2012). It expanded rapidly partly because it widened its membership to include other Latin American nationalities (InSight Crime 2018). Salvadorans joined and perhaps started other Los Angeles gangs, but these were the two that rose to international prominence.

MSS and the 18th Street gang shaped each other's history and transnational trajectory. They were allies in the 1980s. Numerous Salvadoran members had family in the opposing gang, helping to keep the gangs close.

Then in 1989, a brawl broke out at a party. A member of the 18th Street gang killed at least one MSS member with an automatic weapon (Dudley 2020; Martínez & Martínez 2019; Ward 2013). Revenge killings happened later that night. From the perspective of the MSS, "In less than twenty-four hours, the 18th Street had gone from family to archenemy. Neither gang would ever be the same" (Dudley 2020, 86).

The Mexican Mafia also shaped the identity of both groups. The Mexican Mafia came together in the 1950s. It sought to control California's prison systems and became an umbrella group of Mexican gangs (Martínez & Martínez 2019). The 18th Street gang was under the Mexican Mafia's umbrella long before it had its first Salvadoran member. But the Salvadoran-run MSS sought to maintain its independence.

California's entire gang ecosystem was undergoing dynamic changes in the 1980s. Incarceration rates rose, prisons became increasingly racialized, and violence within prisons spiked (Dudley 2020). Such conditions spurred the Mexican Mafia to extend its reach. It sought to control all Latino, rather than just Mexican, gangs (Dudley 2020). The Mexican Mafia thus put mounting pressure on MSS to join their coalition. Inside the prisons, the Mafia ordered other Latino gangs to beat up MSS members. Sometimes such beatings were brutal (Dudley 2020; Martínez & Martínez 2019). Outside the prisons, the Mexican Mafia called for other Sureno gangs to attack MSS in the street. The tactics worked; in 1993 the MSS agreed to become a "Sureno," or a gang loyal to the Mexican Mafia. Mara Salvatrucha thus dropped the "Stoners" from their name and added "13," which is a reference to "M," the thirteenth letter of the alphabet (Dudley 2020). The formal participation in a larger network of organized crime and the difficult lessons of street and prison life changed MS-13's culture and identity. Rather than being a group of hard rockers, they had begun the transition toward becoming, in Dudley's words, America's most notorious gang (2020).

MS-13 and the 18th Street Gang Head to El Salvador

MS-13 and the 18th Street gang arrived in El Salvador in the late 1980s and early 1990s. They came via deportation and transnational migration. About 4,000 gang members with criminal records were deported during these years (Martínez 2016). Many deportees had undergone the familiar pattern of fleeing El Salvador's civil war, experiencing the dislocation of a new culture and a new country in the United States, joining a gang out of desperation, then getting arrested, and ultimately being deported (Dudley 2020).

But after deportation they were still members of their respective gangs; some helped to start new cliques in El Salvador when they arrived (Martinez D'Aubuisson 2022).

Los Angeles gang members also impacted El Salvador through transnational migration, meaning that they simultaneously participated in U.S. and Salvadoran communities (Levitt 2001; Menjívar 2000). Chepe Furia, for example, helped to start the Fulton Locos Salvatrucha, an MS-13 clique in California, in the 1980s. In the early 1990s Furia maintained a transnational lifestyle, continuing his Los Angeles activities while founding an MS-13 clique in El Salvador. Furia was apprehended in Los Angeles and deported in 2003. But he frequently crossed national borders after that date (Martínez 2016). Furia's case illustrates how deportation and voluntary transnational lifestyles were not mutually exclusive: many who were deported simply made the journey back to Los Angeles, perhaps to be deported again or to return to El Salvador voluntarily.

MS-13 and the 18th Street gang quickly became the most powerful gangs in El Salvador. They did so by recruiting local gangs to join them, conducting hostile takeovers of pre-existing gangs (Martinez D'Aubuisson 2022), and spreading into parts of the country that no gangs previously controlled. Such processes made gangs even more ubiquitous in Salvadoran society: by 2018 there were an estimated 60,000–70,000 gang members in El Salvador (Verza 2018), which operate in 247 of the country's 262 municipalities (Martínez, Lemus, & Sontag 2016). The success of MS-13 and the 18th Street gang in El Salvador and other Central American countries is partly explained by cultural superiority (Los Angeles brands have great appeal in El Salvador, whether they are gangs, sneakers, or movies), greater access to guns and money, and formal ties to the Mexican Mafia (and thus transnational organized crime). Many local maras continue to operate in El Salvador, but none have the national presence of MS-13 and the two factions of the 18th Street gang.[7]

With such success, El Salvador became the hub of operations rather than an extension of Los Angeles-based gangs. El Salvador's national MS-13 leadership began serving as the gang's international leadership around 2005 (Dudley 2020). Leaders in El Salvador can thus dictate gang activities in the United States and elsewhere (Silva 2016). The 18th Street gang has greater power relative to governments and other actors in Central American countries than it does in the United States or in Mexico (InSight Crime 2011). And while deportation of gang members from the United States and circular or transnational migration continues, the vast majority of MS-13 and 18th Street gang members in El Salvador have never been to the United States. In fact, Cruz and colleagues (2017) found that less than 1 percent of current Salvadoran gang members grew up in the United States. The authors are careful to mention that their survey is not representative, but the statistic still serves as some indication of the extent to which such gangs have been localized.

The MS-13 and 18th Street gangs are powerful in El Salvador in part because of their ability to infiltrate government and other sectors of society (Martinez D'Aubuisson 2022). Chepe Furia again serves as an example. A Salvadoran congressman stated that Furia was "a mafioso with tentacles in every part of the state" (Martínez 2016, 12). Furia started a company that signed a garbage collection contract with the municipality of Atiquizaya. He became the president of a neighborhood association. The treasurer of Furia's clique was the spokesman for Atiquizaya's mayor. Another clique member was a public prosecutor in the town's vehicle theft division. Furia influenced the regional judicial system: he once asked a judge to release some of the youths in his clique, and the judge consented (Martínez 2016). MS-13 and the 18th Street gang's ability to bend government and business elites to their will has increased over time, and is likely to continue to increase over the next decade (Williamson 2021). This is true regardless of the particular political party or regime that is in power.

New Blueprints of Evangelical Life: The Entanglement Thesis

The stories of these two groups seem to have entirely different orbits. One story is populated by God-talk, holiness movements and church plants. The other is dominated by prisons, violence, and mafias. And yet their trajectories have collided in the lower-class neighborhoods of El Salvador. The intent of this book is to cast light on the nature of their resulting interaction.

How to do so?

The haven thesis is to this point the only conceptual apparatus available for understanding evangelicalism's relationship with society. The continuities within evangelicalism that have endured for more than a century keep the haven thesis relevant; the morgue rule exception is a case in point. But the broader set of evangelical/gang interactions which occupy this book cannot be explained by the haven thesis.

Nor can the haven thesis explain the growing diversity of evangelical interactions with other social groups. This is partly a function of the preponderance of evangelicals in El Salvador. It is also because of the nature of the movement: evangelicalism is notoriously fluid and adaptable (Martin 2002). Given these realities, evangelicalism no longer fits a single model of social interaction: more models are needed.

I propose the entanglement thesis (see Figure I.3). It argues that Latin American evangelicals are relationally and culturally tied to their surroundings and that this empirically observable reality has political, religious, and identity-related implications. The entanglement thesis is intended to help explain how impoverished evangelicals interact with social problems, but it may be applicable to evangelical social interaction in a broad range of social classes and venues. Below, I offer three key components of an entanglement approach.

First, an entanglement approach privileges the geographic and physical proximity to social problems over the cultural distance that evangelical churches might try to create. The entanglement approach assumes that congregations, like all other community-based organizations, act and are acted upon by their local neighborhoods and surroundings. It recognizes the ubiquity of evangelicals in impoverished communities and the empirical impossibility of evangelicals removing themselves from their contexts, even if they remain socially marginalized (Hagopian 2009). Conversely, the entanglement approach recognizes that towns and neighborhoods cannot function without including, at some level, the civil society organizations—evangelical churches—to which so many of their members belong.

To facilitate this, the entanglement model combines congregational analysis with a "lived" or "everyday religion" approach. Richard Wood (2014) has

Figure I.3 Entanglement thesis (created by Adrianna Offutt).

already argued for the importance of combining these two forms of analysis in "zones of crisis" in Latin America. Studying religion outside of institutional religious settings, which is the lived religion approach, reveals how integrated and prominent religion is in Latin American social life. But Wood argues that the formal religious institutions cannot be ignored: they create and legitimate the religious ideas and practices that occur in everyday life.

There are many ways to study congregations, some of which integrate easily with the lived religion approach. The four frames of congregational analysis introduced by Ammerman and colleagues (1997) use three frames—the culture, process, and resources frames—to investigate internal congregational life. These frames can also reveal how outside influences and social problems color worship and decision-making within churches. Ammerman and colleagues' fourth frame, the ecology frame, studies congregational environments and can draw attention to issues such as the scarcity of formal employment opportunities, the strengths and weaknesses of the health, education and law enforcement systems, and (more specifically) how gang members conduct surveillance in neighborhoods. Such observations merge well with lived religion's (Hall 1997; Rubin et al. 2014) interest in the actions and interactions of daily religious life, as such interactions often involve these kinds of environmental components. Analyzing religion both within and beyond institutions thus opens the way for more complete understandings of religious dynamics in the region.

Second, an entanglement approach recognizes the implications of low barriers to entry on evangelical identity and community in impoverished places. Evangelical congregations, as the haven thesis correctly posits, are often effective rescue centers in vulnerable communities. At-risk people—single teenage mothers, for example—are often welcomed and integrated into congregations. Their children may be better off being raised within such congregations, but evangelical membership does not completely change their at-risk status, and their children do not always beat the odds. Evangelical churches can create both sudden and gradual change in people. But not all members experience this, and not in every facet of their lives. Churches cannot and do not remove all threats to human flourishing from community contexts. Such dynamics help explain why so many children of evangelical households do not experience the economic and social lift that is shown in the haven model.

Consistent with the haven concept, the entanglement approach acknowledges that evangelical churches promote codes of behavior that run against typical barrio culture. Unlike the haven concept, the entanglement approach assumes that conformity among attenders to such teachings is uneven. Congregants are often "put in discipline." Violations invoking discipline include domestic violence, infidelity, and drug and alcohol use. But while punishment is frequent, congregants are seldom expelled. They, and their lifestyles, remain in the church. Pastors hope congregants conform to congregational expectations, but for many, this may never happen. An entanglement framework does not assume away this empirical reality; rather it is included as part of how to think about evangelicals in Latin America.

Third, an entanglement approach pays attention to the social networks that connect church leaders and members to the rest of the community. Rather than paying attention to the ties that converts must break when they join congregations (Martin 1990), this approach notes the relationships that continue outside of faith communities. The shift evangelicalism has experienced from extreme minority to being the largest religious category in many lower-class neighborhoods changes the logic of cutting off relationships with non-evangelicals upon conversion, which was essential to creating havens when people were leaving the majority religious culture to enter the early Protestant sects.

Today in impoverished communities, evangelicals maintain important relationships with family, neighbors, co-workers, and schoolmates. Scholars have noticed that evangelicals work within such networks to invite others to church. But too little attention has been paid to the way family networks are structured and the impact non-evangelical members of such networks have on evangelicals. As will be shown in this book, evangelicals do not always have the most influence in their relationships. An entanglement approach examines this side of the equation.

Taken as a whole, the entanglement thesis offers a new way to analyze an evolving religious movement. It offers a counterbalance to the haven thesis while recognizing its ongoing utility. I will return to the lessons that have been learned about evangelicals through the entanglement thesis in the book's conclusion.

Map of the Book

The book is organized in the following way. Chapter 1 is intended to provide some context for the study. It describes the local ecologies that evangelicals and gangs co-habit and outlines the two groups' most prominent, shared characteristics. Chapters 2–7 show different dimensions of evangelical/ gang entanglement. Chapter 2 examines the cosmology that evangelicals and gangs share. Chapters 3 and 4 look at the interlocking nature of family connections and patrimonial systems, respectively. They show how gangs and evangelicals co-populate El Salvador's most basic grassroots social systems. Chapters 5–7 describe evangelical/gang entanglements in local governance, local economies, and within formal organizations. These chapters show the embedded nature of the groups' relational dynamics in major sectors of lower-class Salvadoran society. The book's final chapter reflects on the ways in which the entanglement thesis helps us to understand contemporary evangelicalism and provides policy recommendations based on the book's findings.

1

Inverted Images

Our bus inched its way through the center of Las Palmas, a coastal city of about 50,000 (El Salvador Census 2021). A gaggle of cheerful middle schoolers in Catholic school uniforms crowded into an ice cream shop, escaping the 100-degree heat. Across the dusty street was a bank where residents extract the financial remittances sent from family members in the United States. A young man in jeans, a new white t-shirt, and a baseball cap cocked slightly to one side stood in front of the bank. His arms were crossed. Teardrops were tattooed under his right eye. His posture and facial expression exuded a discomforting combination of defiance and ownership. The people who passed by gave him a respectful berth and kept their eyes averted. On the street corner behind me was a slight, middle-aged man with a loudspeaker and missing teeth. He passionately proclaimed God's love to whomever would listen. Some did listen, others sauntered by, apparently unperturbed by the loudspeaker's low quality, high volume, and occasional screeches.

The scene is typical of "downtown" Las Palmas. The Catholic school provides the city's best education and Catholic culture is most evident among the (relatively) more affluent residents. Evangelicals do better in the poorer neighborhoods. When they emerge in the public square, it is often with a humble appearance (and sometimes a loudspeaker). Gang members tend to emerge from the same neighborhoods to make their presence felt in different ways. Jon Wolseth (2011) noted that the three most prominent civil society organizations in Central America are gangs, evangelical churches, and Catholicism (far outnumbering things like youth soccer leagues or rotary clubs). That holds true in Las Palmas.

The bus chugged past the congested town center and crossed a river that empties into the Pacific Ocean, just 150 yards to our left. Ronaldo, my friend and research partner, and I hopped off near the entrance of Modesto, a lower-class neighborhood controlled by MS-13. The Baptist Tabernacle: Friends of Israel, a megachurch in San Salvador, recently built a church for its local congregation near the entrance of the community. Although still modest, it is

Blood Entanglements. Stephen Offutt, Oxford University Press. © Oxford University Press 2023.
DOI: 10.1093/oso/9780197587300.003.0002

the largest building in Modesto. We could see its roof fade from sight as we walked away from it and into Corinto, a neighborhood controlled by the 18th Street gang. We passed a Seventh Day Adventist church which also houses a small school, and then a typical neighborhood house where we often hear praise and worship in the evenings.

El Salvador's formal institutions seem distant in such neighborhoods. Police presence is less obvious; gang control is more visible. The Catholic Church has no institutional presence; evangelical churches pop up wherever there is space to borrow or rent. Gangs and evangelicals are the dominant culture producers at this grass roots level, where most Salvadorans live.

In this chapter I analyze the shared environment of evangelicals and gangs; I also point to numerous parallels in the organizational strategies that congregations and gang cliques employ. In the first section I outline nine areas of vulnerability that residents experience in lower-class communities, whether they are evangelicals or gang members, or belong to neither group. In the second section I share eight organizational parallels between evangelical churches and gang cliques. My goal is to situate the gang and evangelical interactions that are the subject of the following chapters in a broader environmental and organizational context.

The Shared Vulnerabilities of Evangelicals and Gang Members

Vulnerabilities are embedded in impoverished local environments. They are the product of local histories, state (in)activities, and global economic trends (see Figure 1.1). In this section I highlight nine features of poor Salvadoran communities that simultaneously diminish human flourishing and create conditions in which evangelicals and gangs thrive. They include: food, water, sewer, health, education, family, migration, employment, and political institutions.

Water/Food In; Waste Out

The most basic needs of a healthy community include nourishing food, clean water, and strategies to remove waste. Of these, Las Palmas's local neighborhood economies and social institutions do the best at providing food. Most

BROKEN SOCIAL SYSTEMS

The social systems in El Salvador are poorly equipped to deal with the challenges of everyday life.
Under stress, they break.

HEALTHCARE - LOW QUALITY

El Salvador spends $300 per person on healthcare.
Scarce resources are thinly spread and hard to access.
When they are accessed, they are of low quality.

SCHOOLS - INADEQUATE

Students attend school in half-day shifts and those who
graduate from primary school often have deficiencies in
basic math and literacy skills. Teachers often lack sufficient
training.

FAMILIES - BROKEN

Most households are female-headed. Sometimes
both parents abandon their children. Most
partners are never formally married.

LOCAL ECONOMIES - INSUFFICIENT

Local economies generate low levels of wealth and few
employment opportunities. They rely heavily on remittances from
the over three million Salvadorans who live outside the country.

POLITICAL INSTITUTIONS - DYSFUNCTIONAL

Lack of accountability structures and underfunding leaves
local governments vulnerable to corruption and manipulation
by gangs and other actors.

Figure 1.1 Broken social systems (created by Thomas Hampton).

residents eat three meals per day. Seafood, chicken, tortillas, beans, cheese, and tropical fruit, all of which is cultivated locally, make up the traditional diet. "Pupuserias" pop up in homes and along sidewalks. These makeshift restaurants sell El Salvador's national dish, the pupusa, which is a cornmeal or rice flour tortilla filled with various combinations of beans, cheese, and pork. Salvadorans in all levels of society eat pupusas for breakfast, lunch, or dinner, and frequently multiple times a day.

Food intake is not, however, all good news. Pupusas are nourishing but also usually fried and high in fat. Worse, an increasing share of local diets consist of the soda, chips, and sweets that are sold in local *tiendas*, the storefront shops found in seemingly every third or fourth house throughout these neighborhoods. (That *pupuserias* and storefront *tiendas* are more plentiful than evangelical churches and gang cliques is an indication of their ubiquity.) As the share of fast food in local diets also creeps up and urban residents have little opportunity to exercise, fitness has become a problem. Sixty-three percent of El Salvador's adult population was recently categorized as overweight; more than a quarter of the national population qualified as obese (Owen & Suazo 2014). This is easily noticed in places like Corinto, where in the heat of the day men roll up their shirts to show their *pancito*, or bellies, and teasingly give each other nicknames like *gordo*, which means "fat."

Whereas the food situation in Las Palmas is mixed, the water problems are dire. Residents of makeshift communities (see Photo 1.1), where houses are made from corrugated steel sheets and no city infrastructure exists, get water at distribution sites where trucks from ANDA (the government entity in charge of water and sewerage) make five-gallon jugs available three times a week. Residents of the city's more established neighborhoods do have running water, but the city only turns it on a few days a week. When available, the water's frequent discoloration is rumored to be the result of fecal matter.

This becomes more believable when one walks along the streets of Corinto and notices streams of liquid being emitted from PVC tubes jutting out of the sides of houses. These streams of "black" or sewer water and their noxious fumes travel along open street gutters. Although it does have running water, Corinto does not have a sewer system. The hot sun either evaporates the water as it sits in the open gutters or the water spills out of the gutter and seeps into the ground. Local gardening is thus more precarious than residents appear to realize. This may also compromise Las Palmas's river (see Photo 1.2), which is used for washing clothes and sometimes for drinking water. Energy sapping illnesses, including amoebic dysentery, are not uncommon.

Photo 1.1 Evangelical housing conditions (photo: David Torres Ayala).

Photo 1.2 Environmental vulnerabilities (photo: David Torres Ayala).

Health System

El Salvador's health system struggles to respond to these realities. The country spends about $300 per capita on health care (World Bank Data 2022a). For comparison, the United States spends over $9,451 per capita on health care (Sawyer & Cox 2017) and the United Kingdom spends over $4,300 per capita on health care (World Bank Data 2021a). In Las Palmas, the neighborhood health center provides some services, including preventive health trainings. But its scarce resources are stretched across too great a swath of the city to make much of an impact. There is no hospital; any surgery or serious medical issue has to be addressed in the department capital, which is over an hour away by bus. Even there the quality of medical care is suspect and not always accessible.

Pedro's story is a case in point. He was injured while unloading trucks in a warehouse. He has been waiting for months for the national health insurance system to approve his operation. But he thinks the delay may be a blessing in disguise, as no treatment may be better than mistreatment: another member of his church recently had a tumor misdiagnosed at the same hospital. By the time she was re-assessed it was too late; she passed away a few weeks before my conversation with Pedro.

Gang members are also affected. They are as vulnerable to waterborne disease and inadequate health care as anyone else. Although they are intimidating because of their tattoos and their weapons, gang members are not, as a rule, physically imposing. Rather, they embody the diet, exercise regimen, and health practices that are available in such neighborhoods. Very few gang members exhibit an athletic look; to do so would require more physically empowering environments.

Education System

Schools in El Salvador are underfunded and overcrowded. El Salvador has a pupil/teacher ratio of over 27:1 in primary schools (World Bank Data 2022b). Schools in most lower-class neighborhoods do not have sufficient space to fit all the students, so students go to school in half day shifts. Each shift is about four hours a day. Dropout rates are high throughout the country. Worse, primary school enrollment is actually declining (World Bank Data 2019). Teacher training remains insufficient and school buildings are in various states of disrepair (UNESCO 2009). It is not surprising that on standardized tests, Salvadoran students find themselves in the group of low performing countries in Latin America (UNESCO 2009).

This is just as true in Las Palmas as it is elsewhere in the country. A teacher in a Las Palmas high school stated that when students arrive in his class, they "haven't mastered the basics of the first four levels of math . . . they don't know how to write correctly, their grammar is not good . . . ." Across town at a local elementary built in 1965, the assistant principal provided a litany of problems with their school building, including already warm classrooms that get to temperatures of over 100 degrees because the roof material absorbs heat, problems with the electrical system and the lighting, and no school library. The administrator further stated that "Due to the lack of parental support we have been noticing that children have problems reading . . . ." This includes the custom of pulling primary school children away from class when employment opportunities emerge, such as selling coconuts or washing dishes in a local eatery. Such environmental factors have obvious negative impacts on students' educational performance.

Family Structures

Family structures in Las Palmas's neighborhood also inhibit human flourishing. Many children are raised by single mothers. In some situations both parents abandon a child, sometimes to migrate to the United States, while the child is raised by a grandparent or other relative. The *de facto* way of creating family—many couples are never formally married but live with their *acompanado/a* and thus more easily change partners—means that men and women often have children with more than one partner. Such situations seldom enable children to overcome the poor educational system just described.

Migration

Migration is a common part of Salvadoran life. There are about 6.4 million Salvadorans in El Salvador (World Bank 2022c). There are roughly 2.3 million people of Salvadoran origin living in the United States, making them "the third largest population of Hispanic origin (tied with Cubans)"

(Noe-Bustamente, Flores, & Shah 2019). Salvadorans also migrate to Canada, Mexico, Europe, Australia, and elsewhere in Latin America. This has made El Salvador the "perfect transnational case" (Yelvington 2004), a situation that opens the country up to international resources, but also deprives the country of human capital and distorts important family and other types of relationships. I discuss personal experiences of migration people in Las Palmas have had later in the chapter.

Employment

Migration is high in part because jobs in Las Palmas are scarce. El Salvador's national employment rate was 46.31 percent in 2019 (Trading Economics 2021). Reliable data for Las Palmas's employment rate is not available, but it is likely to be lower than the national average. When I asked people what they thought the best job in the city was, I was repeatedly told that working for the local grocery store was at or near the top of the list. A high school teacher stated that most graduates from his institution "insert themselves in the informal labor market while they look for employment in hotels, gas stations, and grocery stores." The great advantage of the grocery store option is that it comes with a benefits package. It says something about a local labor market when the highest aspiration is to work in the grocery store.

Political Institutions

Political systems in El Salvador are often broken. At the national level, three out of the last four Salvadoran presidents are either in jail or have fled the country due to corruption charges. Various forms of scandal are daily fodder for the national newspapers. The same is true at the municipal level, where governing bodies are chronically underfunded and dysfunctional. Corruption is rampant—two consecutive mayors in Las Palmas (from different political parties) committed serious crimes and were removed from office. Law enforcement is also a notional idea—residents do not really expect the police to prevent crime from occurring in their neighborhoods.

The vulnerabilities embedded in these nine areas, which again are food, water, sewerage, health, education, family, migration, employment, and political institutions, are all causally linked to one another. They are also linked in complex ways with evangelicals and gangs. Religion and violence push and pull on family structures and emigration, for example, just as political systems and health systems shape religion and violence.

Many of these social dynamics will be touched on again and in more depth in later chapters. The point I am making in this section is that the individuals—often teenagers or people in their twenties—who identify as "evangelical" or as a "gang member" are all products of the environment that I have just described. They all eat pupusas. They all live with the threat of waterborne disease. Their futures have all been impacted by suboptimal education. They all recognize the attraction, threat, and opportunity that undocumented migration presents. They are, in important ways and in wide swaths of their social realities, members of the same homogeneous population.

Organizational Parallels Between Churches and Gangs

Within such impoverished environments, congregations and cliques have developed at least eight parallel organizational features. These include patrimonial systems, rituals, local recruitment, income generation, internal codes of conduct, the exercise of community influence, a franchise orientation, and personal transnational connections (see Figure 1.2). Six of these parallels reveal how congregations and cliques operate within their neighborhoods; two parallels show how the two groups engage at the national and transnational levels. Collectively, the parallels tell a narrative of how grassroots groups with very different aims use similar organizational strategies to overcome the environmental challenges that poverty creates.

Local Focus of Operation

Evangelical congregations and local gang cliques are deeply rooted in the neighborhoods just described. This is where their leaders and members are born and come of age. It is where the social conditions help to form their identities. Indeed, those conditions run through congregations and cliques, making congregations and cliques authentically local institutions.

Figure 1.2 Organizational parallels between evangelicals and gangs (created by Thomas Hampton).

Patrimonial Systems

Flourishing as they do in the backwaters of global society, evangelicals and gangs draw on similar combinations of pre-modern and modern forms of social organization. Both groups create pre-modern patrimonial systems, or systems of local authority which are dominated by family structures. Patrimonies remain prominent in places where the state and other modern institutions have failed. In El Salvador, congregations and cliques forge patrimonial systems through real or blood related family ties and through the creation of "fictive kinships" (Collins 2011). Such an approach allows both groups to be patterned with the kinds of social institutions that have always knit Salvadoran communities together.

Sarita, for example, belongs to a Church of God congregation along with her parents, siblings, aunt, and cousins. Sarita and her relatives make up a sizable minority of this small congregation, and those blood connections matter. But she also refers to the other congregants as "brother" and "sister," something Latin American evangelicals have long done. Sarita trusts fellow congregants with intimate feelings and details of her life and is happy to share whatever goods and resources she has with them. The congregation helps Sarita create "fictive" kinships that build trust and tighten congregational bonds.

Likewise, Diego is a member of the 18th Street gang. Two of his brothers are also in the gang with him—it is not uncommon for siblings and cousins to join the same gang. That blood relationship makes the tie between Diego and his brothers even stronger. But Diego has loyalties and obligations to the other gang members that run nearly, and in some respects just as, deep. One gang mantra states that "the brotherhood must be the gang's first virtue" (Strazza 2016, 53).

The leaders of evangelical and gang patrimonies are pastors and *palabreros*, respectively. Both types of leaders are in charge of their kinship networks. Both usually have an inner circle from which they receive advice, but final authority in a community lies with a pastor or *palabrero*. Both may also experience rising leaders within their groups. This can lead to internal competition for the leadership position. Sometimes this is alleviated by encouraging the rival to start his own church or clique. For highly effective leaders of patrimonies, the new groups will still consider the original pastor or *palabrero* to be in a position of authority over them, thus expanding their influence.

Patrimonial systems matter in part because of the transfer of goods and resources, often in the form of sharing, that can occur within them. This is articulated in congregations through corporate meals, lending household goods to one another, and through the relatively better off in their communities providing more of the resources needed to sustain congregational life. For example, Bethel Temple, a small evangelical church in Las Palmas, has a public school teacher in its congregation. Although his income is quite modest, his tithes go further than most of the other members who have informal jobs growing corn and beans on small plots of land or going door to door selling tortillas. Those who do not have a formal job provide "sweat equity" in the form of working with the youth and painting the church walls. Cliques have similar dynamics. Strazza quotes an 18th Street gang member as saying that "what you have, your brother has it too. If you have nothing, neither does your brother" (2016, 54). A feeling of belonging is one of the key attractions of gangs for young people in these communities.

Rituals

Rituals further consolidate congregations and cliques. "Ritual" can mean many things. I understand rituals to be both symbolic expressions of social relations and efforts to interact with the transcendent. Rituals can be found in the context of worship and within everyday life (Durkheim 2008 [1915]; Lindhart 2014). Some examples will help to see how rituals operate.

At one of the local Assemblies of God churches in Las Palmas, congregants participate in worship rituals multiple times per week. They sing praise and worship songs, pray with their hands lifted, and engage in corporate prayer. Usually, one of the congregants gets up and shares a testimony of how Jesus worked in his or (more often) her life. An elder will read the Bible passage, and the pastor will deliver a sermon. Some variations to this pattern are made depending on the day of the week (Wednesdays are a bit different than Mondays, for example), but congregants know and expect these rituals, and by participating in them, they strengthen their own identities as evangelicals.

Other rituals in the congregation confer official status. For the Assemblies of God church just mentioned, and for most evangelical churches in El Salvador, the initial ritual must be a conversion experience. These can be fairly dramatic, causing a marked and immediate change in one's life, or they can be part of a coming-of-age process. But even if it is the latter, most evangelicals can point to a specific moment in their lives where they accepted Jesus as their Lord and Savior. More than singing or praying, this officially makes a person a Christian.

Conversion does not, however, make a person a member of a specific congregation. Baptism is usually the ritual that ushers a person into formal membership. This is done in front of the rest of the congregation and is accompanied by a public profession of faith. The congregation then recognizes the baptized person as a member of their particular congregation. For many churches, the ritual of communion is withheld from people until after baptism. Communion is a further sign of being a member in good standing.

Congregations need leaders in addition to pastors. Such individuals are referred to as *ancianos* or elders, and in some cases deacons and deaconesses. They lead Sunday school classes, direct outreach programs, and help to plan the church's calendar. To become a leader, members are either voted for or in some cases appointed by the pastor. Once they are chosen, they are presented to the rest of the congregation. Often, the congregation will come and lay hands on them, praying that they will be servants of God in their new offices.

Gangs also use rituals to help incorporate individuals into the group. Youths who are not yet in gangs but nonetheless hang around the gang are referred to as gang sympathizers. Being a "sympathizer" is similar to being an evangelical convert who has not become a church member. Sympathizers can be any age but include the very young, perhaps nine or ten years old. Such children are navigating all the vulnerabilities in lower-class Salvadoran neighborhoods, and often feel rejected or unloved in their home environment. Sebastian, for example, was raised by his mother and stepfather, but felt like the neglected brother when the couple had another child together. Sebastian said, "it was obvious, he was the favorite." Relatively unsupervised in his pre-teen years, Sebastian found himself spending time with older gang members and appreciating the attention he received from them.

The names of gangs are among the more important symbols, and the way that gang members speak of their symbols and represent them shows their ritualistic power. MS-13 is knowns as "the letters," and the 18th Street gang is known as "the numbers." MS-13 has a telling phrase: "We owe everything to the letters. We go only as far as the letters allow us." There is an emotional and possibly religious connection to these names. At one point in my research, I was talking to young men who had exited the 18th Street gang. In the course of the conversation, I referenced the "mara" to which they had previously belonged. The question, which was otherwise benign, prompted subtle but clear physical agitation from the young men. The chaplain who helped shepherd them out of the 18th Street gang later explained to me that "mara" was a term for a gang that had come to be predominantly associated with MS-13, especially from the perspective of 18th Street gang members. I did not make that mistake again.

To enter the gang, a sympathizer has to go through an initiation. Multiple pastors told me that this initiation is the gang equivalent to a baptism. For the MS-13, the initiation is comprised of being beaten for thirteen seconds. Although this initial beating varies in severity, it always carries significance. Sebastian stated that entering a gang "is a commitment, it is practically a pact." Gang sympathizers have made no such pact, so the transition to gang member is an important one even though youths enter with low ranks in the organization and without much responsibility or knowledge of the gang's inner workings.

Gang members also engage in worship, although the diversity and variety of rituals and objects of worship far exceeds the more homogeneous (but still lively) evangelical experience. Some gang members engage in Satanic rituals and occult practices. At the inception of MS-13 in California, MSS stood for Mara Salvatrucha Stoners, and members listened to heavy metal music and took drugs, and some dabbled in Satan worship through animal sacrifice (Ward 2013).

This strain of activities has continued in MS-13 and other gangs, becoming in some instances more intense. Some gang members openly admit in court that they kill because they are motivated by Satanic beliefs (Miller 2017). Arlo, an inmate I interviewed who became a Christian and left the gang, affirmed this, saying that when he was in the gang he had gotten involved in "santeria . . . hidden arts, occultism and things like that." Arlo also sometimes worries that he committed the "unpardonable sin" in the process, which, according to the New Testament, is blasphemy against the Holy Spirit. At the same youth prison, a chaplain explained that occult services are normal in many prisons, and in this youth prison there had recently been a human sacrifice.

Other rituals can represent increasing loyalty, status, and leadership within a gang. These include tattoo art, slang, hand signals, secret written code, and graffiti. A teardrop under a gang member's eye, like the one referenced in the opening lines of this chapter, represents a life that the person has taken. Devil horns show up frequently in MS-13 graffiti and tattoo imagery, and a spiderweb tattoo is an indication of lifelong commitment to the gang (Strazza 2016). Violating or defaming such rituals and images can result in death; Oscar Martínez (2016) tells the story of a man who thought he would cover his bases by getting MS-13 tattoos on some parts of his body and 18th Street tattoos on other parts of his body. In response, the gang dismembered him before killing him. Acts of violence are themselves ritualistic. Through such acts, gang members deepen their shared identity and prove their worth and belonging (Brenneman 2012). Strazza (2016) argues that the three rituals that are most important in creating gang cohesion are "la vida loca," tattoos, and violence.

Recruiting Locally
Evangelicals and gangs both recruit. Evangelicals do this through sharing their faith with others. The term "evangelical" is derived from the act of sharing the "Good News," so this is central to the faith community's identity. The message evangelicals share is pretty consistent: Jesus is the Son of God, he died on the cross for the sins of the world, he rose again and conquered sin, he wants to have a personal relationship with you if you are willing

to accept him into your heart and make him Lord and Savior of your life. Pentecostal evangelicals often mention the role of the Holy Spirit and place an emphasis on God's healing power. This message, with nuances between denominations, is what all or most evangelical congregations propagate.

The strategies to do so, however, are quite diverse. These include long-standing approaches, such as going door to door in neighborhoods, finding public spaces to preach to passersby, and boarding buses and preaching to their passengers while the bus goes on its route. Other strategies include vacation Bible Schools and puppet shows for children and open-air meetings for adults. Mass media campaigns are also used, but these are handled by larger churches in San Salvador or its suburbs. Congregational initiatives in lower-class neighborhoods can include showing an evangelistic film from the back of a truck, but more often they rely on the personal touch.

The personal touch frequently involves working through existing relationships. Family networks are especially important. Wives bring their husbands to the faith (husbands do the same for wives, but it is less common). Youths are likely to invite siblings, half-siblings, and cousins to come to church with them. The evangelical message is also transmitted through other types of personal relationships; a person with a close friend in a church is much more likely to join than someone who doesn't (Smilde 2007).

Some pastors in Las Palmas are also able to share their message in public schools. Pastor Vincente is one of those. He uses materials from an international organization that is designed to teach values to children. Some of the values are not specific to the evangelical faith, such as being honest and trustworthy. But Pastor Vincente also shares with students that these are Christian principles and invites children who want to know more about the Christian message to talk with him. In this way, he says, several children have come to faith. (Catholic leaders also have easy access to the public schools in this area.)

Gang recruitment embodies the complicated relationship that cliques have with their neighborhoods. In some cases, gangs extend a caring hand to youths. They offer to buy basic goods that an impoverished family needs, or school supplies for the youth. I have seen the affection that gang members show to young children and the affection with which the children respond. These relational dynamics are a very real part of communities that live under gang control. Because these relationships also often follow family ties, it is not in this sense that different from the way evangelicalism flows through the social networks just described. It is also somewhat logical that such children want to join a gang when they reach a certain age.

Young people can see that gang status is one of the few paths to empowerment in vulnerable neighborhoods. The opportunity to be in a brotherhood, to have people that will be loyal to you even, literally, to death, has a strong appeal. That these new proto-family relations also elevate a person into having local authority is also empowering. It is hard to understate the respect experienced upon entering a gang. I have seen grown men avert their eyes when a teenage gang member passes by, and I have heard multiple stories of the immediate change in behavior toward youths as soon as they enter a gang. Such dynamics are well known and serve as a powerful recruiting tool.

There is also a darker side to gang recruitment. It often includes the provision of drugs by gangs to children who are as young as nine and ten years old. Most current or former gang members I talked to referenced the role of drugs, especially marijuana but also harder drugs, in their path to gang membership. One former gang member believed that drugs are part of an intentional effort at manipulative recruitment. "That's when drugs take a toll on you," he stated. "Those that are more involved in the gang, they use them to brainwash you, and remember that it is a vice, you become an addict." Arlo added that in his recruitment, "It started with drugs and then you go a little deeper, and then they are blinding you, saying that you have to do this to move forward, that you have to do that to climb higher, that's how they guide you to go on that path." For some members of cliques who feel trapped once they are on the inside, there is a strong sense that their friends deceived them about what it meant to be a gang member while they were being recruited.

Income Generation

Congregations and cliques are both self-sustaining. They do not need, and usually do not receive, income from outside their neighborhoods. In fact, the reverse is usually true: a portion of the income received in local congregations and cliques has to be passed up to the national leadership. This empirical reality runs counter to conventional wisdom that assumes evangelicals (and to a lesser extent gangs) have been imported from the United States and continue to be funded by U.S. entities. Both types of organizations do see some of the personal remittance money that flows from the United States to family members in El Salvador. But for day-to-day operations, there simply are no organizational financial flows into local congregations or cliques. Both types of organizations are self-sustaining.

Evangelical congregations' income comes from members' tithes and offerings. In the United States, these terms are nearly synonymous. In El Salvador, giving a tithe, or 10 percent of one's income is the basic expectation, and perhaps obligation, for members. Offerings are viewed as more voluntary in nature. They are a series of one-off opportunities to give, usually for a specific item. If a congregation wants to add on to their building or if they have a ministry to support, for example, they take an offering to cover those expenses. The income from the tithe is usually dedicated to the pastor's salary and other fixed costs, hence the need for offerings if additional costs emerge.

Congregants in Las Palmas are mostly poor, and the tithes and offerings are modest: Templo Belen, for example, posts the previous week's offering on a small blackboard in the back of the church. The congregation of approximately forty attendees usually collects $60–$80 each week. This is not enough to cover the costs associated with Pastor Enzo's salar and building maintenance. So other ways to cover such costs are found. Like many pastors in Las Palmas, Enzo finds other employment. He was for a time cheerfully going door to door selling bread. (This allowed him to be in the community and do some pastoral work along his route.) Another pastor, Benjamin, was an electrician before becoming a pastor; he continues to do electrical work to supplement his income. Building maintenance costs are reduced through some members volunteering to do the work and other members offering the supplies needed. In these ways communities come together to keep the church afloat.

Cliques generate most of their income through extortion. Roughly 70 percent of all businesses in El Salvador pay gangs "rent" money (O'Toole 2017). Gangs extort businesses of all types, although buses have been a particular area of resistance and contestation. In an effort to impose their will on the national transportation system, gangs killed 692 bus drivers from 2011 to 2015 (Martinez and Lemus 2016). This provides some sense of the earnestness with which gangs approach rent collection.

Whereas collecting offerings in congregations has a ritualistic or worship component, rent collection is fairly businesslike. Levels of efficiency and professionalism vary widely from clique to clique. But well-run cliques explain to businesses that they are providing protection for their business, and that the business needs to pay them for their services.

Cliques ask lower ranking members or hire community members (often women) to collect rent money. These emissaries are paid well by community standards. If a business resists extortion, the women report this to their employers. In response, more diplomatic cliques send members to politely explain the gang policy and to clear up any misunderstanding that might exist. For these cliques, it is not until there are repeated cases of noncompliance that violence is used to enforce collection procedures.

Extortion is not the only source of income for gangs. Cliques also own businesses. In Las Palmas these are most visible in the downtown open-air market. The booths on one street have been taken over by the gangs, with MS-13 controlling one side and the 18th Street controlling the other. Drug sales within communities also serve as a revenue source. Extortion, however, remains the most important source of local income for most cliques in Las Palmas and around the country.

Internal Codes of Conduct and External Community Influence

Congregations and cliques both have codes of conduct for their members. For most evangelicals, ascetic norms are enforced through church discipline. Extramarital affairs, alcohol, drugs, and tobacco are almost uniformly prohibited by evangelicals in lower class neighborhoods (some upper-class evangelicals drink socially). There are consequences for violating these norms. If, for example, a church member is found to have gotten drunk, he or she will have a meeting with the pastor or the elders. Usually "privileges" in the church are revoked. This usually includes not being allowed to hold an office in the church and not being allowed to do any teaching. After a period of time, perhaps three to six months, the privileges will be restored. Punishments would likely be more severe and of longer duration for extramarital affairs or drug use. But regardless of the infraction, members are seldom asked to leave the congregation.

Beyond these widely practiced evangelical norms there are rules and regulations that differ from church to church. For some Pentecostal denominations, the reaction against Catholicism is still quite strong. Members are thus not permitted to enter a Catholic Church. This was the case for a Pentecostal woman whose Catholic uncle passed away. She was among a gaggle of women with Bibles and head coverings who waited outside the Catholic Church for the funeral to be over and then joined the rest of the procession as it went on to the cemetery. Some denominations also impose dress codes; one woman explained that when in church and other public settings, she could only wear skirts. These kinds of religious regulations are only enforced by the stricter sects within the larger evangelical movement.

Pastors have a different kind of authority beyond the congregation. Many pastors visit, pray for, and extend various forms of hospitality to any who live nearby, whether their neighbors attend their church or not. Such dynamics often make them loved and respected as they do "God's work" in their neighborhoods.

Cliques' leadership structures help them control the conduct of their members. The *palabrero*, or spokesman for the gang, is usually the leader. Longer serving and more distinguished gang members form an inner circle. A "team-first orientation" often prevails, even among leaders. For MS-13, "individuals who place themselves above the team are considered counterproductive, even traitorous, and must be disciplined" (Insight Crime & CLALS 2017).

Gangs prohibit specific behaviors and semi-formally adjudicate possible offenses. MS-13 members are, for example, prohibited from stealing from another gang member, raping women related to the gang, using crack cocaine, informing on the gang, and under most circumstances, leaving the gang. When these rules are broken, offenders sometimes must appear before the rest of the gang, more or less in a courtroom type of assembly. Sentences issued include fines, disciplinary beating, and in some cases, a death sentence (Insight Crime & CLALS 2017).

Beyond the formal rules and processes, youths just entering the gang recognize that in order to advance they have to perform their duties well. When Erik, a missionary, talks to young gang members and asks them what they want to do with their lives, the most frequent response he reported receiving is that they want to "take" or "obey orders." This implies a form of regimentation that youths accept within the gang structure.

Cliques also have influence in the broader community. Part of gangs' philosophy is that they protect the communities they control. They believe that they want what is best for their own neighborhoods (Insight Crime & CLALS 2017). Gangs have a reputation for allowing outside people and organizations into communities if they believe that there is genuine interest in helping residents. In some cases, gangs have even facilitated social programs. For these reasons, community members who are not affiliated with gangs sometimes approach local gang leadership when they find themselves in need of assistance. Gang leaders provide such assistance, at least in some cases.

National and Transnational Linkages

I began the previous section by claiming that congregations and cliques are fundamentally and authentically local. It is also the case that most congregations and cliques are tightly linked to transnational and national entities. Although they are rooted in their communities and act autonomously, their origins are elsewhere and their identities continue to be shaped and changed by the transnational organizations and movements of which they are part. Evangelicals and gangs share several transnational traits.

Franchises

Evangelical and gang organizations are both comparable to chain store franchises. That is, local entrepreneurs start and/or run a single unit of a larger chain of congregations or cliques.

Most congregations are part of denominations or other types of church networks. In El Salvador's biggest denomination, the Assemblies of God (AG), churches are "self-supporting, self-governing, and self-propagating" (Moody 2018), a long used and worldwide standard for church planters. But as independent as they are, AG congregations also conform to denominational norms, doctrines, and teachings, providing a shared transnational religious identity. Other advantages to denominational membership include legal coverage for buildings and land as well as access to various types of global resources. Not much of this encroaches on a congregation's day-to-day independence.

Denominational networks create fellowship, especially for leaders, at the regional, national, and global levels. I attended a quarterly AG meeting of about twenty pastors in Las Palmas and the surrounding rural areas. It was clear that the friendships in the room had been built and sustained over long periods of time. They discussed challenges in their ministries and their communities and prayed together. Some leaders discussed collaborative efforts between one or two nearby congregations. At the end of the meeting, they hugged each other and affirmed their attendance at the next meeting.

Denominations and other types of church networks allow Salvadoran congregations to participate in global flows of money, resources, and people. When Las Palmas experienced flooding, for example, an NGO connected to the Central American Mission (CAM) partnered with the local CAM church in disaster response. They channeled disaster supplies and conducted training sessions through the church and into the community. Short-term mission teams (STMs) are a particularly popular way to create linkages. Many STMs flow across borders and into El Salvador through denominational channels, but there are also numerous independent church-to-church linkages. Of the million or more North Americans who participate in STMs each year (Wuthnow 2009), thousands flow into El Salvador. STMs are now a global phenomenon, with El Salvador sending and receiving teams from places like Honduras, Nicaragua, Canada, Spain, and India. Other forms of facilitating church partnerships include creating joint Facebook pages and announcing formal "sister church" relationships. They all help to link local congregations into transnational society.

Gangs use a similar organizational strategy. The autonomy of local cliques needs to be emphasized: "The diffuse nature of the gang and its dynamic leadership structure make for a complex picture of the gang's day-to-day operation that varies greatly depending on the place where the gang operates" (InSight Crime & CLALS 2017). But participation in national and transnational gangs is important to cliques in multiple ways.

The MS-13S has a national leadership structure called a *ranfla* (which can be translated as "ruling council"). Most national leaders are incarcerated. They govern the gang by sending orders through leaders on the outside. The *ranfla* oversees programs, or groups of cliques. There may be six to eight cliques in a given program. Program leaders pass down key decisions to cliques that are made at the national level. An example of such a decision is when gangs decided to create a spike in the murder rate in March 2022, when sixty-two people were killed in twenty-four hours (El Faro English 2022a). It would be counter-productive and burdensome for national gang leaders to overly script the day-to-day dealings of local cliques, but somewhat evenly distributing the murder spike across the country showed that national leadership can create and enforce national level policies if they deem it useful or necessary.

Gangs have also developed transnational organizational structures. These help to connect cliques throughout the Western Hemisphere and in other locations around the world. For the MS-13, El Salvador's national gang leaders are also the international leaders. For example, Armando Melgar Diaz, known as "Blue," ran the East Coast Program, a series of cliques in the United States, while living in El Salvador. In 2020, Attorney General William Barr "accused Melgar Diaz of exercising influence over 13 states from El Salvador, including approving of murders," and labeled him a terrorist. Melgar Diaz helped to organize drug trafficking by MS-13 into the United

States and forced cliques in the country to send a percentage of their earnings back to El Salvador. In 2021, when Melgar Diaz was in a high security prison in El Salvador, the United States initiated an effort to extradite him so that he could face charges (Garcia 2021).

Personal Transnational Connections

Evangelicals and gangs also have countless personal transnational networks. I was sitting with a pastor and his friend under a thatched roof structure with no walls, enjoying the ocean breeze. We bought soft drinks and pupusas and gazed out at the waves.

The conversation turned to migration, and I was curious to know if *coyotes*, those who are paid to take people across the border, might be losing business to the immigrant caravans that had recently become popular. The pastor laughed and said no, and then called to Noemi, the cook. Noemi attended the pastor's congregation. The pastor explained to me as Noemi came over that Noemi's daughter, Ruth, had gone with a *coyote* to northern Mexico. She had paid the *coyote* $2,000 for her trip; it would have been an additional $6,000 for safe passage into the United States. Ariana's plan was to stay in Mexico for a time and wait for an opportunity to cross the border. Noemi expressed confidence that Ariana would eventually get there and was happy with the *coyote*'s price.

After Noemi went back to her grill, the pastor and Ronaldo began recounting the adventures of other people they know, mostly evangelicals, as they navigated the long route to the U.S. border. Some made it successfully, some were forced to return. Hundreds of evangelicals from Las Palmas and tens of thousands, perhaps hundreds of thousands, of Salvadoran evangelicals have taken this journey. Those who arrive in the United States maintain close contact with their families back home. They create vibrant, grassroots transnational connections.

Gang members also have personal transnational connections. A minority of these are generated by deportations from the United States of gang members and suspected gang members. Those who return remain embedded in the social relations they created when they were in the United States. "Blue," for example, spent most of his teenage years in Virginia before being deported back to El Salvador while in his early twenties (Garcia 2021). More often, gang members gain transnational connections in the same way that all Salvadorans gain such connections. Loved ones (often parents) live in the United States but proverbially keep one foot in El Salvador. They send their relatives in the gang money, call them regularly, and sometimes even visit. This is a standard part of social networks for Salvadorans; gang members are no different in this regard.

Conclusion

Gang and evangelical identities are largely forged in El Salvador's marginalized communities. The two groups are shaped by the same set of social realities and draw on the same pool of resources. It is thus unsurprising that the two groups have developed distinct but similar organizational strategies and structures.

I have highlighted such organizational similarities, but it is also important to emphasize the *inverted* nature of the two organizational images. Most community residents believe that churches stand for light and hope. Churches are perceived to be doing God's work in the community. Most community members also believe that gangs represent darker forces in the neighborhood. Gangs are perceived to be connected to violence, death, and sometimes Satan. Churches often trade in currencies of charity and love; gangs trade in currencies of fear and violence. In short, the two groups have sharply contrasting messages, activities, and attitudes.

Yet their similar social location and shared organizational tendencies bring them into extremely close contact. The multiple dimensions of vulnerability that afflict people in both organizations, the ways in which state and social systems have failed them, the possibilities of migration that play in their imaginations and the very real transnational connections that they both experience draw these two contrasting groups into a very tight orbit.

In fact, the two groups bleed into one another. How and why this occurs, and the implications of such dynamics, are explored in the following chapters.

2

Shared Cosmologies

Santiago is a twenty-four-year-old Salvadoran with an interesting life history. Santiago's mother left when he was an infant. His father and grandmother raised him, attending the local Assemblies of God church during Santiago's early childhood. Santiago fondly remembers going to Sunday School and being very involved in other children's ministries.

Santiago's father remarried when he was ten. "That's when all the problems started," said Santiago. His stepmother mistreated him. One day he "escaped" from her and started living in the streets. The first time Santiago stole was because he was hungry. "I remember a drunken guy told me to go ahead and steal a bag from an old lady. So I did it and this drunken guy gave me fifty cents. And I bought sour cream and tortillas." Santiago's father was extremely poor, so life in the streets was not terribly different in that respect. But stealing for food introduced a new layer of complexity into Santiago's conception of morality.

When Santiago was thirteen he moved to La Tutunichapa, one of the more violent neighborhoods in the capital city. Santiago did not join a gang, but to make a living, he sold drugs alongside gang members with whom he was friendly, and who believed that Santiago "was like us." Santiago also found a church he liked and regularly attended. For the next two years he became more involved in the street lifestyle and remained an active church attender. "There are many teenagers who do that," Santiago said. "The thing is that we have a need to find a refuge. And the only place that is a refuge is the church. It's always like that." In saying this, Santiago provides a redefined, street level understanding of the haven thesis.

At the age of sixteen, things became dangerous on the street for Santiago. He wanted to leave the lifestyle. Santiago stopped selling drugs and became active in a Christian organization that helps youth groups from El Salvador go on mission trips to other countries. Santiago became excited about going on a mission trip to Belize. Each of the youths had to raise $400 to participate, which the organization helped them to do by organizing bake sales and other

Blood Entanglements. Stephen Offutt, Oxford University Press. © Oxford University Press 2023.
DOI: 10.1093/oso/9780197587300.003.0003

fundraising events. Unfortunately, Santiago only raised $200, so he was not able to go on the trip.

This was a moment of particular insecurity in Santiago's life, and he felt angry, betrayed, and disappointed. "I thought I was trying to change and God was not supporting me. I got upset with God," said Santiago. "I literally threw my Bible away and I told God 'no—you did not want to support me when I wanted to change things for you . . . so no more.'" Santiago stopped going to church and went back to selling drugs. He soon ended up in prison.

When Santiago was sentenced, he declared himself to be close to the 18th Street gang. This determined the penal center to which he was assigned. Santiago believed the 18th Street gang-controlled penal center was his best option in part because he had relatives in the 18th Street gang. Although there was some pressure to join the gang when he arrived, membership remained voluntary. The 18th Street gang accepted him in their prison and he remained formally unaffiliated (although opposing gangs were unconvinced of this when he left prison).

Santiago remained angry at God the first two years he was in prison. "I started to do things against God, against the Bible," said Santiago. But then Santiago found himself in crisis. Some inmates were killed in his sector and he was moved to an isolation cell. The guards tried to pressure him into telling them what he knew. "I was tied up from my arms and my legs to the base of the bed. I didn't have a bathroom and I was only getting one meal a day. The guards would ask me who killed those guys and I didn't know and even if I did, I'd not say anything because I'd get killed." Santiago began to feel like there was no way out.

A Christian inmate was allowed to come speak to him from outside the isolation cell. He read a verse that Santiago still remembers: "Revelation 2:9—'I know thy works and tribulation and poverty (but thou art rich), and I know the blasphemy of them that say they are Jews and are not, but are the synagogue of Satan.' And God talked to my life in that moment. That was it for me." When Santiago got out of isolation, he became a Christian (again). Two months later he was baptized.

The third and fourth years Santiago was in prison he was active in his faith. He ministered to other inmates, hoping to facilitate an encounter with Jesus. In retrospect, Santiago said that God didn't let him go to Belize on the mission trip, but instead sent him to the penal center to do ministry there.

Santiago was released from prison and immediately got a job with a church that has a prison ministry. Life continued to be difficult: gang violence nearly claimed his life shortly after his release—his assumed affiliation with the 18th Street gang did not benefit him in that moment. But Santiago continues to view himself as a missionary, and he hopes that he can eventually serve God overseas. Santiago wants to go "to a place where you can't preach the gospel. A place in which, if they see me with a Bible they will want to murder me. Let's go there." Growing up in a culture of violence may have made such a desire more likely for Santiago.

Santiago's story shows how he and others like him traverse different groups within Salvadoran society. These groups are knit together by a shared cosmology that is characterized by binary ideas such as God and Satan, good and evil, and angels and demons. The cosmology is paralleled by human organizations, principally churches and gangs. Such groups are knit together within communities by what Peter Berger (1967) called primary and secondary plausibility structures. These include families as well as local social organizations, such as schools and churches, which are discussed in the following chapters. This chapter is dedicated to exploring the shared cosmology itself, the existence of which is the first hint that groups within communities are more integrated than the binary ideas it projects.

The chapter proceeds as follows. First, I provide a brief history of El Salvador's cosmology. Second, I describe the main features of the current cosmology, introducing the various supernatural actors and the different ways evangelicals and gang members approach relationships with them. Third, I use conversion as a lens to see the ways in which a shared cosmology helps to integrate the two groups. I then close with some summary observations.

History and Sources of El Salvador's Cosmology

Multiple religious, social, political, and economic factors have helped to shape El Salvador's cosmologies throughout history. In this section I touch, very briefly, on the most salient of these. The intent is to appropriately frame the firsthand accounts of religious worldviews in the sections that follow.

The narrative of El Salvador's cosmology necessarily stretches back to pre-Colombian times, when an ethnic group called the Pipil lived in what is now western El Salvador and eastern Guatemala. The Pipil were likely responsible for the creation of the Cotzumalhuapan civilization of the Terminal Classic period (800–1000 AD). They lived along the periphery of the Mayan empire and were subject to political and economic pressures from the Mayan power centers in the Mesoamerican highlands (Carmack, Gasco, & Gossen 2007; Coe 1999). But the Pipil spoke Nahuat, a language similar to that of the Aztecs. They were thus likely to have migrated from Mexico.

Much of everyday life for the Pipil was influenced by the supernatural. Archeological findings suggest that religious figures, such as the Wind God, the God of the Rising Sun, the Old Fire God, and Quetzalcoatl, or Feathered Serpent—all of which are also of Mexican or Aztecan origin—figured prominently in culture and social formation (Coe 1999). Reliefs show pods of cacao, probably the Pipil's most important crop, sprouting from the bodies of gods and men. A ball game was central to Pipil culture and part of religious ceremony; there are images of players wearing gloves that reach up to celestial deities. Death and human sacrifice are also prominent features of Pipil sculptures and ruins (Burkhart 1996; Coe 1999).

The Spanish arrived in El Salvador in 1524. By the mid-1500s, Franciscans were working among the Pipil. Dominicans, Augustinians, and later the Jesuits also became active in the region. Indigenous groups received the Christian message and often synthesized it with existing beliefs and practices (Burkhart 1996). Some Catholic orders encouraged this as they sought to understand how Christianity fit appropriately into existing Mesoamerican cultures. The consequent folk or popular Catholicism which emerged across Latin America was characterized by "occasional practice, heavy devotion to saints and shrines, and syncretism manifest in everything from the incorporation of pre conquest calendars or deities into Catholic devotions, the persistence of traditional beliefs about healing, and sporadic bouts of reform" (Levine 2009, 128). Popular Catholicism became the norm in the region.

There were some unique aspects of popular Catholicism in El Salvador. The Queen of Peace is a prominent example. In 1682 local merchants found a wood box in a stream and took it to the village of San Miguel. They opened the box to find a beautiful image of the Virgin Mary with the Christ child. Immediately, as the story goes, the fighting and bickering in San Miguel ceased. They therefore called the image the Virgin of Peace. Over a century later, in 1787, a volcanic eruption threatened to cover the town with lava. The townspeople brought out the image and prayed fervently. The lava changed course and the village was spared. These and other miracles prompted Pope Benedict XV to award the image the title of Queen of Peace in 1921. In 1966 it was named the primary patron of the Republic of El Salvador by Pope Paul VI (RFCatolica Radio Online 2015). The Queen of Peace is one of a number of figures that populate the "sacred canopy" of Salvadoran folk Catholicism.[1]

The mid- to late 1900s marked the beginning of the next major cosmological and religious transition: the move to religious pluralism. Daniel Levine perhaps best captures these dynamics. He describes Latin America's contemporary religious scene as "a blooming confusion of churches, chapels, street preachers, and television and radio evangelists competing for attention and vying for members and a share of public goods and public space" (2009, 123). Levine identifies early drivers of this new religious reality to be evangelical street preachers with Bibles in hand, who were "ordinary, often non-white, and barely lettered men using a popular language, who recall the circuit-riding preachers of nineteenth-century North America" (2009, 122). The street preacher Levine noticed in a Guatemalan square in 1968 was not greatly different from the Salvadoran street preacher in Las Palmas fifty years later that I referenced in the previous chapter. The difference in religious context, however, is vast because of the large numbers of evangelical institutions, organizations, and networks that sprang up in the intervening years.

Various streams of Catholicism remain influential in today's pluralistic environment. Liberation theology has dwindled but is still present. The Catholic Charismatic Renewal movement has grown apace. Popular Catholicism has lost some ground, as evangelicalism's "virgophobic" (Levine 2009) and anti-Saint Day stance has reduced popular practices in many communities. But it remains customary to see busts of Mary or Jesus in the back of a pickup truck traveling on the Salvadoran highways to a celebration in a remote village. This is especially so during Holy Week, when there are magnificent processions and floral street carpets in towns throughout El Salvador. Some of today's evangelicals are more open to viewing, if not participating, in such events, within which indigenous practices from pre-Colombian times are sometimes embedded (Burkhart 1996). Such moments perhaps most explicitly tie the various epochs of Salvadoran religious history together.

Two more items of Levine's (2009) analysis of contemporary Latin American religion are worth mentioning. The first is the deeper trends impacting religion, among them migration, democratization, expanded literacy, access to mass media, and reduced barriers to organization and public participation. Levine points out that such trends are likely to continue to open up the region to outside religious influences. They may be connected to Catholic laity choosing to be "Catholic in my own way," meaning that members select some Catholic beliefs and discard others. Such trends may also open space for minority religious groups, both international, like the Mormons, and regional, such as a group called the Israelites of the New Pact, which originated in Peru. Syncretic Pentecostal groups can also do quite well; the Universal Church of the Kingdom of God in Brazil combines local practices such as Umbanda with classical Pentecostal beliefs and practices. From a cosmological perspective, it is interesting to note that most or all of these trends embrace strong interactions with the supernatural and continue to be largely based around the general set of Judeo-Christian cosmological actors. They correspond with cosmological actors discussed by our interviewees, and which I lay out in the following section.

The second is Levine's attention to how violence has shaped religion in Latin America. Social agendas of churches and religious beliefs have been impacted: churches have become advocates for human rights in the region (especially the Catholic Church). Millennarian views are more popular in some particularly violent contexts. Violence also creates needs that churches have shown an aptitude for meeting. Refugees and internal migrants fleeing from violence, for example, often find churches that offer community and basic relief services in their new neighborhoods. Most specifically to the concerns of this book, Levine writes that "violence driven by gangs, drugs and crime . . . remain a central fact of the urban life of the poor. Opting out of this violence by opting into a new community of the saved has been understandably attractive to many" (2009, 138–139).

Violent actors sometimes explore a darker side of the region's cosmology, including the example of Santa Muerte, or Saint Death. Santa Muerte is a vibrant part of contemporary Mexican folk Catholicism, and her millions of followers can be found throughout the Americas and the world. Santa Muerte's origins may have links to Aztecan death deities.[2] She was a relatively minor figure until the beginning of the current century, when religious entrepreneurs began successfully promoting her. Andrew Chesnut (2018) emphasizes the multi-faceted nature of Santa Muerte: people from all walks of life depend on her to be, among other things, a love sorceress, money-maker, and miracle worker. The working class closely relate to her because they feel "she is like us" (2018, 3). Chesnut notes, however, that the media focuses on her connection to the Mexican underworld. They do so with some justification: Santa Muerte is a patron saint of gang members and drug traffickers. Family members of prominent leaders of the movement have been gunned down. People active in criminal activities offer candles, cocaine, crystal meth, and other black market goods to her shrine (Chesnut 2016, 2018). Santa Muerte's embodiment or connection to death is for some a fascination and a point of worship.

The Cosmology's Actors and Attributes

All of this sets the stage for a description of lower-class El Salvador's contemporary cosmology. My subjects did not talk about some of the specific historical cosmological figures mentioned in the previous section. But they did discuss relationships with supernatural beings such as God and Satan. They also talked about miracles, demon possession, and witchcraft. Gangs do not challenge this cosmology's basic framework. Rather, they work within it, often identifying and empathizing with forces of good *and* forces of evil. I provide examples and analysis of each in this section, beginning with the main actors.

God the Protagonist

God is the central actor in the lower-class Salvadoran cosmology. He is the Triune God of the Christian tradition. God the Father, God the Son, and the Holy Spirit were frequently referenced individually and together.

The evangelicals and gang members I talked to assigned specific attributes to the Christian God. Some attributes were mentioned by both groups, others were articulated by just one of the two groups (see Figure 2.1). Pedrita, for example, is an evangelical woman who had to flee her home during the civil war. She continues to live in a makeshift house that was intended as a temporary shelter when she first took up residence in the 1980s. Pedrita explained

Attributes of God

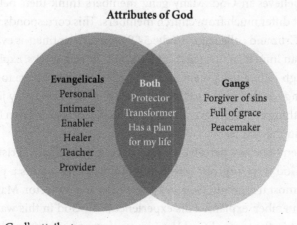

Evangelicals
Personal
Intimate
Enabler
Healer
Teacher
Provider

Both
Protector
Transformer
Has a plan
for my life

Gangs
Forgiver of sins
Full of grace
Peacemaker

Figure 2.1 God's attributes.

that "God is a personal God. You can tell him your most intimate secrets. He wants to share with you and give you instructions, but he does that in a very personal way." When asked to give an example of how this happens, Pedrita talked about interactions she has had with God in her prayer life, and said that "When I don't have anything, God touches people's hearts to help me." Direct communication with God and living in community thus allow Pedrita to experience an intimate God who is at work in her life.

Evangelicals highlighted other characteristics of God, including God as enabler, healer, teacher, and provider of basic goods (especially food). One can see some of these in the example of two sisters, Estela and Rosalie. Neither received a formal education, but their mother tried to teach both daughters how to sow. Estela had a gift for it; Rosalie did not. Rosalie eventually emigrated to the United States, where she has been able to get a wage earning job. Estela stayed in El Salvador. She has operated in the informal economy, earning money through sowing. "It is God who gives us our capabilities," Estela explained. "My sister was not given this ability by God. But if God did not give me [the ability to sow], my children would have suffered." In this example, God used Estela's mother to teach her a life skill she would need. God also ensured that the sister who "stayed behind" had the needed survival skill to do so.

Gang members, for their part, almost universally believe in God. In Cruz and colleagues' study (2017), 95.3 percent of gang members and ex-gang members reported that their relationship with God was important to them. Adrian, who runs a prison ministry, finds a similar reality among inmates. Adrian said that some gang members in prison may openly defy God, but everyone believes in God. Many gang members think their beliefs about God do not differ much from church members. This corresponds to another finding in Cruz and colleagues' study: 54.9 percent identified as evangelicals. Leonardo, an inmate in the penal center where Adrian works, explained that "even though I am a gang member it doesn't mean that I have to believe in satanic things or that I have to follow angels of evil, I personally just believe in God, nothing else. Whatever my faith is, it's in God." I return to Leonardo's story later in the chapter.

Gang members also perceive God to have specific characteristics. These include a God who forgives, who is full of grace, and who is a provider of peace. But most frequently, God was referred to as a protector. Matias, a current gang member, explained his experience with God in this way. "I know that I'm not in the ways of God but I know that he has always taken care of my life and is always up to protect me despite the mistakes of my life. I know that he is always by my side to protect me." Martin, an ex-gang member, remembers that when he was sent by his clique's leader to commit a crime, he would pray and ask God to bring him back unharmed. "We were going to commit the crime and when we came back I said, shoot! We asked God to do this for us. I felt vile and felt more away from him and tried to forget him." But Martin's perception of God as protector was shared by those who also went out with him. I explain in the following pages how this becomes complicated by simultaneous requests to the "Beast" for protection, but such requests do not negate gangs' understanding of God as protector.

Two widely shared understandings of God by evangelicals and gangs are that God can transform people and that he has a plan for everyone's life. God's transformational abilities are a key plank in the evangelical message and a central hope for many gang members who do not wish to spend the rest of their life in the gang. Pastor Berrios summarizes the evangelical position: "without Christ a person becomes a smoker, a drunk, a drug addict, a *marero* . . . the Holy Spirit restores him, changes him, and after being a degenerate he becomes an honest person, a normal person." Every Sunday in El Salvador, evangelicals stand up in churches across the country and provide testimonies of how God transformed their lives. They touch the themes mentioned by Berrios as well as many others. Many gang members concur, and even anticipate such a future change in their own lives. As one current gang member explained, "I have the conviction that I know that someday, maybe with faith, I can return to the way of God, nothing is discarded in this world. Everything is possible while we can believe in Him."

The idea that God has a plan or purpose for everyone's life is related to God's transformational power and is another point about God on which evangelicals and gangs agree. Pastors often reference Jeremiah 29:11 in sermons which reads, "I know the plans I have for you, declares the Lord. Plans to prosper you and not to harm you, plans to give you a hope and a future." Their parishioners take this verse to heart, and sometimes even hang it on their walls at home. Gang members hold on to this belief as well, sometimes with a hint of desperation. Juan reflected on the fact that he and his two brothers had lost themselves in the gang, but, he said, "It is already in God's plan, and God's plan is perfect. I thank God, we are here alive." Matias concurred, saying "I know [God] always has some purpose and all the things he has done in my life are for something good." Several Latin American scholars have noted the aspiration of lower-class youths to "become somebody" (see, for example, Kennedy 2014; Perlman 2010). There is often a belief among lower-class youth in Latin America that God will facilitate that self-realization.

Satan as the Antagonist

In the binary cosmology of lower-class El Salvador, Satan is the leading personification and orchestrator of evil. Gang members and former gang members described Satan in various ways. They reported that Satan or the Beast could control who would be released from prison. Satan could also entice, empower, and even command a gang member to do evil acts. And like God, Satan can be petitioned for protection, which is frequently done when gang members set out to commit a crime.

Some of the most vivid discussions of Satan came with ex-gang members who wanted to act as a corrective to a lack of commentary by current gang members. Emilio, a former gang member, for example, expressed surprise after one such focus group that interactions with Satan were relatively diminished in gang members' remarks:

> I saw how Satan moves in the gangs. I have always said it; the gangs are a work from Satan. They are totally influenced by the enemy. There's no other thing, it is a satanic influence. And this influence makes them murder, extort, and hurt people. So I did experience . . . the Satanism that moves in the gang. Everything comes from the Devil.

But Emilio also acknowledged that many gang members, even those committing crimes, try to stay away from spiritual activities associated with satanism.

It is conventional wisdom that the higher one climbs within a gang's structure the more likely one is to have a closer association with the Beast.[3] I was not able to prove (or disprove) such perceptions empirically. There is, however, evidence that violent crimes are necessary for promotion in the gang (InSight Crime & CLALS 2017), and the capacity to carry out higher volumes of violent crimes is often associated with dependence on the Beast (Martínez 2016). Arlo, an inmate and former gang member, stated that "There are many things people do in gangs, right, you steal, maybe you even have to take a life, things like that, you know, outside of God's path. That's how little by little you start saying you are moving forward, and you continue to climb the ladder, according to the world, according to the devil's blindness." Such reflections lend some support to conventional wisdom.

Satan's influence and touch can also be personal. Emilio stated that "there are many that pray to the Beast before committing crimes . . . they start getting more involved and they say that the enemy asks them for souls and they deliver souls. And then it gets to the point in which the enemy asks for family members, their parents, and children. . . . and that's where the problems come, because they have to kill their own parents, their children, and the satanic rite is more involved in everything." Although relationships with God and Satan can both be personal in this cosmology, the impact of relationships with the two different entities on the individual is obviously quite different.

Part of a relationship with Satan can include human death, sometimes in a ritual manner. Cristian, a young evangelical, lives in a ravine where the local clique has a "punishment house." Cristian explained that the area around the house is a clandestine cemetery, or a place where the gang buries people they have murdered. I visited Cristian in his house, and he pointed to the punishment house as well as the clandestine cemetery. Some nights, Cristian hears screams of people he believes are being killed, as well as other sounds that he associates with Satanic activity. He commented that he does not sleep well on these nights.

Cristian further explained that families of victims often learn where their loved ones are buried. Sometimes they come to conduct rituals associated with a Christian burial; sometimes they exhume the body so that they can bury it in a formal cemetery.

Like gangs, evangelicals also believe in Satan. They too associate violent crime with Satanic activity and believe that the deeper one goes in the gang, the more influenced by Satan the individual is likely to be. Cristian's pastor, for example, was present when I visited Cristian. He reinforced Cristian's account and added details about Satanic gang rituals. The pastor explained that gangs

> kill people and take their brains or hearts and give them to the Beast as an offering. The Devil asks for those violent deaths. In [specific communities] there have been very horrible homicides. Dismembered bodies have been found. They kill under the effect of drugs. Rites are heard in which the victims are being offered to the devil. We know that they have a pact with the devil, because of the barbaric way in which they act . . .

The perspective articulated by Cristian's pastor is the consensus among evangelical pastors in El Salvador. Pastors believe that Satan is active in El Salvador, and gangs are a primary agent of Satan's destructive and violent work in communities. Many pastors believe that they are engaged in spiritual warfare with Satan on a daily basis. The pastors I talked to unanimously believe that God is greater than Satan and will ultimately prevail. But many also fear Satan and believe that gang members can commit themselves to Satan such that they are beyond the reach of evangelical ministries. On the question of Satan's existence and how he manifests in the world, gang members and evangelicals are largely in agreement.

Supporting Cast: Angels, Demons, Witches (Performances of Miracles, Witchcraft)

The cosmic struggle going on in lower-class Salvadoran culture includes a strong supporting cast of both good and evil actors and events. On the good side of the ledger, miracles occur on a daily basis. These happen in all facets of life. Miracles that were reported by subjects in this study healed serious ailments, helped undocumented migrants find safe passage to the United States and helped them navigate the U.S. immigration court system, reconciled alienated family members and friends, and created success in the workplace. Such events were accompanied by dreams, prophecies, and sightings of angels. These kinds of events provide hope and wonder among people feel downtrodden for various reasons.

Healing miracles are the most ubiquitous type of miracles. The largest share of such miracles in this study resolved reproductive health concerns and children's illnesses. Ariana, a community member, recounted an experience she recently had with her son, Hector. Hector was dealing with concurrent maladies, one in his heart and the other in his testicle. Hector visited various doctors and was given "special medicine," according to Ariana, but to no avail. His condition worsened and he was admitted to the hospital. A few days later, Ariana was called to come to the hospital because, she said, Hector was dying. Their church convened an all-night prayer vigil. In the early morning hours, the pastor came to be with Hector and Ariana in the hospital. The pastor began praying for Hector, placing his hand on his head. Then, according to Ariana, Hector "felt an electric current going to his heart and his testicle." In that moment, he began to feel better. Hector eventually returned to full health.

In community-based focus groups, our team gathered together Catholics, non-Pentecostal evangelicals, Pentecostals, Mormons, and people who identified as non-religious. People freely discussed miracles they had experienced in these contexts, including deliverances from internal bleeding, serious arm injuries, troubles during childbirth, and near blindness. Importantly, none of those who participated articulated the idea miracles are not real. On the contrary, it was interesting to hear a participant who identified as non-religious explain that he not only believed miracles occurred, but that he could provide examples of miracles that had occurred in his own life. He proceeded to do so. Miracles are a taken for granted element of life in lower class El Salvador for evangelicals and non-evangelicals alike. Rather than forcing evangelicals to create their own life worlds, belief in miracles further integrates evangelicals into the mainstream Salvadoran cosmology.

The same holds true of the evangelical belief that demons and witches are active in the world. Such beliefs are nearly universal among Salvadoran evangelicals, although there are some differences between denominations regarding the level of vulnerability professing Christians have to demonic activity and witchcraft. A Church of God congregation, for example, teaches that followers of Jesus are shielded from demonic attack. Ana Rosinda, a life-long member of the church, reflected this teaching when she stated, "I don't think it is possible for [demons and witches] to give me problems since God is protecting me." Many churches and denominations in El Salvador agree with this teaching.

Sometimes, though, such doctrinal beliefs are not consistent with evangelical life experiences. Consider the story of Maya, who grew up in, and currently attends, a church that has the same teaching. Maya is thirty-eight years old and has been married to Javier for fifteen years. The two met while working in a funeral home. Now they own a small business that makes and sells tortas and sandwiches on the beach and at sporting events. Their income and education levels (Maya has a ninth-grade education) make them modestly more successful than many of their neighbors in this humble community.

Maya and Javier went through a traumatic spiritual ordeal several years ago. One Saturday night Maya was sick and in bed. Javier, who began to cry as he told his part of the story, was by her side, praying for her and "laying hands" on Maya's stomach: it was swollen such that she appeared to be pregnant (she was not). That is when Javier felt a demon in Maya for the first time.

The two got very little sleep that night, but Maya decided she needed to go to church the next morning. The congregation was already praying for her, she said, but when they heard what happened the night before they convened a special prayer meeting. Maya felt like there was something moving around in her stomach as they prayed. Then "something talked in me but it was not me." The voice of the demon, according to Maya, said "I want to talk to Javier." The pastor indicated to Javier that he should ask the demon what he wanted. The demon responded by laughing very loudly. So Javier told the demon that Maya's body did not belong to him: it belonged to Jesus. Javier then commanded the demon to leave Maya's body in Jesus' name. The demon laughed again and then became still.

This was the beginning of a week-long struggle with the demon. Maya went to the church each day and the church elders anointed her with oil. Maya reported that throughout the week she could feel the demon moving around in her stomach. On the seventh day, in the midst of the prayer meeting, Maya's body levitated. The church elders saw this and began to pray with even greater fervor. Maya's body stopped levitating. Javier and Maya said they then heard what sounded like a shot from far away, and Maya said she began to experience what felt like contractions. She believes in that moment that "through the Holy Spirit I was operated on, because I felt pain across my belly. And in that moment the demon came out."

Maya and Javier were clearly still shaken by these events even after several years had passed. I asked if they knew why the demon possessed Maya. They weren't sure, and they acknowledged the teaching in their church that followers of Jesus cannot be demon possessed because they are already covered by the blood of Christ. But they felt, regrettably, that somehow it worked differently for them. The couple have long suspected that witchcraft was at play. "There are people around here that are involved in witchcraft," said Javier. "We think maybe someone was trying to kill [Maya] with this." Since the exorcism, Maya's health has been good and there has been no recurrence of demonic activity.

Evangelical pastors and other leaders often shape ministry strategies in ways that reflect the presence of demons and witches in their cosmology. Erik, for example, reported praying about why his church had been successful in reaching one gang-controlled neighborhood but largely unsuccessful in reaching the neighborhood immediately next to it even as his church was strategically situated on the gang boundary (see Photo 2.1). Erik said that neighborhood was controlled by a different clique, and as he prayed, it occurred to him that a different demon or spirit oversees that neighborhood. Spiritual warfare in the form of prayer was needed to combat that spirit, as well as spirits in other nearby communities. So, Erik said, "we divided all the people [in the congregation into prayer groups] by communities and we believed in God taking down the spiritual walls that were there. And we really began to see success in the communities." Demons and witches are very clearly part of the evangelical cosmology.

Gang members in this study also had experiences with witches and demons. Many claimed that witches and demons can be detected visually. Humans who practice witchcraft can of course be seen. There are also spirits, for lack of a better word, that sometimes appear. One former inmate, for example, explained that in his prison many inmates told him about a witch who occasionally appeared. She looked like a dwarf and "lived" in an area near the bathrooms. The former inmate also said that others in the prison reported seeing a demonic manifestation in the form of a snake. The snake had the ability to come in and out of the prison. Not everyone in the prison saw these apparitions, but it seems that most believed that they were visible.

Many gang members further believe that humans who practice witch-craft or sorcery have unusual abilities. One of these is teleportation. Emilio

Photo 2.1 Church at a gang boundary (photo: David Torres Ayala).

recounted that a fellow prisoner, Andres, would go to a corner of the cell, curl up, and ask two fellow gang members to watch over him, as he was "going home." Emilio explained that Andres' "witchcraft was about leaving his body there but his soul would go to visit his family. When his soul would come back he would say [things like] 'well I found my wife and son doing this and that.'" Andres reported using teleportation to visit people he loved, but I heard stories of others who employed similar skill sets to exact revenge or commit other types of crimes. Martin, for example, explained that witches had the ability to kill a person outside the prison if the witch was given a personal belonging of the intended victim. Gang members, Martin reported, used this technique to kill girlfriends who were being unfaithful, and he knew of at least one attempt to kill a gang informant using this method. The attempt failed, according to Martin, not because the witch didn't possess such powers, but because the witch was unable to procure an article of the informant's clothing or other belonging through which the act could have been performed remotely.

Another sphere of these kinds of beliefs for gang members is that demons are manifested in modes of thought and behavior. As noted in the previous chapter, some gang members are drawn into gangs through enticements that include drugs, alcohol, and/or sex. Several intoned that the introduction of vices into their lives had a dark spiritual element that changed the way they thought and acted in life more generally. Matias explained that "if we . . . do evil, that is where the demons act. They may not act in a way that you can see. But rather they are in the mind and in the heart of a person." In this sense, many gang members believe the locus of demonic activity is in the psychological sphere. The effects can be severe, as mental health is affected. Matias, for example, reported dealing with demonic attacks that gave him suicidal thoughts.

While such narratives show witchcraft and demonic activity to clearly be part of gang culture, not every gang member engages in these activities. Miguel, for example, is a current gang member. He grew up in a Pentecostal church, where he heard a testimony of someone who had been a sorcerer but who had converted to Christianity. The ex-sorcerer recounted the kinds of activities in which he was involved when he gave his testimony, the impact of which stayed with Miguel even as he transitioned into gang life. As a result, he says, he avoids all forms of witchcraft and other similar activities to this day. Likewise Martin, an ex-gang member, told of some members of his clique who sought help from witches. But he gives thanks to God that he never went with them and remembers others in his clique who also stayed back. But both Miguel and Martin have no doubt that demons are real, and that witches and sorcerers wield considerable power.

Mobility within the Cosmology: Conversions

Conversions between churches and gangs, and vice versa, further help to reveal the shared cosmology of the two groups. The understanding of conversion in the haven thesis is that converts to evangelicalism come into a new cosmology, with a new set of beliefs and a new understanding of who God is and how to relate to him (Gooren 1999; Lindhart 2014). I argue that converts remain within the same cosmology; they simply switch or double up on allegiances.

Some examples may help to show how this works. In this section I revisit Santiago's story, which appears at the beginning of this chapter. I pair it with the examples of Miguel and Leonardo, both of whom were briefly referenced above. Together, these stories show some of the tragedy of how youths encounter obstacles to human flourishing within the context of the lower-class Salvadoran cosmology.

Miguel grew up in a strong evangelical home; his parents helped to pastor their church and he attended multiple services each week. But Miguel explained that as he grew, "my mind was changing and my body asked me for other things." Miguel joined the gang, an act which he understood to change his religious identity: he says he is not currently a Christian. Miguel did not, however, stop believing in God. When I asked what he currently thinks about God, Miguel said, "to be honest I'm with one foot on one side and one foot on the other because, just as I like it, I really don't like the street itself, but I like Christianity, but I feel I'm not ready maybe, I don't feel fit to be a Christian yet, but many times I do, you feel the call, but we 'harden our hearts'[4] [grimaces and chuckles]." For now, Miguel remains in the gang and in prison.

Leonardo's story is similar. He was raised by his mother and his older sister, who is an evangelical. Leonardo's sister regularly took him to church, for which he appears to remain grateful (his mother did not attend). As mentioned in an earlier section, Leonardo rather adamantly stated that he believes in God and that gang membership does not affect such beliefs. Given his strong position on this, I asked Leonardo how he was different from the person right next to him in the focus group who had recently left the gang to convert to evangelicalism. He paused to consider the question. Leonardo then explained that "I have not yet fully accepted; I have not given my heart to God . . . I think [God] exists because I've seen things he's done in other people and he's done in me too. All I need is to take that step, give my heart and soul to God completely. That's all I need." For Leonardo, this distinction seemed to be a rather fine-grained point, even though it was what kept him in the gang.

The life trajectories of Santiago, Miguel, and Leonardo share some important features. They all absorbed the evangelical cosmology in their early childhoods.[5] Their caretakers involved them in congregational life. As Santiago, Miguel, and Leonardo became older children, and still while they participated in their faith communities, each made a transition, for different reasons, to street or gang life—the process began for all three before their fourteenth birthday. Santiago, Miguel, and Leonardo then experienced first-hand some combination of the life altering impacts of engaging in violent crimes, abusing mind altering substances, having harmful sexual encounters, and other similar behaviors. The effect of these kinds of activities on people at such a young age is profound.

Through it all, the basic ideas about the identity and nature of God and other actors in their cosmology were not significantly challenged, and in some respects were reinforced. Miguel and Leonardo believed (to different degrees) that their status as Christians was suspended when they achieved the status of being gang members.[6] Santiago's story was a little different: because he did not formally join a gang, there was not a clear competing claim on his loyalties. He more easily held onto his Christian identity.

But in the lower-class world of evangelicals and gangs, claims on identity do not always determine beliefs, practices, and spiritual encounters. As gang members, Miguel and Leonardo attend and participate in evangelical worship services and other activities sponsored by the prison chaplain. Miguel and Leonardo pray to God and are prayed for by pastors and other spiritual leaders. In short, they continue to believe in, have discussions about, and attempt to communicate directly with the God they were taught about in their early childhoods. All of this is true even as they currently choose the gang as their primary allegiance, and thus categorize themselves, even if a bit reluctantly, as non-Christians.

Santiago eventually also rejected Christianity. His attempt to more closely affiliate with the church ended with the trauma of his exclusion from the mission trip. Santiago then left the church and discarded his Christian identity.

He was soon incarcerated. In the midst of these social network and identity transitions, Santiago did not stop believing in God, Satan, miracles, angels or demons. Rather, Santiago sought to change his relational location within his still taken-for-granted cosmology by distancing himself from God and the church.

Now, further on in their life narratives, the attitudes of the three young men toward God had developed different variations and commonalities. Santiago was frustrated and feeling rebellious: he began actively trying to offend God (he did not specify what actions he took in this regard). Miguel seemed full of regret and guilt about the path his life has taken. Leonardo essentially presented himself as an evangelical Christian. He only created a distinction when directly asked to do so. All three attitudes are common in the lower-class Salvadoran environment. The crucial similarity between Santiago, Miguel, and Leonardo, and one that is also broadly shared among similarly situated Salvadorans, is that they all believed God wanted them to return to him, to use the evangelical language that the three youths speak. This basic belief is often an important precondition in the gang-to-evangelical conversion phenomenon.

Miguel and Leonardo were at this point in their journeys when I talked to them. It may be that they eventually transitioned back out of the gang and into the church. If they did, such a transition could be permanent, but it could just as easily be temporary. Regarding the latter, gang re-entry for converts to evangelicalism can happen quickly: Adrian, a prison chaplain, explained that youths "let themselves be carried away by emotions, and they can accept [Christ] in that moment. If they have been carried away by emotions, when they go back to their circle and are under pressure again . . . they will revert back to their old life."[7] Or gang re-entry can happen weeks or months after a conversion experience, as economic or social pressures convince ex-gang members that the tools of survival offered by gangs have greater utility than those offered by churches. All of these pathways seem open to Miguel and Leonardo.

Santiago transitioned back to Christianity before I talked to him. I tracked his post-(re)conversion life over a three-year period. Santiago's return to the church appears to be permanent, which is also a common experience. After Adrian described conversions of gang members that don't last, he stated that "the opposite can also happen. They hear God's word, they believe it in their heart, and they actually convert . . . I'm telling you because I've seen it, and I see the difference [in their lives]." This experience is strongly supported by the extant literature (Brennman 2012; Cruz et al. 2017; Flores 2014; Wolseth 2011).

Some pastors have programs to make it more likely that youths will stay out of gangs. They attend to the psychosocial needs of exiting gang members through counseling and religious ritual. Churches sometimes use material developed by Alcoholics Anonymous or similar types of organizations in these efforts. Religious rituals are used by leaders to more solidly anchor converts in the church. These include having other church members gather to pray for new converts; those who pray often place their hands on the person for whom they are praying, physically reinforcing the relational and spiritual connections they are trying to make. As with all new members of the faith, pastors try to get gang members involved in ministries that allow them to engage in pro-social behavior. Eventually, former gang members are encouraged to be baptized and take communion. Such efforts assist (but are not foolproof) in permanently relocating gang members toward God within the Salvadoran cosmology.

On the other side of the spectrum, completely disingenuous conversions of gang members are on the rise. This has become commonplace enough that in some communities, pastors report that gangs no longer allow their members to leave the gang if they become evangelicals. As one pastor explained,

> Five years ago, when a "marero" wanted to leave the gangs, he spoke with his leader and the only reason needed to give them was to belong to an evangelical church, but under their supervision. For a while now, that is no longer allowed, because many of them have cheated, they have said they have become evangelicals only to disguise themselves and commit crimes again without the authorities suspecting them. They have gone to collect "rent," already being out of the gangs . . . For this reason, they have even been killed. Before, the authorities respected the "mareros" who became evangelical, but now they know that some "mareros" have the Bible in their hands when they go to ask for the "rent."

There are many incentives for gang members to fake conversions. One of these is that it enables gangs to infiltrate many other sectors of society, including the church. Another incentive for incarcerated gang members is that it can increase their chances at a commuted sentence. Adrian, the prison chaplain where I met Miguel and Leonardo, has learned to watch for signs of this in his ministry. Adrian believes that ultimate proof of conversion is when members of opposing gangs can work together in church ministries. This is one of the reasons that, once out of prison, Adrian's church seeks to bring former gang members from different gangs into close proximity with one another.

Finally, it is worth noting that evangelical youths in El Salvador do not have to join a gang to experience movement into and out of congregations. Many youths are pulled away from congregational settings by other attractions, only to return. One pastor explained the way this works in the coastal town of Las Palmas. "We are a tourist city. There is a lot of paganism, drugs, alcohol, and prostitution. . . . There are young people [in our congregation] who in a year reconcile up to seven times, because they do feel the need to seek God, but there is so much temptation here." This is another wrinkle in the entangled nature of evangelicalism with society: it isn't clear how such behavior patterns are distinct from many non-evangelical youths in San Diego.

Conclusion

Salvadoran evangelicalism exists within in a larger historical narrative. When evangelicalism emerged in El Salvador, it was simultaneously a rupture and a continuity of the existing religious cosmology and culture. The element of rupture can be seen in the way community members understand that conversion "is a bridge to a different life, a kind of forward-looking contract between the convert and the church (and its leaders)" (Levine 2009, 134). It is true that evangelicalism maintains its own faith distinctives and its own subcommunities within a pluralistic society. Such observations are empirically validated; they accurately portray part of Salvadoran reality.

However, the idea of continuity is often lost in descriptions of evangelicalism. It should be recovered. Evangelicalism's original success was also due to its ability to map onto the existing Salvadoran culture and worldview. It shared a logic of social organization with the Pipil culture (Bueno 2001), which is more fully explored in the chapter on local authority and competition. Evangelicalism also shared an overlapping set of cosmological actors with Catholicism: most of the Judeo-Christian actors appear in both Christian cosmologies. Evangelicalism found a foothold in El Salvador because of, not in spite of, these pre-existing cultural affinities.

Evangelicalism's contemporary social location is very different from those early historical moments. As prominent local culture producers, evangelicals now help to shape public perceptions of deities and other cosmological actors in communities. What helps to make this possible is the ongoing cultural resonance that evangelicalism has with other cultural products (even if tensions exist with other producers). These other products continue to emanate locally from the various expressions of Catholicism and an enduring, though subtle, indigenous cultural orientation.

Gangs share this partially evangelical, broader community cosmology. They too are strong local culture producers. But gangs operate on a different side of the same cosmology; they do not seek to create a new religion.[8] Thus, while differences in tone, emphasis, and religious practices may be promoted by elements within gangs, no major changes to the Judeo-Christian cosmology are seriously considered. This helps to explain why the vast majority of gang members state their enduring belief in God (Cruz et al. 2017).

Maya's experiences capture the shared cosmology well. Her interactions with a demon correspond with other accounts of demonic activity and witchcraft uncovered by this study. Some of these narratives came from evangelicals and others came from Catholics, who together recounted miraculous events and times when spirits disturbed their sleep, apparitions appeared, and illnesses were caused by or at least connected with spiritual activity. Other narratives referencing witchcraft and demons came from gang members and ex-gang members, who discussed various ways to use Ouija boards, demonic images on cell phones, and inmates asking witches to place spells on enemies or traitors. None of these stories contradicted a shared set of presuppositions about the supernatural; all of these understandings mesh well with the evangelical perspective in El Salvador on these issues.

Shared beliefs about transcendent beings are also what facilitate the ability of (particularly younger) Salvadorans to slide in and out of different positions within the cosmology, from gang to evangelical, and back again to gang, or vice versa. Instead of sliding back and forth, some try to maintain a double affiliation. With either strategy, Salvadorans can come to a point where, like Santiago, they make a more durable and decisive commitment. But even when this is the case, they do not lose belief that actors and practices in other parts of the cosmology are real and have power. Understanding these cosmological linkages is essential to understanding the linkages in corresponding human institutions.

The entanglement thesis intends to highlight evangelicalism's cultural continuity and the shared, community wide cosmologies. Such dynamics have implications for all sectors and institutions of society. The implications of evangelicalism's impact on society are poorly understood precisely because of the long-running assumption of evangelicalism's siloed orientation. This study focuses on the evangelical/gang relationship. But it does so by taking into account the presence of both in other social institutions. Families are among the most intimate of these. It is to those I now turn.

3

Complicated Family Networks

Families are the most basic and organic social system in lower-class Salvadoran neighborhoods, as they are in most societies. The way that families are structured helps to determine many aspects of Salvadoran culture. Families help to shape meaning in communities. They establish and reflect the local moral order. Families provide systems of communication and can form the basis of neighborhood power and authority. In short, families do much to determine what society looks like and how it is organized.[1]

Most of the relevant scholarship implies that evangelical families have effectively cut ties from other families in the community and function in very distinct ways from families in mainstream Latin American culture (Martin 1990). Authors argue that evangelicals endorse and often practice lifelong fidelity in marriage and create stable two-parent households (Brusco 1986). When scholars acknowledge family ties that stretch outside local faith communities, they are usually pointing to the opportunities for evangelicals to recruit relatives to the faith, especially women who help convert their partners and other men in their lives (Martin 1990; Steigenga & Smilde 1999). This narrative reflects what may have been more true at the beginning of the movement and what evangelicals themselves think *should* be true about their families. Sometimes these evangelical aspirations are realized.

But often they are not. The empirical reality of lower-class El Salvador is that most evangelical families are part and parcel of larger and very complicated community family systems. Many couples in lower-class Salvadoran neighborhoods never formally marry. Rather, they "accompany" each other for a time. They may have children while they are together, but often the relationship doesn't last. Both parties then find different partners with whom they may also have children. "Weak" nuclear family ties proliferate as a result, creating extensive social networks within and beyond communities, including transnationally. Santiago, for example, reported in an interview that he had nineteen siblings, counting children that both his mother and father had with other partners. Some of Santiago's siblings also now have partners who can also claim a family relation with Santiago, and whose own family

Blood Entanglements. Stephen Offutt, Oxford University Press. © Oxford University Press 2023.
DOI: 10.1093/oso/9780197587300.003.0004

networks, in a more remote sense, are part of Santiago's family networks. Santiago can leverage, and be leveraged by, all of these relationships in different ways and to different degrees.

In this chapter I explain the role family systems play in entangling evangelicals with the broader community and particularly with gangs. To do that, I present five findings concerning evangelical/gang interactions in extended family networks and analyze the (often fractured) family units within evangelical congregations. I then consider the social implications of how families are structured in lower-class Salvadoran neighborhoods and close with some ideas about how this changes our understanding of Latin American evangelicalism.

Evangelicals and Gangs in Family Systems

Family systems draw evangelicals and gang members into what are often intimate relationships. Five findings from my research nuance this claim: 1) evangelicals and gang members populate the same families; 2) evangelicals and gang members within the same families often find ways to support one another; 3) conflict can emerge between gang members and evangelicals within families; 4) children in evangelical households who grow up within a gang environment often become gang members; and 5) gang members often seek out evangelical organizations for help in raising their own children. These findings build on each other and are intended to tell part of the story of how, and the extent to which, evangelicals and gangs have become entangled.

The story of the Mendez family is woven into the points that follow. The Mendez family shows the complexities created by family relationships in contemporary El Salvador. To tease out the Salvadoran realities more fully, I buttress the Mendez example with other cases from my research. Some of these reinforce the "ideal type" that begins to emerge from the Mendez example, while others show different ways that elisions of identity and relationship between evangelicals and gang members occur.

Evangelicals and Gang Members Populate the Same Families

The Mendez family has lived in Las Palmas for generations. They witnessed the evangelical movement as it began to grow in the 1970s and 80s; some family members joined evangelical churches. El Salvador's contemporary gang system rose a decade or two later; once again, some of the Mendez family got involved. The Mendezes thus count within their family church members and pastors, gang members and leaders of local cliques, and family members who are caught betwixt and between. In this section I introduce four members of the Mendez family. I tell their stories with the intent of showing how family members live into different categories along the evangelical/gang spectrum, even as they maintain their family identity.

Ana is a member of the Mendez family, a life-long evangelical, and a leader in her church. You can see her part of the Mendez family tree in Figure 3.1, and her photo in Photo 3.1. Now in her mid-forties, Ana oversees the Sunday school program, serves on the leadership board, and often leads the singing during worship services. She engages in a church-related activity almost every day of the week.

Ana is also poor. She lives in a one room house with a porously covered patio. The roof and the walls are made of corrugated steel sheets, which amplify the heat in Las Palmas's already steamy environs. Seven relatives live with Ana, including her mother, two of her teenage daughters, her baby granddaughter, and two cousins. I heard some of Ana's story as I sat, sweating, just inside the door of her house on a 95-degree day. Although Ana pointed a small fan in my direction, it felt like it was well over 100 degrees.

Ana attends the Good Shepherd church, led by Pastor Enzo. Enzo and Ana grew up together in the Good Shepherd, which at that time was pastored by Enzo's father. Ana's father, a brick mason, was an elder in the church. Ana's mother, however, did not like the church. Although her father remained an elder at Good Shepherd, Ana's mother eventually took the rest of the family to a nearby Pentecostal congregation. When Ana was in her late teens, the pastor of that church raped her. Adriana, Ana's oldest daughter, was born as a result.

Ana never married after that, although she "accompanied" a man named Hector for a number of years. Hector and Ana had two daughters together. But Hector drank and occasionally became violent. Eventually the two separated but they still see each other. Hector comes to church occasionally, where I met him one Sunday morning, and where Ana hurled some friendly insults at him. He laughed good naturedly and somewhat shyly stayed in a gaggle of men on the other side of the room.

Alejandro is Ana's "nephew," although technically he is Ana's first cousin once removed. Alejandro is highlighted in Figure 3.1. His mother, Erica, is

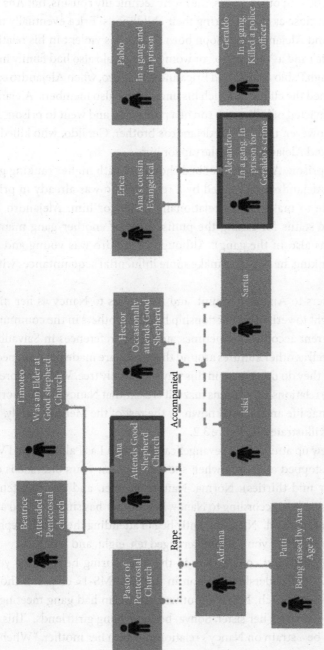

Ana and Alejandro's Part of the Mendez Family

Figure 3.1 Ana and Alejandro's section of the Mendez family (created by Thomas Hampton).

Genogram lines that appear in Figures 3.1–3.3 follow standard conventions as described by Hartman (1995)

an evangelical who grew up in the same neighborhood as Ana. The two were "cousin-sisters"—in other words, they were technically cousins, but Ana and Erica were as close as sisters during their childhoods. Erica eventually married Pablo, and Alejandro was soon born. Pablo was violent in his relationship with Erica and a "mujeriego," or womanizer. Pablo also had family in the gang. Although Pablo abandoned Erica and Alejandro, when Alejandro came of age he joined the clique in which his uncles were also members. Alejandro was then convicted of killing the son of a policeman and went to prison. Ana explained, however, that it was Alejandro's brother, Geraldo, who killed the policemen, and Alejandro took the rap for him.

While in prison, Alejandro rubbed shoulders with higher ranking gang leadership. Alejandro was helped by a relative who was already in prison and was able to make things relationally easier for him. Alejandro also gained some status for taking the punishment of another gang member (Geraldo was also in the gang). Although Alejandro was young and still quite low ranking, he began to make some influential acquaintances within the gang.

Nancy refers to Ana as her aunt, and Ana refers to Nancy as her niece. When I sought to verify this relationship by asking others in the community, I heard different accounts. Sometimes aunt/niece references in Salvadoran culture (as well as other cultures around the world) are made between people even though they do not appear in this way on a family tree. While the precise nature of the relationship remains fuzzy, it is clear that Nancy is an important person in Ana's life and is well known by the rest of the Mendez family. Her family tree is illustrated in Figure 3.2.

Nancy grew up attending an evangelical church in Las Palmas called Vino Nuevo. She stopped attending when she was thirteen years old (she is currently in her mid-thirties). Norma, Nancy's mother, and Nancy attended church together but, according to Nancy, her mother has since "turned away from the things of God." Nancy recently began attending the Good Shepherd church, with her three young daughters aged ten, eight, and four.

Nancy's brother and cousin were in the gang during her teenage years; her brother had a leadership position in the local MS-13 clique. Although Norma attended church, Nancy's brother and cousin had gang meetings in her house. Nancy and her sister, Sonya, became "gang girlfriends." This fact continues to be a strain on Nancy's relationship with her mother. "When my brother and my cousin had meetings in our house, she never stopped men from approaching us, on the contrary, she told them that they could use us as

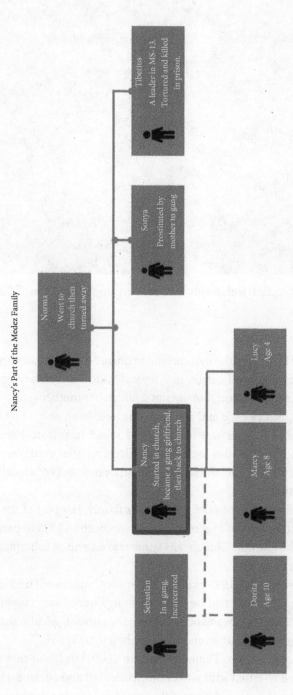

Figure 3.2 Nancy's part of the Mendez family (created by Thomas Hampton).

Photo 3.1 Evangelical with family members in gangs (photo: David Torres Ayala).

they pleased," Nancy recalled. According to Enzo, Norma actually prostituted Sonya in order to pay off a debt. In a separate interview, Nancy agreed that Sonya served as a prostitute, but did not confirm her mother's role.

Regardless, Nancy's life and relationships have been shaped by the gang lifestyle. Nancy's brother was tortured and killed in prison. Nancy's boyfriend and cousin were also incarcerated. These realities exist alongside the fact that Nancy is also known and cared about by members of a local evangelical congregation.

Jaime is a fourth member of the Mendez family. His part of the Mendez family tree can be seen in Figure 3.3. Jaime was born in 1975 to parents who were part of the Catholic Church. His father was an artisan fisherman, a trade that he taught to Jaime.

Jaime's father died in 1995 but his mother continues to sell seafood on the pier. Jaime remembered that he and his siblings were "were taught to go to mass. We were taught that we should pray to the saints. Logically, that was the teaching that our parents had and they taught it to us as well."

But Jaime converted to Pentecostalism in 2000. His life at that time was "a mess." Jaime wrestled with addictions to alcohol and cocaine. He started drinking at age fourteen; he was introduced to cocaine some years later.

Jaime's Part of the Mendez Family

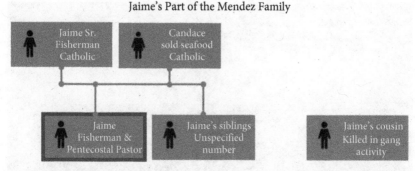

Figure 3.3 Jaime's part of the Mendez family (created by Thomas Hampton).

Jaime made some enemies during this time who subsequently tried to kill him. He also twice attempted suicide. Jaime said that "I was in a very difficult part of my life, in marriage, in family, in health, economically. Then it was on January 15 of the year 2000 when, um, Christ found me and rescued me from the life I was carrying."

Jaime was not recruited into a gang even when he was involved in illicit activities. This is partly a function of his age. Jaime was involved in that lifestyle in the 1990s, when gangs did not yet have a strong presence Las Palmas. Still, the Mendez family experienced its first gang-related tragedy in these years. Jaime relived that memory during our interview, saying that, "in the year '96, May 10th of '96, one of the first that died from the MS was my family. He was a cousin of mine, he was 16 years old . . . since he was younger, he respected me, I even talked to him, telling him to stay away from it, but one day he arrived with the two letters here [he points to his chest] . . . he was very young."

After Jaime's conversion, he began attending the Church of God. He had a radical life change; he shook off his multiple addictions and became drug and alcohol free. He continued to fish for a living and eventually became a leader in the church. In 2010, his pastor, Angel, chose to start a new church in the community, and Jaime served as his assistant pastor. Then in 2013 Angel emigrated to Guatemala and Jaime took over the duties of being the head pastor. You can see a photo of Jaime in Photo 3.2. Jaime continues in this role and the church has grown under his direction, although he continues to supplement his income through artisanal fishing.

Ana, Alejandro, Nancy, and Jaime are all in the same family. Ana and Jaime are highly committed to their respective churches. Alejandro is in prison

Photo 3.2 Evangelical pastor with family members in gangs (photo: David Torres Ayala).

and likely headed deeper into gang life and networks. Nancy is pulled in both directions. One can see through the Mendez example that community ecologies exert pressures on family systems, even as families stretch across religious and social divides.

Evangelicals and Gang Members Who Are Part of the Same Family Often Find Ways to Support One Another

Family systems that stretch across the evangelical/gang divide are constituted by different kinds of relational experiences. In some cases, family relations remain warm and supportive. Some examples can elucidate how this works.

In the Mendez family, Ana and Alejandro have always been close. Alejandro asked Ana to bring him clothes, food, toilet paper, and so on while he was in prison. She was happily doing so on a regular basis. In doing so, Ana joined countless evangelical women who tend to the needs of loved ones in prisons and jails across El Salvador. I saw this play out at the Las Palmas jail, where women, many of whom have their heads covered in the custom of conservative Pentecostal denominations, buy basic goods at a nearby shop

and stand in line in the afternoons for the police to register their goods outside the jail and then take them inside.

Jaime also speaks affectionately about his incarcerated family members,
and he believes the sentiment is reciprocated. He noted that "one [of
them] is serving 35 years of prison, and the other one is serving 10 years
of prison . . . but the respect that they have for us, with respect to us being
Christians, in the family, is very great." Perhaps in part because of his family
experiences and previous personal experiences, Jaime keeps himself open to
relationships with other gang members. I asked Jaime what would happen if
a gang member wanted to attend his church. "We are open," he replied. "Of
course we are. Because we believe that the church of Christ is the place they
can be transformed, with the help of God." Jaime is willing to engage in such
ministry even though, he explained, there are risks for the gang member
and for the church involved. Such risks are attached to the zone that they
are working in and the possibility that someone from another gang might
become aware of the relationships that they are forming. Still, Jaime recently
helped a youth leave the gang and join the ministry team of a church in a
nearby town.

The Rivera family provides further insights into how evangelicals and
gang members in the same family support one another. The Riveras live in a
one lane shanty town that grew up alongside an old railroad line. Their home
experienced an upgrade in 2015 when a U.S. missionary named Erik raised
funds for a housing project. Hoping to build relationships in the community
as well as to provide some much-needed shelter, Erik asked youths to help
in the construction of several homes. Carlos Rivera agreed to help, as did
his cousin and two of his best friends. All four youths were in the local gang,
and Erik was able to get to know them as they worked together to build the
modest, but still much improved, homes.

Carlos's local gang clique nonetheless remained active in gang activities.
Two years after the housing project, Erik took me to visit Carlos. Carlos's
aforementioned cousin and two best friends had recently been arrested for
burying a young woman alive. Carlos was rumored to have participated in
a separate murder. Carlos's brother was in the midst of serving a thirty-year
prison sentence (which began before the housing project), and his sister had
been released from juvenile prison the day before my visit. Several months
before our conversation, Carlos had made the mistake of going into an opposing gang's territory. In reprisal, the opposing gang cut off his left hand and
the thumb on his right hand. Carlos thus embodies the violence that marks

contemporary Salvadoran gang life, and many of his closest family relations are deeply connected to gang life and activities.

Several members of the Rivera family also go to church. Carlos's mom, Ana Louisa, was regularly attending Erik's church, which is just a mile or so outside the shantytown, at the time of my visit. She was in a small group Bible study which consisted of women with whom she said she had a lot of *confianza*, or trust. Carlos's niece, Isabella, was enrolled in the Christian elementary school that Erik started and participated in the dance worship team at the church. According to Erik, Isabella is thriving in the school and church environment, and is one of the best students in her class. Carlos himself occasionally attends Erik's church—he came impeccably dressed to one service I attended. Erik reported Carlos had even prayed to give his life over to Christ. Seven months later, Erik related that Carlos had come to an evening church service, where "he told me, crying, that he wants to leave the lifestyle. There are so many problems and sometimes he feels like taking his life." But Carlos has remained in the gang. His family networks root him firmly in both church and gang relationships.

The support that runs in both directions between Carlos, Ana Louisa, Isabella, and others in the family is obvious. If Carlos were to leave the gang, his mother would likely support his decision. She knows first-hand that gang life can take her children away from her. But meanwhile, Carlos appears to be loved and trusted by everyone in his home, including his mother. Being in the gang brings protection, income, and status to a family that experiences multiple dimensions of vulnerability—Carlos's amputated hand is a constant reminder of the implications of that vulnerability. Just as Ana Louisa's church and Isabella's Christian school are part of her context, so too is Carlos's clique. It is part of how the world works. Ana Louisa will continue to love, support, and care for her son. Although it is many other things, being part of the gang is also a way that Carlos loves, supports, and cares for her.

Other evangelicals showed a deep respect for actions or complicated choices made by family members who were in a gang. In one example, a small child in a church-based ministry loved his uncle, who was in the gang. He proudly talked of his uncle being his "hero" at the church, according to the pastor. Then the uncle was killed in gang related violence, and the child was devastated by his loss. In a second example, the leader of an evangelical NGO reported a conversation with a youth in a partnering church. The youth has a brother who is a gang member, and he was asked how he perceived his brother. "He is my hero," the youth said. Surprised, the conversation partner asked why. "Because I grew up in an abusive home," he said. "My father stopped beating my mother the day that my brother joined the gang." This hints at not just the complex motives for joining a gang, but also ways in which intra family violence can create alliances between evangelical and gang member siblings against a common enemy or problem.

Conflict Can Emerge between Gang Members and Evangelicals within Families

Inasmuch as support runs between gang and evangelical family members, significant problems can also arise within such families. While this is true of almost all families, the structure of lower-class Salvadoran family systems and the religious and gang identities that circulate within them create distinct ways in which conflict is played out.

The Mendez family provides two points of reference. The first is a conflict that centers around Alejandro, Ana, and Alejandro's uncles. The latter are not part of the Mendez family but are related to the Mendezes through Alejandro and his parents. Alejandro's uncles live about 100 yards away from Ana, in the same community. They sell drugs in the area and wanted Alejandro to use his access to the gang leaders in prison to facilitate their business interests. Alejandro, however, was unhappy with his uncles. He felt that they had not helped him at the time of his trial, and now they were just trying to use him. So he refused, which made his uncles angry.

It was during this time that Ana was bringing basic hygiene items to Alejandro in prison. Alejandro's uncles noticed and told Ana to stop helping Alejandro. But Ana felt a loyalty to Alejandro, so she continued with her visits.

Alejandro's uncles believed Ana was openly defying them. They threatened her and told her to leave the community. (They also threatened to harm her pastor, an indication of the importance of church in Ana's life.) For Ana, leaving the community was not easy. She could stay out of the community for a few days at a time, but her economic and family realities created significant obstacles to a permanent move. She recognized the risk of staying but was also irritated that she had been ordered to leave; she decided to continue to live in her home and to continue to take basic hygiene items to Alejandro.

The situation escalated. Alejandro's uncles threatened to kill Ana's daughters. Ana began to pay the local clique money so that she could continue to live in the community. A clique member entered Ana's house and took her phone to see if she had made any calls to the police. Ana had not taken that chance; in any event, it was not at all clear to her that the police could improve her situation. It seemed that the gang was increasingly angry with Ana, and she wondered if there were problems that extended beyond her relationship with Alejandro. She could not be certain. Ana finally stopped helping Alejandro, hoping this would alleviate some of the pressure that was taking a toll on her well-being.

Pastor Enzo and others in the congregation were aware of Ana's predicament. Enzo took me to visit Ana in her home, but when we arrived at the community and phoned ahead, Ana explained we would be at risk if we tried to enter. Although the gang tracked her movements, Ana was permitted to leave the neighborhood. We met her in a nearby shopping plaza. Pastor Enzo encouraged Ana to continue to pray and stated that God would show her a way out of her problem.

A way out did eventually present itself. Following through on advice from a neighbor, Ana made an appointment with a gang leader with a higher rank in the gang than Alejandro's uncles. He lived in a neighboring community. Ana hoped to demonstrate that the source of her problems was that she was actually helping a gang member (Alejandro). Ana hoped that the leader would look favorably on her actions and order a reprieve.

We learned the next day that Ana's visit was a success. The *palabrero*, or gang spokesman/leader, viewed Ana's assistance to Alejandro favorably. He told her that if she was helping one member of the gang, then she was helping the whole gang. The leader said that the gang would no longer bother her or her children. He informed the clique in Ana's neighborhood of this immediately.

That night at prayer meeting, Ana got up and radiantly shared that God had faithfully delivered her from the problems that she was having in her community. The fifteen or so people in attendance knew Ana's story and celebrated with her. It was interesting to hear Ana explicitly say it was God who had solved her problems; perhaps she felt that God had worked through the *palabrero* to bring the crisis to an end.

A second conflict within the Mendez family is related to the first but highlights the relationship between Ana and Nancy. It came to light that during the conflict, the gang was willing to pay for information about Ana. Nancy would occasionally make up lies about Ana so that she could earn money from the gang. This in turn made Ana's life more difficult.

Ana confronted Nancy when she learned what had been happening. Nancy confessed. Angry at first, Ana soon switched tactics and tried to draw Nancy into attending her church. This was a natural decision for Ana, who regularly asks people to come to church with her. Ana felt that her family relationships would improve if Nancy left the "things of the world" behind and allowed Christ to change her life. Nancy, having some knowledge of the faith from her childhood and being in the midst of some other difficulties in her life, agreed. She began attending regularly with her children and the pastor even trusted her with a "cargo," or a responsibility, in the church.

About a year later, Nancy stopped attending church. In the midst of a life of poverty and abuse, Nancy's personality had developed some hard edges. There was some friction between Nancy and another church member, who possibly had a similar life story and similar personality traits. Nancy resumed some of her previous illicit activities in the community, according to the pastor, who also said Nancy could come back to the church any time she wished. But at that moment, Nancy was not interested.

Children in Evangelical Households Who Grow Up within a Gang Environment Often Become Gang Members

Lower-class Salvadoran communities bring youths together from all social categories: evangelicals, Catholics, gang members, and so on. Teens get to know each other in classroom contexts, in places of work, and in the neighborhood. Thus, in gang-controlled communities, nearly everyone is touched in some way by the gang element of the youth culture. Many young people become curious about gangs even if they are not ready to join. An option for such youths is that they can become "affiliated" with a gang, or become a gang "sympathizer." This usually involves more friendly relationships with gang members and helping the gang out in little and usually informal ways. Without full gang membership, such youths can also be fully involved in churches or other parts of the community. They thus help to extend the gang's range of influence and facilitate social networks across social divides, including between gang and church.

The way such dynamics can impact children in evangelical homes can be seen in the story of Adriana Mendez, Ana's oldest daughter. Adriana was an outgoing teenager when I met her. She was very active in the church youth group and, like her mother, on very good terms with the pastor and his family. Adriana also had extensive social networks in school and the community. It is not surprising, and perhaps almost inevitable, that she knew gang sympathizers and members, keeping in mind that she has family members who are themselves gang members. Being socially situated in this way is fairly typical for an evangelical youth in a lower-class Salvadoran neighborhood.

Things became more complicated when Adriana started dating Ronaldo, a classmate who lived in an adjacent neighborhood. Ronaldo attended a Pentecostal church. He was also perceived as being sympathetic to the 18th Street clique that controlled his community. This romantic relationship generated a response from some classmates who were also members of the MS-13 clique that controlled Adriana's neighborhood. Adriana showed me texts she received from them: mixed into what looked like normal teenage banter and teasing, the texts had more serious lines telling her to stay out of the city center. Because Ronaldo was not formally a gang member, she hoped this would pass over.

Adriana's relationship with Ronaldo got more serious. She became pregnant with Ronaldo's child. Ronaldo had no interest in the child and disappeared from the scene, but Adriana had been drawn into the circle of friends in his community. This created questions about her own relationship with the 18th Street clique in that neighborhood (was she a gang sympathizer?) and seriously compromised her relationship with MS-13 in her own neighborhood.

Adriana dropped out of high school, had her baby, and then started attending a different school about an hour away. MS-13 did not allow her to continue in her original school. Adriana finished high school while continuing to feel pressure from MS-13. She moved to another town, also about an hour away, but she left her baby with Ana to raise. MS-13 did not permit Adriana to re-enter her old neighborhood, and Adriana did not see her baby for the next three years. She did find a job, began to "accompany" a new boyfriend, and found a new church. Her life stabilized. (Ana, however, continued to raise the child.) Ana was happy for Adriana, commenting that Adriana had fallen into the wrong circle of friends while she lived in Las Palmas, and she had done a good job of making a fresh start.

Adriana never entered a gang herself, but her story makes it easier to see why children raised in evangelical homes and churches comprise such a large share of the gang population. How large a share is a matter of speculation. Paul Glader (2015) cites Salvadoran journalists and pastors (and stated that none of the above could provide a source for the statistic) as saying up to 60 percent of gang members come from evangelical backgrounds. In my research I heard estimates ranging from 40 percent to 70 percent. Precise numbers may never be available, but evangelical households clearly produce gang members with remarkable frequency. That is partly because the journey from evangelical home to gang member is a short one (metaphorically and literally) and is embedded within the context of (often lifelong) community relationships.

Evangelical parents and guardians display a wide variation of attitudes about their children entering the gang. Some try to do whatever they can to keep their children out of the gang. For example, Juan and his brothers were raised by his grandmother, a devout evangelical. The grandmother saw that her grandsons were becoming friendly with MS-13 members in the rough urban neighborhood where she lived. This frightened her, so with her limited resources she undertook the arduous step of moving them to a neighborhood across the city and into an opposing gang's territory. Much to their grandmother's dismay, this only changed the trajectory of Juan and his two brothers from "letters" to "numbers"; it was not long before they became members of the 18th Street gang.

Sometimes the panic and desperation are greatest among pastors who worry that their own children will enter a gang. A senior manager of an evangelical NGO recounted a conference he attended for pastors with gang ministries. He spoke of one pastor who had ministered extensively to gangs. But in the conference this pastor was "just in tears [as he] shared how his son got recruited into the gangs, and how devastating that was for him. And just the efforts [he had made] to avoid that . . . and so the guy is out there in the fight, but in the end, his son got recruited."

I also spoke with gang members and ex-gang members whose parents were pastors or in leadership positions in churches. Emilio is a former inmate and ex-gang member. "My dad was a preacher of the Word of God," he recounted. "My mom was always involved in the things of the church. They always instilled in us Christian values." Emilio remembered the trauma, particularly of his mother, when she began to realize that Emilio was engaging in gang activity. One night after being out with the gang, Emilio related, "I came home and I was drunk. My mom and siblings got together and prayed for me.

I remember my mom's words, she said 'Lord I cannot do anything else with him, I lift him up to you and ask you to do what you want with him.'" Miguel, introduced in the previous chapter, is a current gang member and inmate. He told me that his parents were co-pastors of his church and his brothers also helped with church programs—it is "practically a family church," he said. "I used to go to the services, attend Sunday School classes . . . ." He knew his family felt that his decision to enter a gang was anathema to their aspirations for his future.

But other evangelical parents and guardians permit or even openly support the gang activities of their children. This is partly explained by the simple reality that parents breathe the same social air as their children. They too have social networks that include gang members and sympathizers. The parents see their community for what it is, and are realistic about the options in front of their children. This is the reality even for dedicated and lifelong evangelicals. Ana, for example, was concerned when Adriana's relationships drew her closer to the gang, but she was neither surprised nor did she take active steps to limit Adriana's social life. This could be because, from Ana's perspective, this is what social life looks like in El Salvador, and it is no different than the current reality of Ana's own family. It is perhaps even more true for parents who have only recently begun to explore their evangelical identity. Ana Louisa Rivera did not mention seeking to restrict Carlos or her other children from gang activity in any significant way. This continued to be the case as she found her way into a congregation and a Bible study group. Even if she were able to do so, which is not likely, there are no indications that Ana Louisa was attempting to withdraw herself or her children from those networks.

Woven into these underlying social realities are the economic and perceived security benefits that can accrue to families of gang members. As one pastor explained, "I am ashamed to say it, but some mothers and fathers, although they claim to be evangelical, are glad that their gang-member children bring money from the rent to their homes. They say, 'how good is this, I don't work and this boy keeps us, this is a blessing.'" Feelings of power and security also often accrue to parents or guardians of a gang member. It is worth remembering that evangelicals live in vulnerable contexts who are naturally drawn to feelings of security. Thus, the conveyance of otherwise unattainable economic and perceived security benefits keeps many evangelical parents open to gang membership for their children. A significant portion of evangelical parents may be swayed by such incentives.

Gang Members Often Seek Out Evangelical Organizations for Help in Raising Their Own Children

Just as there is a contingent of evangelical parents who are pleased when their children enter gangs, there are parents who are in gangs but who do not want their children in the gang. Gang members' interest in raising their children in evangelical organizations provides a reverse perspective into the intimacy and overlap that evangelicals and gang members experience in communities.

Several pastors reported efforts by gang members to bring their children into church programs. One such pastor reported a conversation he had with gang members, in which he encouraged them to leave the gang. He reported that the gang members replied: "No, pastor, we can't free ourselves of this . . . but . . . do us a favor. Help our children to not go through this hell." The pastor works with an NGO to provide extensive programming for children in his church. He brings gang members' children into these programs and maintains an ongoing dialogue with the parents in the gang.

The logic articulated in the gang members' response to the pastor offers another insight into how gang members often perceive themselves. As explained in the previous chapter, many gang members understand themselves to have chosen the path of darkness or of Satan. Many have personal regrets about the choices they have made, and they want their own children to make different choices. Erik, the missionary who has built the relationship with the Riveras, taps into this logic as he works with gang members. One afternoon I was walking with him as he was handing out flyers for a children's Bible School in the Riveras' neighborhood. We happened upon some of the members of Carlos's clique. After exchanging pleasantries with them, Erik asked them to give the flyers to their younger siblings and reminded them that they don't want their siblings to turn out like them. The gang members willingly took the flyers and nodded in assent. It remains true, however, that children of gang members who attend programs in evangelical institutions sometimes still join the gang.

Nuclear Family Units in Evangelical Congregations

In describing the intersections of families, evangelicals, and gangs, I use a frame of analysis that takes broader family systems into account. This approach shows that most extended families with evangelical members look different than the way scholars have described nuclear family units that constitute evangelical congregations. (As noted earlier, scholars usually depict such families as two-parent households that are largely separated from "worldly" culture.) The data I have presented is in some respect complementary, rather than contradictory, to the established paradigm.

However, the data I collected on family units within congregations also presents a different picture. Most such families were single-parent households, often headed by women who became mothers in their teenage years. A diverse number of congregational and family factors account for such dynamics. Those that deserve a closer look include the attraction congregations have for single mothers as well as the ways in which evangelical women experience domestic abuse, infidelity, and emigration.

Evangelical churches in Latin America have long been effective at drawing single, often teenage mothers into their congregations. Contrary to the popular myth of the "judgmental evangelical," such mothers often experience the warmth of community when they enter a congregational environment, and their children often benefit from supportive programming and relationships. Such families are not, however, able to simply drop all the risks that accompany impoverished, one-parent households. They remain exposed to many of the same social problems that make them vulnerable outside of their faith communities. The gang, after all, still likely controls their neighborhood.

Sometimes evangelical women show the agency necessary to separate themselves from abusive relationships. Consider Raquel, who is in her mid-thirties and attends church with Ana at the Good Shepherd. Raquel had a conflictive relationship with her husband even as they had three children together. She eventually decided to leave him. In reflecting on that decision, Raquel said, "My husband was no longer for me . . . God gave me the strength to move on." Nina, now in her fifties, has a similar story. Her partner, Elmer, physically abused her. Several years ago, Nina decided she had had enough and moved out. Since then, she has lived a few doors down from her old house, where sometimes her grown children stay with her.

Migration further helps to pattern many family units within congregations. Stephania is an evangelical who lives in a rural area outside of Las Palmas. Her husband emigrated to the United States seventeen years ago, and she has not seen him since. He sends her money to support their son, who at the age of twenty was preparing to migrate to the United States as well. Stephania knows the trip will be dangerous, but, she said, "God will help him." Migration has thus played a primary role in creating Stephania's family dynamics.

In addition to single mothers who are coming into congregations, some evangelical men and women do not conform to the evangelical marriage ideal; they continue to have children with multiple partners after they become evangelicals. This has a generational effect within the church: some children who grow up in evangelical homes replicate this way of doing family when they are adults. Although there are evangelicals who do stay with one partner and create stable two-parent households, others perpetuate the standard approach to family networks that can be found in lower-class Salvadoran neighborhoods.

Pastor Enzo's own family serves as an example. Enzo and his wife, Dinora, come from two-parent evangelical families. Three of Dinora's brothers are pastors or missionaries. I met pastor Enzo when his third child, a daughter named Gracia, was a cheerful but shy eight-year-old. When Gracia was sixteen, she and her boyfriend became pregnant. Pastor Enzo and his wife were devastated. Dinora, the pastor's wife, briefly considered kicking Gracia out of the house. Enzo informed the leaders of his denomination, who said that because of the pregnancy, his own position needed to be reaffirmed by having the congregation vote on whether or not he should continue as pastor. The congregation did so, overwhelmingly. It appears that Gracia and her boyfriend are, for now, going to stay together. But it is important to keep in mind that two-parent evangelical households are not always replicated by the children that grow up in them.

The Social Implications of Lower-Class Salvadoran Family Systems

Families simultaneously serve as social glue and as the source of serious social problems in lower-class El Salvador. This matters to evangelicals because, as the data in the previous two sections has shown, the identity created by family systems helps to create evangelical identity within this context.

Families as Social Glue

The families in this study are not structured conventionally. Nonetheless, they serve as the most basic social networks in communities. Some of the most basic family ties are still important, including parent–child and sibling

Table 3.1 References to family relations in Families Code Group

Number of references to parents	242
Number of references to children	92
Number of references to siblings	53
Number of references to spouses	35
Number of references to grandparents	35
Number of references to extended family	35

relationships. This is true even if children do not grow up in a home with their parents.

References to specific family relations in the Families Code Group,[2] which was created from the data for this study, is revealing. As seen in Table 3.1, references to parents were far more frequent (242) than to any other familial tie. Not surprisingly, mothers were mentioned more than any other specific family member (ninety-six specific references to mother, ninety-two references to father, and fifty-four additional references to parents in general). This is particularly interesting given that no one under the age of eighteen was interviewed in this study, although life narratives of adults frequently began with discussions of events that happened during childhood. One pastor involved in prison ministries commented on the respect gang members have for their mothers: "they always respect their mother. It is curious that they . . . have a tattoo of her, or they always talk about her as someone highly respected, someone who can put them in, let's say, their place, or someone they can listen to for advice." Mothers were the central family figure in this study.

The second most frequently referenced family relation was to one's children (ninety-six times). This was followed by references to siblings (fifty-three times). Spouses, grandparents, and extended family members (a combined total of aunts, uncles, cousins, nieces, and nephews) were all referenced considerably less (thirty-five times each). Interviewers seldom asked direct questions about a specific family relationship; these terms mostly emerged organically as interviewees shared about their lives. All references were counted; it did not matter if they were positive, negative, or indifferent in nature.

Although claims made from this data analysis must remain modest, the data serve as another indication of the way that meaning is distributed within families. It points to a diminished role for spousal relationships. It

Table 3.2 References to family relations by gender

Number of explicit references to female family members	215
Number of explicit references to male family members	183

shows an emphasis on maternal relationships, with grandmothers, but not grandfathers, playing a strongly supportive role (thirty-three references to grandmothers and only two references to grandfathers). Women were more prominent in discussions about families in general: Table 3.2 shows how many more times women were specifically referenced than men in the Families Code Group (215 to 183). It seems that the older men get, the more absent they are in the data—brothers were actually referenced far more than sisters in this group, and mothers were only mentioned four more times than fathers (absent general references to parents). Mario Vega, pastor of Elim, a Salvadoran megachurch, agreed with other social commentators when he stated from the pulpit that El Salvador has become a matriarchal society that is still marred by machismo. The discursive analysis of the Families Code Group supports such a claim even as it affirms the tremendous importance and meaning that families possess. The family in lower-class Latin America is still "the main space for the reproduction of social order: it is the place *par excellence* for the accumulation of economic, social, and cultural resources as well as for the transmission of these elements across generations" (Ulmann, Maldonado, & Nieves 2014, 125).

Families as the Source of Social Problems

Social problems arise from family systems that are constituted in this way.[3] Representatives that I talked to from multiple social institutions, including NGOs, schools, and health clinics, viewed families as a social space in which poverty, violence, and other social problems originate. Gloria, a Salvadoran who is employed by an international evangelical NGO, did a study with a colleague on "protection and risk" factors in Salvadoran communities. Gloria and her colleague found that while families serve as a protection factor, "intrafamilial violence makes a strong contribution to social violence . . . If a teen grows up in a family where there's violence, his or her behavior is going to be violent in and out of the house. That's just the pattern they see." Nestor, a math teacher in a public elementary school in El Salvador, stated that family structures in vulnerable neighborhoods create a drag on children's performance in school. "A good percentage of families in these communities are disintegrated . . . That reality of our students, at some point, lowers their academic performance," he said. Likewise, Raymond, a health clinic employee in the community, noted that one of the clinic's biggest challenges is caring for pregnant women. He identified teenage pregnancies as part of this issue, as well as men who do not permit their pregnant partners to go for their checkups.[4] Similar comments were voiced by others who interact with El Salvador's family systems on a regular basis.

Pastors also see families as a source of social problems. One pastor shared about a time when some teenage girls approached him after a church service and told him they were being sexually abused. Sometimes the perpetrators were

> their own fathers, and sometimes their stepfathers . . . [these girls hated] not only those who raped them but their mothers [because] when the daughters said to their mothers "mom, your husband is touching me," mothers said to them "you are the one who flirts." [The daughters] said "how can it be that my mother does not defend me, and defends her husband?"

Pastors are aware that such issues are in their communities and in their congregations. Some pastors are also the perpetrators of sexual violence. It is important to note that the examples presented here are just a smattering of a broad spectrum of damaging social dynamics that are caused by and/or circulate within families, evangelical and otherwise.

Conclusion

This chapter tells a different story than the one scholars typically present of Latin American evangelical families. By focusing on family systems and networks that run across and beyond lower-class Salvadoran communities, and supporting that analysis with more typical looks at nuclear family units within evangelical congregations, the lived reality of families comes into clearer focus. The key elements in this narrative center around social networks and identities.

Social Networks and Identities

The social networks in this study are complicated sets of family relations. Basic family ties, including parent–child and sibling relationships are still foundational. But spousal relationships are diminished, while relationships between half-siblings, half-cousins, step-aunts and uncles, and the like carry increased importance and are found with higher frequency. Evangelicals and gang members populate, propagate, and replicate these systems. In doing so, they create cross-cutting dynamics.

On the one hand, family ties connecting evangelicals and gang members create social cohesion within communities and open opportunities for greater understanding between the two groups. Sibling connections between evangelicals and gang members can be mutually advantageous. Early in life, this can be especially so in abusive homes. Evangelicals and gang members can unite against a common threat in such cases. Evangelicals need physical protection that gang members provide. Gang members gain from the emotional and spiritual support that evangelicals bring to them and other victims in the family. Later in life, sibling connections can be a needed source of communication in the community between groups. Gang members and evangelicals openly speak of the respect they have for each other within the context of such relational ties.

Romantic relationships can also emerge between (usually) male members of gangs and (usually) female evangelicals. Erica, Alejandro's mother, and Adriana, Ana's daughter, had relationships of a similar nature. I heard stories of other unions that occurred between evangelicals and full gang members. Evangelical parents of daughters entering such unions, much like parents of youths who enter gangs, have varying reactions to such developments.

Family connections between the two groups also create vulnerabilities. Relatives of gang members can be asked to collaborate with gangs regardless of their religious affiliation; not all evangelicals are empowered or inclined to refuse such pressure. At other times gang members can simply turn on their evangelical family members; this is a universal family dynamic, but one made more dangerous in a culture of violence. Violence also is inflicted on gang members themselves, sometimes in their home environments. Bullets intended for gang members too often hit younger and unaffiliated siblings or other family members. These children are often part of Sunday School programs or other church activities. Gangs can also decide that evangelical family members have learned too much about their crimes. A related dynamic is the concern some gang leaders have that loyalty to family can trump loyalty to the gang. In these instances, an order can be given from within the gang for the individual to kill his or her family member (Martínez 2016).

Identity is the second key element in this chapter. Family identities complement, contrast, and conflict with evangelical and gang member identities. The families introduced in this chapter demonstrate the conflicting loyalties and complicated intimacies that family relations create. They show the ways that family identities can both override and submit to religious and gang identities.

Family history and the intensity of one's religious identity can factor into the extent of evangelical/gang entanglements. Pastor Enzo and Pastor Jaime, for example, are both committed to their identities as evangelical leaders. But their family histories are different. Enzo is the son of a pastor who followed in his father's footsteps early in life, and whose siblings have all remained strongly in the church. Jaime is a first generation convert whose personal history passed through the local drug and alcohol scene. Not surprisingly, Jaime has greater family ties to gangs. Likewise, Ana has been deeply committed for most of her life to her religious identity, whereas Ana Louisa (Carlos's mother) only recently started attending church and Bible studies. The two women have different dispositions with respect to their family ties to gangs. Ana works toward moving some of her family members out of gangs and into churches; Ana Louisa appears more firmly embedded in gang-centric relationships and seems more likely to be drawn out of her evangelical identity than to draw her children out of the gang. Such examples speak to the variety of attitudes and social locations that exist in the midst of evangelical and gang ties.

Concluding Thoughts

The evangelicals populating the families in this study are often humble people with good intentions. Their possessions are few, and yet they share what they have with other members of extended family. These evangelicals visit family members who are in prison. They invite unwed mothers into their lives and their congregations. They are often unwed parents themselves, and their children often become teenage parents. These evangelicals are motivated by faith in many of their family interactions; they want other family members to experience God's love.

The evangelicals populating the families in this study have problems. They are shaped by past physical, mental, and sexual abuse, much of which occurs within families. Such evangelicals must work through those life experiences and the resulting issues in ways that standard narratives of evangelicals forget. Their religious beliefs and practices do not always completely free them from the scars of such memories; sometimes these evangelicals replicate abusive patterns in their own families. More than anything, this study shows that families, life, and religion are complicated. The entanglement theory attempts to account for such realities.

4
Competing for Local Authority

Lower-class Salvadoran towns are crowded with actors and activities. Signs promoting mayoral candidates pop up during election season, stands in the open-air markets vie for customers, restaurants post their signs as close to the road as possible, churches stage noisy services, police pickup trucks drive by with semiautomatic weapons in plain sight, and gang-crafted graffiti reminds the visitor about what might be happening behind the scenes.

Some such actors are simply trying to eke out a living and do what they can to get past another day. Some, however, are looking to exercise authority in communities. To do this, people need power, which is an item that comes in many currencies and is produced and retained in various ways.

It does not take too long to see that in many lower-class neighborhoods, three groups most want to influence community culture and events: evangelicals, gangs, and the police. In this chapter I thus ask: How is authority distributed and contested among different groups operating in the same space (evangelicals, gangs, and the police)? What are the effects?

I argue that the forms of social organization used to establish authority in communities are both traditional and modern. Evangelicals and gangs extend the family structures discussed in the previous chapter to establish patrimonies. Patrimonies serve as power bases for *caciques*, or community leaders (pastors and clique leaders), who compete with each other for community influence. Police enter this fray from a power base that is outside the community. Whereas evangelicals and gangs are grassroots organizations with "bottom up" strategies, the police force is an extension of the state and it attempts to exert power using a "top down" strategy. The triangulation of the three groups is marked by differing objectives, the exercise of different forms of power, and by frequently violent encounters. Especially for evangelicals and gangs, such competition is part of a broader set of complicated relational dynamics.

Blood Entanglements. Stephen Offutt, Oxford University Press. © Oxford University Press 2023.
DOI: 10.1093/oso/9780197587300.003.0005

Traditional Forms of Authority

Traditional ways of organizing and governing communities persist in El Salvador. The contemporary actors are new (evangelicals and gangs), but the organizational and cultural patterns they inhabit are ancient. Two such cultural patterns are particularly relevant for contemporary evangelicals and gangs: that of *caciques* and patrimonies.

Caciques

The traditional leadership form of the *cacique* is employed by evangelicals and gangs alike. David Bueno (2001) explains that the notion of a *cacique* predates European presence in the Americas. Arawan-speaking tribes referred to traditional chiefdoms using this term. In pre-Colombian Mesoamerica, tribal units were governed by a paramount chief (the Pipiles in El Salvador were under the sway of Mayans in the Guatemalan high lands), but *caciques*, or local leaders, were chosen by, and from within, their communities. Once chosen, *caciques* had to be loyal to the paramount chief, but they could govern more or less how they pleased: a *cacique* was "not bound by laws outside his domain" (Bueno 2001, 178), which gave the leader considerable latitude in determining local laws and governance.

Other characteristics of *caciques* help elucidate contemporary leadership dynamics in El Salvador. Friedrich (1965) describes the *cacique* as a leader who possesses authority from a strong local source, protects his "citizens" from outside exploiters, serves as a political broker, possesses coercive powers, is essentially self-employed, and contains access to a legitimizing office or position. Such authority is constantly being negotiated, and there are, according to Friedrich, only very rare moments when *caciques* are not beset by rivals vying for influence within a given town or territory.

Bueno (2001) argues that *caciquismo*[1] is one of a number of cultural traits that tie Pentecostals to the earlier Pipil/Mayan culture. Focusing particularly on rural areas, Bueno argues that, like the original *caciques*, who "were trained to lead public worship and to intercede with group deities" (2001, 178), Pentecostal pastors are religious leaders whose authority naturally encompasses more than narrower (often Western) notions of religious life. In spaces not controlled by formal authorities (read: neither the state nor the

Catholic Church), Pentecostal pastors, "through membership-citizenship structures" (2001, 178) assume many of the same roles of the cacique.

Strong similarities accompany some differences between local gang and evangelical *caciques*. Both are part of national and international authority structures but have considerable latitude to determine clique or congregation behavior at the local level. Like evangelical pastors, clique leaders control members of their own group and also seek influence within the broader community. There are some organizational differences between the two: one clique controls a given territory, for example, which is more like Catholic Church polity (although with different territorial boundaries). There are likely to be multiple churches within a given clique's territory, and thus multiple evangelical *caciques*, but each with different levels of influence at the community level. The concept of *cacique* is also useful in understanding rivalries between pastors of different congregations and between leaders of rival cliques, but that is beyond the scope of the current argument.

Patrimonies

Patrimonies are logical extensions of family networks. As referenced in the first chapter, evangelicals and gangs both forge patrimonial structures. Patrimonies are antecedents to modern bureaucracy and remain common in places where states fail. Collins (2011) describes two types of patrimonies: 1) patrimonial households and 2) non-household based patrimonial alliances, such as ad hoc warrior coalitions. The latter are melded together through a socially constructed sense of kinship, or a "fictive kinship."

Evangelicals and gangs in El Salvador are hybrids of these two patrimonial forms. Family structures are critical to both groups. But both groups also build their social networks beyond blood relations while seeking to maintain the same level of cohesion and loyalty. Congregations are successful in doing so in part through their use of a variety of rituals and symbols, including referring to one another as brother and sister. Cliques accomplish fictive kinship ties through different (although, as described in Chapter 1, often parallel) sets of rituals and symbols. Their semi-military form of organization (Insight Crime & CLALS 2017) tightens relationships and ensures loyalty and obedience.

Because patrimonies are part of El Salvador's cultural DNA, the ability of evangelicals and gangs to take on patrimonial forms gives them legitimacy.

They become natural and often even taken for granted social categories and sources of authority in their neighborhoods.

Within communities, evangelical and gang patrimonies experience tremendous overlap. The entangled family dynamics that emerged in the previous chapter are also true, and true to a greater extent, for evangelical and gang patrimonies. A crisis in Honduras brought this reality into stark relief. In 2012, a fire raged through an overcrowded prison near Tegucigalpa, killing some 350 inmates (Navarro 2012). A representative of just one evangelical organization reported that their ministry was serving over 100 children who had lost a relative in the fire. "Really, we have so many connections with kids that lost somebody," an organizational representative said. "I am not saying fathers. It was a combination. It could be brothers. It could be a lot of things." Many other churches and organizations had similar relational connections to the fire's victims. Such ties, and the feelings of personal loss the fire created within the evangelical community, brought into stark relief the overlapping memberships and meaning systems of the two patrimonies.

The Relationship between Caciques and Patrimonies

Patrimonialism and *caciquismo* are closely related. *Caciques* are the heads of patrimonies; patrimonies serve as a power base for *caciques*. Friedrich notes that the constellations of local power in southern Mexico over the course of several decades were fluid, and thus *caciques* were socially located and interfaced with political movements and entities in different ways over time. But they were consistently rooted in family structures. Friedrich noted that, "since 1924, the competition for power has been largely between groups defined through natural and ceremonial kinship, and political leadership has been to a significant degree a specialized function of leadership within such kinship networks" (1965, 192). Caciques, he argues, provide such leadership.

The ability of caciques to manifest differently in different socioeconomic and political environments helps to explain why caciques populate evangelical and gang leadership positions in contemporary lower-class Salvadoran communities. Although *caciques* remain rooted in kinship and fictive kinship networks, they build out from there within the most relevant contemporary social entities. This is how the *cacique* form has remained powerful for centuries.

It is equally accurate to say that contemporary grassroots movements utilize these existing cultural forms of organization to pattern their communities. They modify the way *caciques* work to suit their own specific needs in the process. Bueno argues that Pentecostal "emphasis on extended family structures goes beyond a geographical locality, and consolidates a new power base by introducing new loyalties and priorities" (Bueno 2001, 175). Such adaptation creates a different social constellation than the ones Friedrich studied, but families and family extensions remain foundational. Although Bueno doesn't use the same language, he affirms the idea that Pentecostals use non-household based patrimonial systems that have been extended by fictive kinships. The *cacique*, or local pastor, serves as the leader of a local patrimonial system.

Community members operate within a multi-polar leadership structure. They likely participate at some level in multiple patrimonies, and they have no problem respecting the various authority figures simultaneously. An Assemblies of God pastor explained, for example, that "in [gangs] you can find young men who are the sons of Christians and even of pastors . . . so they know that you should respect spiritual leaders." Such gang members do so while maintaining their fidelity to the leader of their clique. There are other reasons why gang members acknowledge pastors' leadership—gang members that did not grow up in evangelical homes also respect pastors. But the overlapping patrimonial memberships are nonetheless an important variable. Such feelings make the collaboration discussed in the next chapter more understandable but does not negate the intense competition explained in this chapter.

Stronger and Weaker Caciques

Not all *caciques* have the same level of authority. This is true for evangelicals and for gangs. Some pastors rise to the level of being a *cacique* in the broader community, whereas the influence of others is confined to their own congregation. This is a critical point, and one that helps to determine the variation in ways that pastors are treated by gangs. My research strongly indicates that pastors who are older, who have larger churches, and who have more resources to provide the community, be they from their own congregation or from outside sources, have greater social standing with gang members.

Age may be the most important of these factors. Thirteen pastors agreed to share with me in a one-on-one interview about their interactions with gangs (this excludes pastors in focus groups and other forms of interactions I had with pastors). As illustrated in Figure 4.1, seven pastors were in their fifties and sixties and tended to have larger churches. (I considered churches with roughly 100 members or more to be large—remember that the pastors I interviewed were operating with scarce resources in marginalized neighborhoods). Six pastors were in their thirties and forties, and their churches tended to be smaller. All of the pastors I interviewed in their fifties and sixties either had only had affirming things to say about personal gang interactions or they had mixed things to say about their personal gang interactions. Conversely, all but one of the pastors I interviewed in their thirties and forties either only related personal threats or other forms of violence gangs had inflicted on them and their families, or they had mixed things to say about their personal gang interactions.

Such data are far from conclusive, but data from the focus groups I conducted, from my less formal conversations with other pastors, and from my ethnographic research also points in this direction. It is also consistent with other work on *caciques*, as Friedrich (1965) noted that older, popular *caciques* were often accorded a special, affectionate name ("Tata" or father). In short, there are strong indications that younger, less established pastors may be effective leaders for their congregations, but they are more vulnerable to gang violence, threats, and general disrespect.

An example may help to see how pastors extend their influence beyond a specific congregation. Pastor Enzo is in his mid-forties and has a small but well-established church. Enzo is not well known throughout Las Palmas and has been subjected to gang threats. But as I walked around the neighborhood closest to his house with him, I saw how he might earn *cacique* status in the future. Enzo knocked on doors and chatted easily with the neighbors, none of whom on this occasion attended his church. He asked Pedrita, a resident,

Pastors' Reported Experiences with Gangs

Age	Negative or Mixed	Positive or Mixed
30s and 40s	5	1
50s and 60s	0	7

Figure 4.1 Variation of gangs' respect for pastors by pastors' age.

where she was going to church these days, and then they both talked about others they knew in that congregation. When Enzo saw Olivia, another resident, he asked about her nieces and nephews and listened thoughtfully to the various family concerns that she had. Finally, we stopped in to see Ricardo, a charismatic Catholic. Ricardo was an extrovert and provided an impromptu sermon that began with the miracles of Jesus and covered various Old Testament characters, with Enzo interjecting at times to provide additional insights. There were many smiles and much enthusiasm as the two conversed. Everyone we visited was grateful for the opportunity to chat with Enzo, and in both the manner in which his neighbors addressed him and in their nonverbal communication, they exhibited gentle forms of deference. Although he was not their pastor in a formal sense, they still acknowledged his pastoral role.

Such relationships and deference are important when community decisions need to be made or conflict arises. It is in these moments when people who are seen to have authority in the community step forward and exercise their power. Pastors almost by definition serve this role for their congregations, and so have influence for a smaller set of community members. But when evangelicals run up against other community groups, particularly gangs, those pastors who have authority beyond their own congregations become particularly strategic.

Competition and Conflict between Gangs and Evangelicals

Competition marks the complex relationships between evangelical and gang *caciques*. Much of the literature on evangelicals and gangs, including this book, highlights collaborative and productive elements of their relationship. But that is not the whole story. Conflict and violence also characterize relationships between the tightly intertwined groups and their leaders. The prize at stake is ultimately community influence.

Evangelicals and gangs desire different types of influence and use different strategies to attain their goals. Evangelicals want to dictate spiritual and cultural elements of the community; gangs want to establish territorial and economic control. Gangs use hard power; evangelicals use soft power. Such differences create important spaces in which the two groups can collaborate, as I explain in the next chapter. But religious, economic, and political

Contested Relationships: Gangs, Evangelicals, and Police

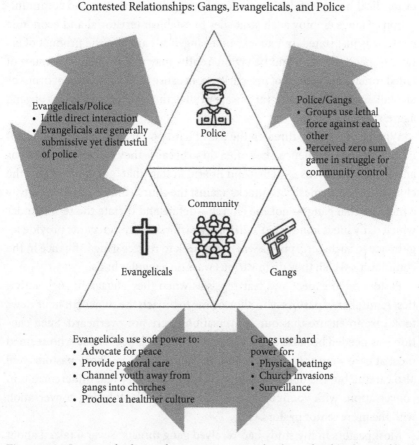

Figure 4.2 Contested relationships: gangs, evangelicals, and police (created by Thomas Hampton).

influence always overlap in everyday life: such points of intersection create the dangerous conflicts that exist alongside collaboration. Figure 4.2 depicts the primary ways in which gangs and evangelicals approach the contested nature of their relationship, as well as how each group interacts with the police (a topic covered later in this chapter).

Gangs' Hard Power

Gangs use hard power against evangelicals. This includes the use of weapons such as guns and knives, physical beatings, invasions of churches and evangelical homes, and surveillance of evangelical activities and communications. Gangs employ such strategies to establish territorial and economic control, as just stated, but attacks on evangelicals are also the product of erratic teenage thinking and behavior. Youths may react violently because of failed romances, feelings of insecurity, or because of the influence of drugs or alcohol. Evangelical pastors are aware of all of these potential sources of gang aggression.

When gangs use or threaten the use of hard power for the rational goal of increasing their influence, they often do so because they perceive churches as anti-gang institutions. Ardalan and Boerman state that "gangs often view the church as their nemesis. . . . attacks against the church are intended to convey a message that gangs—not the church—define and dictate the terms under which daily life is conducted" (2016, 3). Pastors and congregants provide legitimacy to such perceptions when they seek to reduce gang influence in the community, which they do in various ways on a regular basis.

Pastors often expect and fear reprisals when they engage in such activities. A number of pastors who allowed me to broach the subject in interviews took care to ensure that our conversations were not overheard. Such caution was needed because of pervasive gang surveillance. Those who seemed most at ease were the older, community-level *caciques*. Those pastors were also careful, but the observable anxiety that was a very real undercurrent in conversations with younger pastors was not as evident during conversation with the more senior pastors.

Most pastors in my study had received gang threats. Several talked about the balancing act that responding to such threats necessitated. Pastor Luis, for example, explained that when a gang member recently threatened him, he acknowledged to the gang member that he knew he was now in danger. Pastor Luis also expressed to me the fear that he experienced because of the threat. But Pastor Luis, like many pastors in similar situations, did not want to appear able to be bullied and did not want to run from the gang. Such a response would reduce their leadership status in the community and within their own patrimony. Thus, while acknowledging the reality of the gang member's power, Pastor Luis respectfully informed him that he wasn't going to leave the community. Instead, he told the gang member, "I am going to keep doing what God is telling me to do." I heard similar refrains from pastors several times in my research. This is one way in which pastors absorb gangs' efforts to manipulate and intimidate them, and continue to do their jobs.

Sometimes gangs make good on their threats against pastors, especially those who are young and/or who have smaller churches. During one of my research trips, a twenty-two-year-old pastor was killed by gang members in the department of Ahuachapan. A Salvadoran newspaper reported that shortly before his death, the young pastor had several verbal clashes in public spaces with gang members (Laguan 2018). I was not able to learn why this particular pastor was killed: several pastors in my study reported surviving direct confrontations with gang members. But when such pastors are threatened they are aware of cases such as the twenty-two-year-old pastor just mentioned. When threatened, pastors must include the possibility that they might also be killed into their calculus as they consider their next steps.

Violence from previous gang activities can sometimes follow gang members who convert to evangelicalism and become pastors themselves. A pastor in Las Palmas recounted the story of Santiago, an ex-gang member who became a pastor. After some time, a member of an opposing gang saw Santiago and told him he was going to kill him. Santiago explained to the gang member that he had left gang life behind and was now a pastor. The member of the opposing gang responded by saying he wasn't going to kill him that day, but he might kill him later. A month later, Santiago was dead.

Pastors' families are not immune to gang violence. In some cases, pastors' families are targeted; in other cases, violence finds pastors' families much as it does other members of the community. For example, Pastor Enzo had a middle school aged daughter who saw a drug transaction at school. Those involved in the transaction told her that she shouldn't come back to school. Enzo and his wife decided to take their daughter out of the school, and she completed her education in a cosmetology program. Enzo did not believe that his status as a pastor would provide sufficient protection for his daughter to continue in the school once she had been threatened.

Lay members of evangelical patrimonies are also subjected to gang violence. Benjamin, a pastor of an Assemblies of God church in Las Palmas, explained to me that he was walking with teenagers who had attended his church after an evening service when they saw two men shooting another man. Benjamin directed the boys to run with him, and they found a hiding place until the shooting stopped. In this case, they avoided harm. But the same pastor lamented that "the husband of a member from my church was murdered right in front of her house." Pastor Jose, a Baptist pastor in a different community, also deals with gang violence on a regular basis. He recounted a time when a group of boys were drinking liquor, and they told one of the youths of the church to come over because they had something to give him. "Then they hugged him, and they put a knife in his back. He fled to protect himself in the church." This is where, presumably, he felt most safe and protected. But, the pastor said, the youth died before they could get him to the hospital.

Examples in my research correspond with multiple other reports of gang violence against evangelicals. Ardalan and Boerman (2016) referenced a Pentecostal youth who repeatedly told MS-13 members that joining the gang was wrong and against the values of his church. The gang threatened him, shot at him, and killed his uncle. In a different case, gang members entered an evangelical church with the intent to assassinate a church member. The pastor attempted to detain the gang members, but they reportedly assaulted him in front of twenty-five church members. The gang members eventually found their intended victim and shot him to death in the pastor's house (La Prensa Cristiana 2019). In a third report, gang members waited for people to come out of a church service and then shot them in front of the church (U.S. Department of State 2018). Such incidences affirm in the minds of evangelicals that gangs can and will use violence against them.

In the face of such pressures, pastors seek ways to cope. One example of this is the support they seek from other pastors. Pastors in Las Palmas formed a Whatsapp group, where they share prayer requests. One pastor, for example, shared that his church had been burgled three times. Pastors also cope by changing their church calendars. The evangelical practice of having evening services almost every weeknight is being reworked in some communities. Moody noted that in order to conform to gang curfews and to avoid problems at night, "many churches in rural areas now hold their services in the early afternoon, in spite of conflicting work schedules, so that the congregants can be in their homes before dark and not have to face danger to and from church" (Moody 2020). Another evangelical leader concurred, saying that people feel safer when they stay home. He stated further that, "many [pastors] are no longer having evening meetings . . . [and] some have been conducting their meetings behind closed doors for safety."

Evangelicals' Soft Power

Evangelical *caciques* cannot and do not fight back with the use of force, but they do use various forms of soft power. Nye's classical definition of soft power is "the ability to get what you want through attraction rather than co-ercion or payments" (2004, i). Like other religious leaders in other contexts (Byrnes 2021), evangelical *caciques* use the soft power tools of attraction, opinion, and moral authority to exert power over gang leaders.

Pastors use these tools to mute the effects of gang aggression and to change the prevailing community culture. Specifically, pastors try to 1) re-duce the likelihood of violence against themselves, their families, and their congregations; 2) provide pastoral care for community members, in-cluding for those traumatized by violence both inside and outside of gangs; 3) channel youths away from gangs and into churches; and 4) produce "cul-ture" that they view to be healthier and more empowering. These are all pro-social goals. Self-interest is also evident: successful efforts in these domains result in more influence for the pastors who work within them.

My research revealed numerous examples of pastors who used soft power to reduce the likelihood of violence against themselves, their families, and their congregations. Pastor Jaime, for example, reflected on a recent gang threat he received. The threat came, he said, "because of economic reasons. They asked for a specific amount of money, which we did not have." As Pastor Jaime explained to the gang that he would not pay the extortion fee, he used moral and spiritual language in order to argue that violence should not be done to him or to members of his congregation as a result. The gang members were receptive to Pastor Jaime's message, perhaps because they accepted him as person who is connected to God and, as such, a religious authority. As Pastor Jaime gratefully put it, "God helped us to find grace before them."

Pastors spend much of their time outside of formal church services pro-viding care for community members and congregants. In a culture of vio-lence, this often means that pastors care for trauma victims. They listen to their stories, pray for them, proclaim God's love for them, and seek to in-corporate them in safe and loving social networks. Samuel, for example, was shot by a gang member in front of his son, Esau, a teenager. In Photo 4.1, you can see the scar where the bullet entered Samuel's side as well as the scar running up his mid-section from the ensuing surgery. Esau also appears in the photo. They are the brother and nephew of Pastor Enzo. Esau suffered significant trauma from the event. Although his father survived, Esau con-tinued to experience depression and had trouble sleeping. Pastor Enzo, like most pastors in lower-class El Salvador, does not have any formal training in trauma counseling, but he consistently checked in on Esau. He also encouraged Esau to participate in the church youth group and ensured that

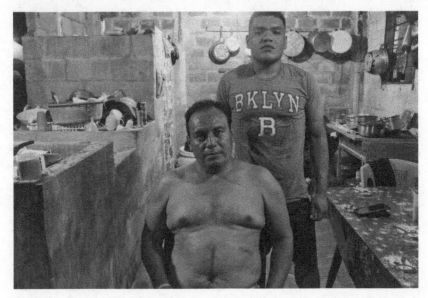

Photo 4.1 Evangelical shot by a gang member and his son (photo: David Torres Ayala).

other church members made him feel welcome and valued. I periodically saw Esau over a three-year period; Pastor Enzo's efforts and regular involvement in the church community appeared to have a positive impact on his well-being.

Pastors also care for gang members who are traumatized by the violent acts they commit. This happens within neighborhoods: pastors told me of gang members, especially early to mid-teenagers, who come to them in tears and anguish after they commit a violent crime. Pastors involved in prison ministries also engage such issues. Such ministries are often more systematic than the community encounters just mentioned. Pastor Adrian, for example, uses a twelve-step rehabilitation program. He hopes that those who go through the program leave the gang and join a church. It may be that gang leaders do not interfere in such ministries because they appreciate such care for their members. This in spite of the fact that such programs can siphon human resources away from gangs and into churches.

Pastors and other evangelicals also exercise soft power by producing culture in communities. Sermons, Bible studies, youth groups, and other church programs can all be seen as cultural artifacts produced by churches (Wuthnow 1994). Evangelicals promote a youth culture that includes (often goofy) youth group activities, Bible studies, and worship songs. Gang culture production, other hand, is built on sex, drugs, and violence, and is referred to as "la vida loca" (Strazza 2016). While Salvadoran evangelicals incorporate songs, books and other resources produced in the United States, they often feel like Hollywood and other mainstream mass media producers (Lindhart 2014) are in league with gangs, and both are working against them.

Undaunted, pastors often try to compare evangelical culture favorably to street or gang culture. Pastor Jaime preaches about his complicated personal history. He shares with audiences, who are often youths in the midst of making difficult life decisions, that he was empty and miserable when he was taking drugs and engaged in other illicit activities. Pastor Jaime then shares that God and the church can offer a better, more fulfilling, more edifying way. This message of hope is repeated by pastors throughout the country and the region. It is a direct and consistent effort to use moral authority to create a different social imagination for community members than the one that is produced by gangs.

Pastors are also sometimes able to win battles against gangs over graffiti. This is especially true if the graffiti is close to the church. Violating gang symbols by covering over graffiti is, under normal circumstances, an act of disrespect to the gang. Gangs often retaliate using violence. Enzo, however, decided to fade out MS-13 graffiti directly across from his church. (Enzo appears in Photo 4.2 opening the church door across from the washed out graffiti.) He then requested a meeting with the local *palabrero* to ask if he could permanently remove it. In a nearby community, evangelicals painted over 18th Street graffiti and wrote "God loves you" next to it, as shown in Photo 4.3. I was not able to talk to gang members about these two incidents, but community members reported that no retaliation had occurred.

In sum, the competition between evangelicals and gangs is one which pits different forms of influence and different strategies to exercise power. If death tallies determined the winner of this competition, the outcome would be one sided. But sides are fighting for the ability to control the community and its culture. In this sense, both groups are embattled and thriving.[2] Because multiple social spheres are in play and evangelicals and gangs value such spheres differently, it is not entirely a zero-sum game; both sides may simultaneously experience a modicum of success. The conflict, however, remains real: it is important to acknowledge the trauma and persecution that many evangelicals experience at the hands of gang members along the way.

Photo 4.2 Contested graffiti across from church entrance (photo: David Torres Ayala).

Photo 4.3 God loves you graffiti (photo: David Torres Ayala).

The Failing State, the Failing Police

Police are a third actor in the competition to gain power and authority in communities. In fact, modern understandings of governance assume that the state *should* monopolize the use of force in communities and provide governance (Weber 1946). In lower-class El Salvador, the state clearly does not hold such a monopoly. Still, the state is better funded than either evangelicals or gangs, and its influence is such that any serious conversation about power and authority needs to take them into account. So where is the state? How is it attempting to retain relevance? I covered the state failures of the mayor's office, the schools, and public health services in Chapter 1. In this section I focus on the police: the part of the state that most directly competes for authority in local communities. (Please refer back to Figure 4.2 to see how police relate to evangelicals and to gangs.)

The National Civil Police of El Salvador (PNC) has struggled to enforce the rule of law and protect Salvadoran citizens since its inception. The PNC was created in the country's national peace accords in 19992. But negotiations did not result in the creation of a strong, accountable entity. According to Hector Silva Avalos, a former Salvadoran diplomat turned scholar/journalist, "The UN warned time and time again of the risk that the PNC was born contaminated or without effective tools to clean itself up, while certain foreign officials took note of the lack of political will of successive governments to build an independent and professional public force. As they predicted, institutional weakness took its toll." Systemic weakness is a foundational reason that the PNC is vulnerable to infiltration and is ineffective in protecting its citizens (Alonso 2016; Malkin 2015; WOLA & IUDOP 2020).

Low human capital within the police force aggravates such systemic problems. Members of the police force are "poorly paid, they're poorly trained, and . . . a great majority haven't even finished elementary [school]," according to Sidney, a U.S. State Department contractor who has done police training in El Salvador. Police cadets attend a police academy, and U.S. funding and personnel support El Salvador's police training efforts. The United States spent $140 million to bolster El Salvador's system in 2017 and "is involved in almost every layer of El Salvador's efforts to cauterize the near-constant gang violence" (Watkins & Kohut 2018). Even with U.S. resources and personnel, Sidney characterizes cadet training and in-service officer training of police as minimal. He argues that trainees retain very little of the training they do receive, in part because the PNC does not monitor trainees or provide training reinforcement.

The poorly educated police also lack effective law enforcement tools. For example, in 2018, there was only one crime lab that receives bodily fluid from a crime scene in the country, and without D.N.A testing, evidence such as bloody clothes cannot be matched to victims or suspects. "Prosecutors can request D.N.A. testing through a medical examiner, but the results aren't stored centrally and can't be easily searched. For a country that had nearly 4,000 homicides [in 2017], the implications are staggering" (Watkins & Kohut 2018). Such examples point to the severe institutional limitations law enforcement in El Salvador faces. In lower-class communities across the country, such issues are even more glaring.

One of the biggest problems for police that surfaced in my research is that most residents perceive them as outsiders in the communities. Location assignments for police officers occur at the national level (municipalities do not control any police units). Officers can thus be deployed anywhere in the country; most do not work in their own communities. "That's by design," explained Sidney. "If the gang members know where they live then they will be targeting them in their home." Such a policy may create needed safety for police and their families (just how safe is a matter of debate: numerous officers still feel so threatened that they flee the country (Seiff 2019)). But it also creates a problem: police are outsiders in the communities they seek to serve. Whereas gangs and evangelicals are woven into communities through their patrimonial systems, local police officers patrol communities that they do not know and in which they are not trusted.

The PNC has piloted community policing strategies intended to help police gain trust in communities, but lack of institutional commitment has minimized their impact. "[If] you form a little group of 10 officers and [say] OK, you're our community police guys. . . . But the other 2,000 guys continue to, you know, do business as usual and abuse civil rights, then there's not going to be any change," explained Sidney. "I think that's one of the biggest things I encountered, was the resistance from the operational arm to actually accept some of the things [U.S. trainers] were trying to do." The resulting distrust of officers at the local level is hard to overstate. I spoke with numerous community members about the local police in El Salvador. Not a single resident expressed confidence in the police. This is part of the larger distrust in public institutions that is endemic throughout the Central American region (Brenneman 2016a).

In spite of community policing initiatives, police violence and abuse trended upward during this study. From 2014–2017, investigations carried out by the Internal Affairs Unit of the Salvadoran police increased in almost every area. They investigated more cases of theft (140 in 2014 to 166 in 2017), injuries (350 in 2014 to 434 in 2017), unlawful search and entry (twenty-one in 2014 to seventy-one in 2017), and police threats (eighty in 2014 to 210 in 2017) (WOLA & IUDOP 2020). These are just the numbers of incidences that were investigated. Numbers under the Bukele administration were not available at the time of this writing, but most observers expect that the real numbers for such police behavior increased during this time, even if the Internal Affairs Unit became may (or may not) have become less attentive.

Police and state failure is not isolated to the local level. There have been whispers of shadow forms of national governments throughout the region for decades. The illicit economy is so strong throughout Central America, and formal state institutions so weak, that these reports must be taken somewhat seriously. The problem is historic: William Stanley (1996) described how elites in the 1980s and 1990s used state organisms to coerce and manipulate their rivals. The problem is also contemporary: multiple reports show ways that powerful families or individuals capture various state institutions and use them for their own, often illicit, ends (The Economist 2021).

The state, due in part to significant external backing, is thus chronically failing but unlikely to completely fail. International funding is enormous: El Salvador received over $300,000,000 in official foreign development assistance in 2019 alone (World Bank Data 2021b). Such resources are evidence of the international system's commitment to maintaining the Salvadoran state's viability. Total state failure or irrelevance is thus unlikely. Still, corruption, infiltration, and competing entities at every level reduce the state's effectiveness such that competent governance and policing of lower-class Salvadoran communities remains beyond its grasp.

Evangelical/Police Relations

Evangelical/police relations in this study were characterized by low levels of direct interaction, evangelicals' general sense of submission to the police, and high levels of evangelical distrust for the police. Low levels of direct interaction could be observed as I walked around neighborhoods, rode the bus, and went to church with evangelicals in Las Palmas. In seven years of ethnographic research I saw very little direct evangelical contact with police even as the two groups were often in close proximity. Don Ignacio, who is Pastor Enzo's father-in-law, for example, lives right next to the jail. One day we were relaxing on Don Ignacio's front porch, when a police truck drove up to admit someone they had arrested into the jail. I began discretely taking photos of the event, which obviously was taking place in the public sphere. But my actions made Enzo uncomfortable. He reminded me a couple of times that if the police saw me they might confiscate my phone. So I put my phone away. Although we often spent time on Don Ignacio's porch, I did not see any pleasantries or hostilities shared between the police guarding the jail and Don Ignacio's family. I also did not hear about any close family relations who were police in any of my interviews. Rather, unless I brought up the topic, there was simply very little discourse by evangelicals about police in my study.

Such evidence is not conclusive. Police do exist in El Salvador, and they are embedded in social relationships. In 2017, there were roughly 26,000 total police personnel in El Salvador (WOLA & IUDOP 2020). But because police usually go to work in communities where they do not live, they are not embedded in local life and relationships. And it is likely that in their home communities and in their family relationships, other parts of their identity are more important than their professional identity. This leads police officers to punch below their weight with regard to relational impact in poor communities.

Of the three groups—evangelicals, gangs, and police—police are significantly outnumbered in lower-class communities by the other two groups. Keep in mind that there are more than twice as many gang members than police in the country. Most of an estimated 70,000 gang members "work" in the communities in which they grew up, creating higher concentrations of gang members in lower-class communities. Evangelicals are also concentrated among the lower class and often make up more than half the population in marginalized neighborhoods. In contrast, police are dispersed across socioeconomic classes and, if anything, are more likely to be concentrated where wealth needs to be protected. The resulting difference between the intimacy (violent or not) of evangelical/gang connections and the relational distance of evangelical/police connections is striking.

In spite of the relational distance, no evangelicals in this study expressed open defiance of the police. Evangelicals do not directly compete with police and they do not issue public declarations against the police. Erik, the

Assemblies of God missionary, related a story about being confronted by a gang member for allowing the police to have an event at his church. Erik explained that he allowed the police in the church "because the Bible tells us to respect those in authority over us and they are the authority. So it comes back to the Bible, it is not because I want to." This sentiment remains prevalent among evangelicals.

Underneath this conformity to official teaching, however, lies great distrust. I asked Pastor Jose what he thought of the police in the station located just a few yards from his church. Jose waved his hand dismissively. When Pastor Enzo was threatened by gang members, he did not go to the police. He did not think the police would or could do anything to help him. When the 22 year old pastor mentioned above was murdered, the media reported that a police officer had also threatened to kill him after he saw the officer smoking marijuana with known gang members (U.S. Department of State 2018). Many other similar examples of negative interactions and opinions with local police officers appeared in my research. These underscore the statistics of reported investigations of police indiscretions listed above. There were a couple of positive mentions: pastors noted gang members scattering when they saw police or they witnessed police officers arresting people who committed felonies, but these were very few. With respect to productive law enforcement and civic activity more generally, most pastors assume that local police units are usually irrelevant.

War between the Gangs and the Police

The conflict between gangs and police has been described as a low intensity war (Partlow 2016). The groups have similar goals and employ similar strategies. They both want to establish territorial control and monopolize the use of force within communities. Gang strategies include armed confrontations, assassinations, and infiltration of the police and other state entities. Police strategies include community sweeps, mass incarcerations, extrajudicial killings, and physical abuse and intimidation tactics. Violent encounters are frequent, and both groups have incurred heavy casualties.

The police/gang relationship is complicated by backroom deals between the Salvadoran government and national gang leaders. After Bukele came to power on a tough-on-gangs platform, it came to light that he brokered agreements with imprisoned national gang leaders before and after he was elected (Martínez et al. 2020; Papadovassilakis 2020). Bukele gained a re-duction in homicides after he took office, although forced disappearances increased significantly. There were also reports that Bukele released four of MS-13 top leaders from prison, all of whom were facing extradition to the United States (Garcia 2022). I heard from members of the diplomatic com-munity and community members that some police are frustrated by Bukele's deals. In Las Palmas, a community member reported that police have orders from the central government to stay away from some of the communities in which gangs are strongest and not to respond to emergency calls in conflict zones between the gangs.

MS-13 also allowed Bukele's party to campaign for the midterm elections in the communities they controlled but did not allow the other political parties to campaign in some of their communities. This allowed Bukele to take control of Congress (Williamson 2021). In return, gang leaders in prison were given additional visitation rights, including having meetings with gang members outside of prison as well as family members. It was also reported that during the coronavirus pandemic, the government provided special as-sistance to people in need. MS-13 was given the ability to hand out that as-sistance in their communities. "That gives them huge amounts of capital and clout in those communities where they operate" (Williamson 2021).[3]

Such negotiations cast a shadow on the legitimacy of the government; they are also a window into the extent of gangs' power in the country. According to Mark Fazzola (2020), Bukele "has acknowledged that the gangs essentially run a 'parallel state.' He said there are about 70,000 gang members who have 'de facto power' to conduct shakedowns . . . ." Yet Bukele also uses his Twitter feed to play up the idea that he is pushing the gangs around and making them bend to his will. It is not clear how such clandestine deals and confusing mes-saging at the national level impact gang/police dynamics in communities, but it does not seem to reduce hostilities or violence between local actors.

Two issues perhaps best capture gang/police dynamics. The first is use of violence by law enforcement against gangs. El Salvador's Ombudsman reports that state police committed 116 extrajudicial killings between 2014 and 2018 (Human Rights Watch 2021). Experts universally believe that the real number is far higher than that, and most believe that such killings increased under the Bukele administration. Early in his presidency, Bukele encouraged "the use of lethal force by security forces . . . even when not a measure of last resort" (Human Rights Watch 2021). Some argue that Bukele's use of extrajudicial force has created a net increase in violence in El

Salvador even as official homicide statistics, which do not count homicides in instances involving confrontations with security forces (Asmann 2019), decreased in the first years of Bukele's presidency. It seems clear that Bukele made informal agreements with national gang leaders *and* used the military and the police to shoot and kill gang members. There is significant doubt, though, that increased police violence leads to reduced gang violence in the long run (Brenneman 2016a).

Pastors and other community members are aware of violence by police or other members of the state security apparatus against gangs. Pastor Adrian, for example, has seen police brutality firsthand in prisons. When the topic came up, Pastor Adrian shook his head and winced. He then explained the severity of the beatings security guards can mete out to inmates. On the streets, police raids can also result in police violence. Pastor Erik described pickup trucks full of police armed with semiautomatic weapons entering humble neighborhoods. Sidney stated that during such raids police "go down the street, see a couple of kids, pull over and knock [them] on the head, slap [them] around. Maybe they weren't in the gang but maybe [the police] just helped them get a little motivation to join the gang." These are regular occurrences in many communities across El Salvador.

The second issue that helps depict police/gang dynamics is gang infiltration of police. According to one report, 480 gang members infiltrated El Salvador's police and armed forces between 2010 and 2015 (Yagoub 2016). Gangs infiltrate mayor's offices and local law enforcement branches, and either penetrate or manipulate the judicial system (Martínez 2016). A former mayor of Apopa, a city just north of San Salvador, was convicted of providing money transfers and access to vehicles to the 18th Street gang during his term in office (Albaladejo 2018). This, most believe, is symptomatic of how local governance and law enforcement is compromised by gangs throughout the country.

Gangs use multiple strategies to maintain their presence within El Salvador's security forces. Gang leaders send members who do not have tattoos and do not yet have police records to apply for police and military jobs. Sidney reported witnessing this in police cadet training. He said his Salvadoran counterparts knew of specific cadets who were gang members, but for political reasons they could not remove them from the program. "So, what they did," said Sidney, "is they had a graduation for the normal cadets and then they had a special graduation for the cadet gang members. And these folks [were then] dispersed out into the units across the country. So that's where you had active gang members working in a police uniform." Gang members who were successful in infiltrating the military, said Sidney, were able to steal specialized weapons. In both cases, gang members were learning police and military tactics and sharing that intelligence with their gang leaders. "So, it was a pretty well-orchestrated intelligence operation by the gangs," he said.

Gangs also seek to compromise police information systems. Clerical positions are often those that process information. Sidney explained that gang leaders send "females to get jobs . . . as administrative aides inside the police department." Community members I talked to were confident that any information obtained by the police went directly to the gangs. This was why no resident I talked to trusted the police enough to report a gang related incident to the police.

Corruption is a third infiltration strategy. In addition to the gang members who are part of the police, police officers who are not gang members may essentially be on the gang's payroll. The low wages police receive make them susceptible to the "carrot" of receiving gang payments. Police also often have families who make soft targets for gang members, so they are susceptible to the "stick" of violence if they do not cooperate with gang members. Such conditions make it fairly easy for gang members to bend individual police officers to their will (Calderon & Silva 2016; Silva 2014).

Conclusion

In answer to the question of how authority is distributed and contested by evangelicals, gangs, and police in communities, I have argued that distribution of authority in lower-class Salvadoran neighborhoods spreads across traditional and modern forms of social organization. As has happened consistently in recent centuries, basic yet flexible forms of traditional social organization, namely patrimonies that are led by *caciques*, take on the trappings of contemporary social groups. Such groups, in this case evangelicals and gangs, modify traditional social forms to better fit their values, goals, and motivations. These groups are embedded in local communities and their memberships are interwoven with one another. Leaders and members of opposing groups often clash, however. Such conflict can be caused by efforts to reduce the influence of the other group in the community and can often include violence.

The police, as an extension of the modern state, also compete for community authority. Their efforts are weakened by their community outsider status. Police are also constrained by lack of resources, poor training, and low human capital. Still, the police remain a viable entity due to significant external financial resources and the backing of the international community. The result is a state security apparatus with which gangs and evangelicals must contend, but which shows chronic weakness.[4]

What are the effects of such distribution and contestation? First, evangelicals, gangs, and police have proven to be highly resilient. One group can achieve gains at any given time, but none of the groups are ever in any danger of elimination. Because of differing goals and strategies by evangelicals, and because of clandestine deals at the national level between the state and gangs, conflicts between any two of the three are not staged within a zero-sum game. The competition for authority within the community had thus reached a contentious period of stasis or perhaps stalemate before Bukele initiated large scale mass incarcerations and military level sieges on entire towns in 2022. It is possible that he is, at least temporarily, changing the way authority is distributed in communities.

Evangelicals, gangs, and police thus co-exist, but recurring and sometimes intense violence is a primary negative effect of their ongoing competition. The numbers of people who are dead, the dangers to youths and children, the communities under constant surveillance, and the threat and execution of police raids adds layers of constant stress on community members. Residents adjust to the pervasive culture of violence, but the underlying trauma can have long lasting effects.

Evangelical congregations are impacted by the competition for authority in unexpected ways. First, the competition draws evangelicals more deeply into the community. Far from escaping society, evangelicals are key players in the fundamental struggle for community authority and identity. Second, the competition also sets evangelicals in a more awkward position with law enforcement. When evangelicals aspire to their own ascetic standards they are usually well within state rules and regulations. In other contexts, this makes for friendly relations with law enforcement agencies. But in lower-class El Salvador, the social location of police relative to the community, and thus to evangelicals within the community, helps to create a less amicable dynamic. Third, the culture of violence makes traumatized individuals receptive to the soft power and culture production that evangelicals offer. Pastors are strategically placed to offer spiritual guidance to troubled youths and counseling to people who have had highly traumatic experiences. The latter has become an important part of social outreach by evangelicals in spite of the fact that most pastors have little to no formal training in counseling.

Competition for local authority results in unexpected alliances. More intimate interactions generally occur between evangelicals and gangs than between police and either evangelicals or gangs. This leads to forms of collaboration in community governance that are discussed in the next chapter, but which occur in the midst of the ongoing competition and violence just described.

5

Unusual Alliances
in Community Governance

Nicolas is the pastor of Luz y Vida, one of Las Palmas's larger congregations. Nicolas is in his early sixties; he has been a pastor for thirty-seven years. The church, made of cinder blocks, is on an unpaved road, and those who attend usually walk or ride their bikes. Most have tenuous employment situations and have had little formal education. It is a church of and for the poor. Although Nicolas is neither highly educated nor wealthy himself, the congregants look to him as their leader.

Nicolas talks to me pleasantly in his small and sparsely decorated office. The office doubles as a storage area for the church's sound equipment. This creates foot traffic as we chat; people are preparing for an evening service. The sanctuary has a cement floor and feels like a small warehouse; about 150 plastic chairs are placed neatly in rows. A keyboard and a podium grace the stage. I learn later, when I stay for the service, that the sound equipment magnifies but also distorts every (not very melodious) note that is played.

Nicolas is optimistic about the impact evangelicals are having on the community and El Salvador. "The [evangelical] church itself is gaining ground, taking the authority that it should have," he explained. He and other evangelical pastors, for example, orchestrated a march through the city of Las Palmas to celebrate the 500th anniversary of the Protestant Reformation. The march went through Las Palmas's main streets and then ended with a worship service in central park, right across the street from the Catholic Church.

Nicolas believes evangelicals should use their authority to help lift Las Palmas communities out of poverty. He attracts funding to the community from international organizations, and his own church contributes in modest ways to anti-poverty initiatives. The church has a food drive, for example, where they collect groceries and distribute them in the community. Nicolas explained that the previous week's food donations were allocated to people who were in need but who were not connected to the church. Such

Blood Entanglements. Stephen Offutt, Oxford University Press. © Oxford University Press 2023.
DOI: 10.1093/oso/9780197587300.003.0006

occasions allow the church to be a blessing to community members beyond the congregation.

The neighborhoods around Luz y Vida are largely controlled by gangs, and Nicolas has nearly daily interaction with gang members, gang leaders, or children of gang members. Nicolas reported that he has been able to bring young men out of gangs and into his church. Such young men need a deep form of counseling because, Nicolas says, "an ex-gang member comes from murdering people, he made a pact with the devil." Nicolas believes that evil envelops youths when they are in a gang environment.

But Nicolas is not blind to the leadership role gang leaders play in lower-class communities. "The gang is an organization, and the church is also organized. The gangs, the church, we are recognized as authorities," Nicolas explained. I asked Nicolas to explain this idea a bit more, and he began to share stories about evangelical interactions with gang leaders. For reasons that can only be guessed, Nicolas was careful not to claim any of the interactions he recounted as his own.

Nicolas shared the story of a young man named Eli, who had been a gang member but had converted to evangelicalism. While in the gang, Eli stole $3,000 of the gang's money. He also developed a rap sheet, and the police were looking for him. The police found Eli before the gang discovered his theft from them, and Eli was sent to prison.

The gang eventually found out about Eli's theft, explained Nicolas, and prepared to carry out the normal punishment for such an offense: death. Eli contacted his pastor and asked, "'Pastor, what do I do?'" In response, the pastor formed a delegation and visited the gang leader, who was also in prison. The delegation asked the gang leader "not to kill [Eli] because he was already converted to Christ," said Nicolas.

The gang leader explained that the delegation was too late: the order for Eli's death had already been given. The pastor responded by saying "'you have the authority [to revoke the order],' and [the gang leader] said 'what [Eli] did deserves death in our organization.'" The pastor persisted. He said, "We will collect the money he took and give it to you so you don't kill him." The gang leader said that would not be sufficient. So the delegation offered the money he took plus interest, if Eli's life could be spared.

"After all that," said Nicolas, "they reached an agreement. The gang leader said, 'give me the money. We will give him a good beating. It is possible he will be left with fractures, but he won't die.'" The delegation recognized that they would not get a better offer, so they agreed. The sum that was owed was a tremendous amount of money for the delegation. Such a price can simply not be paid for every young man who the gangs wish to kill. But, Nicolas explained, in addition to Eli having recently come back to God, "the parents of that young man were members of the church. In the end the church paid the money that this young man had stolen, and [the gang] gave him a good beating inside the prison." The gang leader and the pastor had negotiated what justice would look like for Eli. In the end, events played out in a way that was acceptable, or at least not the worst-case scenario, to all parties involved.

Nicolas's story occurs within the context described in the previous chapter. That is, pastors and gang leaders have significant authority within communities as they sit on top of traditional ways of organizing society, and as modern state institutions experience chronic failure.

In this chapter I take the story a step further by asking: How does community governance function in such scenarios?

I argue that, in the presence of, and often in competition with, broken state institutions, some evangelicals and gangs collaborate, usually in ad hoc ways, to provide a (distorted) form of community governance. Numerous questions emerge in the face of such a claim, such as: how does this square with the hostility and violence many pastors feel from gangs? Which evangelicals are partnering in governance with gangs? Why might some pastors be willing to partner in governance with groups they view to be under the influence of Satan? As answers to such questions emerge in the following pages, I further argue that moral logics, presented by one group or the other, undergird the ability of the two groups to understand each other and work together in a shared context.

What Do Governments Do?

To build such an argument, I need to proffer an understanding of what governments do. Tomes have been written debating the proper functions of government. Constitutions and other guiding documents have been inscribed with overlapping but differing opinions. My interest is not to blaze a new trail in governance theory, but to work with widely accepted categories of government responsibilities.

Weaver, Rock, and Kusterer (1997) provide such analysis. Working within the mainstream ideas of classical liberalism, they explain the role of governments in developing countries and provide detailed lists

Functions of Government	Provided by Gangs	Provided by Evangelicals
Protection and security	Protect territory, organizations, and individuals from non-gang violence.	Protect people from gang violence and gang recruitment; protect youths in gangs from police violence.
Establish and Enforce Rules	Boundary-crossing restrictions and other territorially specific rules.	Ascetic practices.
Judicial Services	Sentencing and punishment of offenders of gang rules.	Advocacy for reprieve/leniency when gangs seek to punish community members.
Production and Distribution of Public Goods		Provide education programs, disaster relief, healthcare, and spiritual & socio-emotional support.

Figure 5.1 Functions of government provided by gangs and evangelicals.

of government responsibilities and services.[1] From these, four general categories of government functions emerge. Governments need to: 1) provide protection and security, 2) establish and enforce rules, 3) produce and distribute public goods, and 4) provide judicial services. Collecting taxes is also a government function, but I address this in the chapter on the economy.

The roles evangelicals and gangs play in fulfilling these functions at the local level are determined largely by the source, strength, and type of power they wield. As was established in the previous chapter, both groups have local authority because of their patrimonial systems and the *cacique* approach to local leadership. The two groups distinguish themselves from one another by the forms of power they exercise: hard versus soft power, and the social locations of their power: "street" versus "church." These similarities and differences help to pattern a still dizzying variety of interactions between evangelicals and gangs in each of the governance categories explored below. A summary can be found in Figure 5.1.

Protection and Security

Protection within a specific territory can be the legitimating service patrimonial systems provide (Collins 2011). This can also be said of nation states and mafias, both of which offer protection for a fee (Tilly 1985). Protection

Protection and Security

Gangs	Evangelicals
Protection for individuals	Protection from gang violence
Protection for businesses	Protection from gang involvement
Protection for churches	Protect gang members from the gang
Protection for NGOs	Protect gang members from police

Figure 5.2 Provisions of protection and security by gangs and evangelicals (created by Thomas Hampton).

is thus a service to be offered and a way to further consolidate power. It is thus logical, if somewhat surprising, that stories of gangs protecting people, businesses, NGOs, and churches surfaced in my research. This logic extends to the stories I heard about ways in which evangelicals protected members of the community, including gang members (see Figure 5.2).

Gangs Offer Protection

Although people fear gangs, they also seek gang protection. This includes evangelicals. Ana's story, recounted more fully in Chapter 3, illustrates this. As an evangelical, Ana went to the local gang leader to seek protection from her uncles, who were in the gang. Protection was granted, and her life improved immediately.

Pastor Nicolas also recounted an example of a woman who benefited from gang protection. He explained that Gloria, a woman in the community, was the victim of spousal abuse. She was searching for a way out, and a friend suggested she to go to the police. After considering this, she said "no, because this neighborhood is full of gang members, and if I go to the police then the gang will come to me and demand to know: 'what am I doing with the police?'"

With this in mind, Nicolas explained, Gloria decided to take her case to the gang leader. The gang responded by sending two members to visit her husband. "They went as friends," Nicolas said. "They talked to him, but as they left they said, 'Look, just one thing, do not hit your wife.'" Nicolas explained that although the message was delivered politely, Gloria's husband knew it had teeth. "That man knows that if he hits [Gloria] again, they will kill him, they will not put him in jail. That's what he understands, they're not coming to take him to jail, they're going to come and kill him." Such a deterrent is, to Nicolas's way of thinking, more likely to keep Gloria safe than the deterrents the police might offer. The examples of Ana and Gloria show (among other things) how individuals can benefit from gang protection.

Businesses, and evangelicals who work in businesses, also benefit from gang protection. Samuel, for example, works at a warehouse that pays an extortion fee to the gang, or what the gangs refer to as a "protection fee." Samuel is an evangelical and the brother of a local pastor. He has developed a working relationship with Andre, a warehouse delivery man and a gang member. "[Andre] has a leadership position in his clique, and he is very *tatuado* [has a lot of gang tattoos]," Samuel explained. "I don't ask him who he has killed. If you know something, you are now an accomplice." As an office holder in the clique, Andre is likely involved in the arrangement the gang has with the warehouse.

One day, some things at the warehouse went missing. When the gang learned about this, they consulted the warehouse manager. "'Let us look into it,'" they said, according to Samuel. After a few days, they came back and told the manager he did not have anything to worry about—they "took care of the problem." Samuel does not know the details of how this occurred, but he does know that since that incident, nothing else has gone missing. As an evangelical, he feels the need to be careful around gang members, but he also feels that both he and the merchandise he handles are protected by the gang.

Churches also often experience protection from gangs. Pastor Enzo, for example, said that the local gang leader came to visit his church unexpectedly. It "had to do with the fact that some kids were playing on the church roof, and they ruined some of the roofing. So someone told [the gang leader], and [the gang leader] told the kids to knock it off." The gang leader just came by to let Enzo know that he had taken care of the issue.

Other pastors reported similar experiences. I asked Santiago, an older pastor in a different neighborhood, if he was able to walk around his community in safety. He explained that the gang ensured his safety wherever he went. He then volunteered that "[The gang members] even take care of the church building." Santiago also said that gangs sometimes ensure safe passage for those who attend church events: "We celebrate different activities at the church. So they have told me that they would not mess with the people that visit my church." Santiago added that "We didn't approach them. It was actually them that got in contact with us" to create this arrangement. Santiago appreciates the extension of this kind of protection; it is also likely that the gang gains legitimacy as it protects a respected pastor and congregation.

It should be noted that the complicated nature and wide variance of security arrangements between gangs and churches means that pastors can also feel extremely threatened by gangs. I walked through a community with an older pastor with a large church, a *cacique*, who was on friendly terms with the neighborhood gang members. We passed a house church which had a dirt floor and walls made out of corrugated steel sheets. The *cacique* commented that the pastor of that church was probably too afraid of gang members to ever have a conversation with one of them. Pastors in such situations are much more likely to be victimized.

But the age of pastors and the size of their churches does not explain all the variance. Some of the same pastors who reported examples of being protected by gang members also reported personal threats from gang members. Only a few evangelicals I talked to experienced consistently positive interactions with gang members. Churches are robbed in El Salvador, and church buildings have been used by gangs as drug sales points. In the previous chapter, I discussed the willingness of some gang cliques to kill people coming out of a church service. While none of this negates the evidence just presented that gang leaders often extend protection to evangelical people, businesses, NGOs, and churches, it does complicate the way such protection needs to be contextualized and perceived.

Evangelicals Offer Protection

Evangelical pastors seek to ensure the well-being of community members. This can mean addressing spiritual or psycho-emotional concerns, but pastors can also seek to provide physical protection. Such efforts can include protecting congregants from gang violence, deterring youths from gang involvement, and protecting gang members from gang and police violence. Unfortunately, such efforts are not always successful.

Pastors seek to protect congregants from gang violence in very practical, day-to-day ways. Benjamin, an Assemblies of God pastor in Las Palmas, recounted an evening in which he was walking home with some youths after a church service. Along the way they encountered two gang members shooting a man. Benjamin directed the boys to run with him, and they found a hiding place until the shooting stopped.

Pastors also try to protect youths by steering them away from gang membership. Pastor Jose shared an example of Bernardo, who was in his church, but who had decided he wanted to be part of a gang. There are unwritten rules, or moral logics, in Jose's community that gangs cannot jump youths into the gang who are fully part of a church. When Jose heard that Bernardo had joined the gang, therefore, he went to talk to the gang leader. "They already had him inside," said Pastor Jose. "But I talked to them for two hours and they released him." Bernardo didn't appreciate Pastor Jose's intervention and tried to join a second gang. But, said Jose, "the same thing happened. [The gang leader] knew that he belonged to the church, so he was released."

Eventually, Bernardo found a clique that did not know he was part of the church, and Jose was not aware that he joined it until too much time had passed. Then the events that Jose feared began to play out. "After a year [in the gang], they asked him to kill the stepfather in order to become a [full member]," said Jose. "However, he didn't have the heart to do it." Knowing that his failure to complete the mission put him in danger, Bernardo didn't want to leave his house. But "one day, his girlfriend asked him to accompany her to go to the market. We believe that the gang sent her. Being on the street, he was put in a vehicle and murdered because he did not obey the order to kill his stepfather," said Jose. This example shows the extent to which Pastor Jose went to protect Bernardo. It also shows that, in spite of their best intentions, violence often finds people that pastors seek to protect.

While I heard more reports of pastors trying to protect community members from gang violence, numerous pastors also reported efforts to protect active gang members. The "rescue motif" that Brenneman (2012) discusses is part of this dynamic: pastors create exit strategies from the gang for youths who wish to convert. But there are times when pastors protect gang members even as they remain in the gang.

Police sweeps often create such dynamics. Police sweeps are widely viewed by community members as violent incursions by heavily armed outsiders. One evangelical leader reported that when police raids occur, pastors will sometimes hide gang members. A second evangelical leader I spoke with affirmed this notion. He noted that it makes sense for pastors to protect young people that they have seen grow up in their community, some of whom may have attended their churches. But it is not just pastors who help gang members in such situations: Wolseth (2011) describes one of his subjects being chased and shot at by police, and then escaping when an older woman slyly incorporated him into an evangelical worship service. Such instances demonstrate the intimate community linkages between church goers and gang members.

Establish and Enforce Rules

Gang leaders and pastors are able to set and enforce many of the rules of daily living in lower-class Salvadoran neighborhoods. Sometimes they work in ways that look almost coordinated; this happens when mutual interests or mutual enemies draw them together. At other times evangelical and gang rules push in different directions; this can result in violence against evangelicals.

Evangelical Rules and Their Impact on Gangs

Evangelicals want young people, including gang members, to stay away from vices such as violence, drug and alcohol abuse, and extramarital sex. They believe such actions dishonor God and have negative impacts on human flourishing. They are, more simply, sins. Within congregations, pastors are able to discipline those who engage in such activities. At the community level, pastors have only soft power options of suggestion and persuasion. Still, pastors go to great lengths to reach people with this message. Although not everyone who hears the message restrains from such behavior, the underlying moral logic makes sense to them. The impact pastors can have on gang members themselves is incomplete, but often surprising.

Pastor Gustavo, for example, argues that church leaders and parents need to engage youths so that they stay out of gangs and choose productive patterns of behavior. "I've seen what [gangs] do," said Gustavo, who is in his sixties. "I've put myself in positions of danger, to be honest. And what has to be done is you have to persuade them and encourage them. I have a lot of trust in these young people, so I've approached them and a number of them have been rescued from these problems." To the extent that Gustavo can be persuasive, and the extent to which he can convince people that the moral logic of evangelicalism should be adhered to, he is able to enforce evangelical standards.

Pastors who have enough influence also try to restrict sinful activities on or near their properties. This can mean restricting gang movement in these areas, at least while church programs are being conducted. A Baptist Tabernacle pastor, for example, has a church ministry for children that meets during the weekdays. He explained to gang leaders that because the church does not have a sports field, the children have to play on the street. So the pastor asked the gang leaders to refrain from letting their members go through the street during those times. In large part, the gang members honor this request. "They have respect," explained the pastor. "They do not interrupt [the children's ministry]. With some of them, we have had conflicts, but we have stopped them. I ask them: 'What is your problem?' They reply: 'No problem, Pastor!' And they proceed to use a different street." One can see in this example moral authority being acknowledged, and obeyed, even among gang members.

Erik tries to establish a more permanent violence and drug free zone around his church property. Gangs do not always adhere to this policy, as Erik related a story of a man who was killed right in front of the church. The perpetrators "came up and shot him three times, took a picture of him with a cell phone and ran off," said Erik. The victim was not an evangelical, but his wife was a member of Erik's church. "I went to the gang members from that area, and I was fuming," said Erik. "And I told them, 'how dare you do that.'" In response, Erik said, "they apologized, you know, [they said] 'I'm sorry for this.' I said 'if you would have told me I would have gotten him out of the community...' They told me, 'you don't know where he comes from or what he's done ... So, we killed him, that's what we do.' So they felt a valid excuse for killing him."

Erik's story reveals two different sets of rules and two different sets of enforcement policies. All of the actors understand both sets of rules and recognize their legitimacy. On this occasion, the gangs enforced their rules at the cost of violating the pastor's rules. They apologized, but they maintained their right to enforce their rules as well as the method of enforcement (murder) that they chose to use. In this case, while soft power was recognized to be legitimate, hard power won out.

Still, soft power could not be completely silenced. Erik later reported saying to them, "I'm not happy as a pastor. This is my area. You are in my area. You are treading on my people. I don't want that." In an environment where many people avert their eyes when they are in the presence of a gang member, such discourse reveals Erik's social status in the community. Erik nonetheless maintains a humble posture, saying that, "I'm not anybody important or anybody brave. But I've done that out of a holy anger. Because it makes me mad." How much difference Erik's protests made in curbing future acts of violence is not clear, but this kind of discourse constitutes, and thus in some way shapes, community culture.

Gang Rules and Their Impact on Evangelicals

Gang rules for communities have different motivations and seek to achieve different ends than evangelical rules. Nonetheless, sometimes gang and evangelical rules align. For example, some evangelical churches, such as the Apostles and Prophets denomination, maintain strict dress codes for their members. Women must wear skirts; men must wear shirts with collars and long pants. This style of evangelicalism does particularly well in rural areas, where, says Moody, some gang rules in some communities "are similar to the legalistic rules of the conservative Pentecostal churches, prohibiting women's use of pants or the cutting of hair for women," (Moody 2020). Cliques that institute such rules may intentionally imitate those of local evangelical churches.

In other instances, evangelicals may benefit from gang rules even if there is not a corresponding evangelical rule. In the early days of the coronavirus pandemic, for example, gangs enforced a quarantine in their communities. One national gang leader released a recording that said: "We don't want to see anyone in the street. If you go out, it better be only to the store, and you better be wearing a mask" (Linthicum, O'Toole, & Renderos 2020). Gangs also modified the extortion payments that people had to pay, especially informal vendors, because they recognized sales made by such vendors during the quarantine period would dip (Martínez, Martínez, & Lemus 2020). This was a rare occasion in which the gangs chose to enforce a state issued decree, but it matched up well with their interest in providing protection for their communities. Many evangelicals lived in the affected communities.

Gang leaders were not, however, motivated solely or even primarily by public health concerns in their communities. Gang leaders stated to the media that they were worried Salvadoran hospitals would not treat gang members who became seriously ill, and that gang members would be last in line for scarce resources such as ventilators. One national gang leader also expressed concern that increased police presence could appear in the communities they controlled as part of state efforts to enforce the quarantine. By enforcing the quarantine themselves, gangs believed they could show such a move as not necessary (Martínez, Martínez, & Lemus 2020). Enforcing the quarantine thus became an occasion in which gangs could serve their own interests and demonstrate their considerable power, with the felicitous side effect of reducing COVID-19 incidences in the communities.

Evangelicals do not benefit, and are not in favor, of all gang rules. One of the biggest impositions on daily life for many community members, including evangelicals, is gangs' regulation and restriction of movement. In addition to monitoring who enters and exits the communities they control, gangs may also regulate movement within such communities. Walter, an Assemblies of God pastor, explained that in the neighborhoods around his church, "when someone enters a zone [the gang] will ask for their documents. And if they see that they are from a rival zone, . . . right there they kill them. They make that person disappear . . . ." The constant surveillance, the strict regulation of movement, and the violence used to enforce boundaries creates fear for many residents, including evangelicals.

Some who live under such conditions are forced give up jobs that are located in opposing gang territories. Others, desperate for income, try to keep their jobs. This is more feasible, although still risky, for people who work in locations that are distant from their homes—cliques are sometimes less concerned and less knowledgeable about opposing gang territories that are not adjacent to their own. One evangelical I talked to is in this situation. He lives in Las Palmas but works an hour away by bus. He said that every night, when he re-enters his community, he thanks God when he is not killed.

Evangelicals can sometimes use their soft power to massage boundary rules and to help those who suffer losses in employment or are otherwise negatively affected. A leader of an international NGO reported that some of the churches they work with have opened up ongoing dialogue with gang members. This has allowed them to ask for, and to receive, permission for children to cross gang boundaries to participate in the NGO's programs. Sometimes there is less intentionality: Benjamin, a younger pastor in Las Palmas, lives in one territory, but his church is in another. Each day he simply crosses the boundary. While he does so warily, to this point gangs have allowed him to cross.

Where such concessions are not granted, pastors try to alleviate the negative impact of such regulations. One pastor, for example, talked of a youth in his congregation that had to leave his job because it was across the gang's border. The pastor said that he found a new job for the young man within the gang territory.

Evangelicals and Gangs against the Rules of the State

In areas of life where evangelical and gang interests coincide, leaders of both groups endorse certain rules. Perhaps the most uniting theme for evangelicals and gangs is that they do not like some state-created and police-enforced regulations. Gang resistance against the state is obvious and further elaboration here is not needed. The case of evangelical resistance is more nuanced, and stems from the historic marginalization they have felt, not least because of linkages between the state and Catholicism. Evangelicals' social location has thus led them to operate outside the spheres of formal state and cultural regulations (Bueno 2001).

As they negotiate life and governance with gangs in lower-class communities, some evangelical pastors are frustrated by a law that criminalizes collusion with gangs. Although I never asked about this issue, several pastors and other evangelical leaders volunteered to share their concerns. At stake is the ability of churches and NGOs to do ministry in the community, including among gang members and their family connections. Funerals of known gang members, for example, draw significant attention. Erik said that, "If you're working with the gang members you have to be super careful. The government will come back and pinch you . . . they can accuse you of being part of the gangs or helping them out and pastors have been accused of that. I don't know if [those specific] pastors are helping them or not." A local pastor from a different community could not clearly articulate what the law stipulated, but he expressed clear frustration with the dynamics it created. While that pastor backed away from service projects that incorporated gang members, it is likely that some pastors choose to continue with gang interactions that are in violation of the law. They may do so with a clear conscience because they do not think the state has sufficient legitimacy to make such a law in first place, and they know that such a law cannot be universally enforced.[2]

Formal pronouncements by national evangelical leaders reinforce such grassroots evangelical sentiment. Mario Vega is the senior pastor of Elim, the largest megachurch in El Salvador and among the ten largest churches in the world. Vega is one of the three most important evangelical leaders in the country (Offutt 2015). Elim is located in Soyapango, a lower-class part of the capitol city's urban sprawl. Numerous pastors within Elim were previously gang members, and Vega has "worked extensively with the country's main gangs," (Papadovassilakis 2020). When the Bukele administration announced the Territorial Control Plan and claimed that it would eliminate or greatly reduce gang presence in communities, Vega was among the plans skeptics. (This was Bukele's plan when he came into office in 2019: not the state of exception he announced in 2022.) According to Insight Crime, Vega

> referred to the Territorial Control Plan as a "tool for publicity," with "no innovations" compared to the hardline policies of previous governments. He told InSight Crime that El Salvador's reduction in homicides is rather part of a region-wide behavioral change which has seen gangs in the so-called Northern Triangle countries of El Salvador, Guatemala and Honduras unilaterally decide to cool down killings, which in turn has driven down the homicide rate across the region in recent years. (Papadovassilakis 2020)

By making such comments in the press, Vega positioned himself as a critic of a government policy which is surely also unpopular with the gangs.

Provide Judicial Services

The provision of judicial services generates perhaps the most direct and intentional collaboration between evangelicals and gangs. This includes the adjudication of disputes and decisions about appropriate punishment for those who violate community rules. Such collaboration occurs organically; there are endless combinations of actors between which disputes emerge and equally endless ways in which pastors and clique leaders pattern their discussions and shape decisions about such disputes. Generally, though, the process involves the probing and negotiation of strength and type of authority that the parties possess, as well as the presentation of, and acceptance or resistance to, moral logics.

Dispute Resolution

Particularly influential pastors often adjudicate disagreements between gangs and others in the community. This is especially likely when pastors are over fifty and gang leaders are in their teens. Pastor Daniel, for example, is in his sixties and has pastored the same church for over thirty years. Current gang members in the community have known, or known of, Daniel since they were young children. Although Daniel talks disapprovingly of gang activities, he maintains a fatherly disposition when talking about specific gang members that he knows.

UNUSUAL ALLIANCES IN COMMUNITY GOVERNANCE 131

Within this relational context, Daniel explained that he often settles problems between gangs and other members of the community. Gang members call families in the community and ask them to pay "rent." Families sometimes feel the fee is too burdensome. In these cases, Daniel said, "the family would look for me . . . even [if] they were not from the church. They would look for me to help them," said Daniel. Daniel has conversations with families to understand the situation. Then, said Daniel, "I would talk to [the gang members], and [the gang members] would make it right." In other words, if Daniel advises the gang to reduce or eliminate the extortion payment required from the family, they often act accordingly. Daniel is thus able to maintain a form of relational balance and sense of good will within the community.

Such dynamics highlight Daniel's status of *cacique*. His authority is derived from the moral and religious sphere, but it extends to other areas, including civil disputes with economic implications. The gangs trust Daniel enough that they submit to the decisions that he is making, even when he argues against actions they have taken and in favor of others in the community.

A different set of dynamics emerges when conflict arises between congregations and gang cliques. Evangelicals caught in such conflict may seek guidance from national level leaders. Nicolas, the pastor mentioned in the chapter's introduction, recounted the experience of Eduardo, another pastor in his denomination. Gang members shot Eduardo's car eighteen times, which left him both terrified and bewildered because, Nicolas explained, "gangs don't do those things." Such acts fell outside of Nicolas's understanding of gangs' moral logics.

Pastors in Eduardo's community and denomination discussed the attack. Since it was aimed directly at a pastor and was of such a violent nature, the pastors felt it would be better not to try to manage the situation at the local level. Rather, Nicolas said, "we spoke to (the head of the denomination to which Nicolas and the pastor belong) and told him what happened." The denominational leader, according to Nicolas, sent a delegate to the prison to talk to a national gang leader about the incident. The gang leader said he did not know about the hit and assured the delegate (who was also a pastor) that he respects pastors and no orders are issued to do anything against them, "unless they have problems with the gang." He promised to investigate what had happened.

The delegate returned to the prison a short while later. According to Nicolas, the gang leader said, "I've found it, it is a little group that's apart.

Tell the pastors to forgive me, but those fellows who riddled the pastor's car, I will give orders to remove them." The delegate understood the gang leader to be saying that he would have them killed. According to Nicolas, the delegate replied, "we do not want that, just make sure it doesn't happen again." The gang leader consented, and afterward the gang member responsible for the shooting personally apologized to Eduardo. For Nicolas, the lesson to be learned from this experience is that if congregations run into problems with local cliques, "you can look for communication, a solution." From his perspective, most or all misunderstandings between evangelicals and gangs can be worked out. The patrimonies, entangled as they are, can peacefully coexist.

In a third kind of arbitration, pastors seek to tell gang members that they are guilty of negatively impacting community members. The goal is to allow community members to live without excessive gang harassment. Erik, for example, has set up meetings with gang leaders to discuss gang treatment of children. "I met with them at a respectful level and I asked them, 'please don't harass the kids on the way to school. Please let these young people that are going to church go to church and quit trying to influence them. . . .'" Erik explicitly named his moral authority during the meeting. He told the gang leaders that "God's brought me here to do what I'm doing." With this as a preface, he asked the gang members to let him make a difference in the lives children who are often the younger siblings or cousins (children within the overlapping gang/evangelical patrimonies) of his conversation partners. Erik reported that the meeting was very positive, and he believes it helped to make the community more open.

Other pastors also reported confronting gang members about their treatment of community members. Pastor Jose referenced Pedro, a security guard who was working near his church. A gang member was harassing the guard and issued a threat against him. Pastor Jose began to look into the situation and learned that the security guard had been in the gang, but then petitioned the gang to leave so that he could become an evangelical. Pedro did not, however, fully convert. Instead, "he kept drinking and asking for rent on behalf of the gang," said the pastor, but Pedro then kept the money he collected for himself.

These are serious offenses from gangs' perspectives. The pastor, however, saw the human element in Pedro's case. He believed that Pedro was simply a young man struggling to find his way in a difficult environment. So Pastor

Jose said he "confronted the situation, I went to talk seriously with [the gang member] and told him please, do not disturb [Pedro]." The gang member backed away from his threat. Pastor Jose did not challenge the gang's moral logic; to some extent he seemed to agree with it. But in his intervention on Pedro's behalf, he convinced the gang that their adjudication of this logic should take a broader set of variables into account. All parties knew, however, that if Pedro continued with the offending behaviors, he would encounter more and serious problems with the gang.

Sentencing

The previous example also relates to the second set of judicial services that gangs and evangelicals sometimes negotiate: sentencing. Gang violence is often intended as retribution for a violation of gang rules or disrespect of gang members. Gangs often (but do not always) meet to calibrate the level of violence that should be used for a given offense.

Evangelical leaders sometimes have sufficient moral authority in communities to influence such deliberations. Typically, their efforts are intended to reduce or commute the sentences determined by gangs. Nicolas's story at the beginning of the chapter about the youth who stole money from the gang is a case in point.

Another example came from Pastor Jose about Gerardo, a youth who ran away whenever he saw gang members. This aroused the suspicions of the gang; in that neighborhood running could be interpreted as a sign of disrespect. "Running away is dangerous because they can kill him," explained Jose. The gang began to chase Gerardo whenever they saw him. So Pastor Jose went to the gang leader. "I asked him: 'has Gerardo done something to you? Why do they persecute him?' He answered: 'he runs away.' I asked them not to kill him and not to pursue him anymore. They obeyed and no longer persecuted him." Jose indicated that such conversations are a regular part of his communication with the gang leader. "This is how we do it . . . we face them, we sit with them and ask them what happens to [those they punish], why they [in this case] are chasing them." The status implied in such conversations is that of a *cacique*.

Other cases are more serious, and church leaders may take on risk to themselves when they inject themselves into decision making processes. This was the case for Sito, a child enrolled in a church-based ministry. One day Sito was kidnapped by the gang and taken to one of the gang's "punishment houses" to be killed. Angela, the pastor's wife, learned what had happened and rushed to plead for the child's life, taking Manuel, the director of the children's ministry, with her. The gang leader did not immediately capitulate and made threats against Angela and Manuel. But the two persevered, and eventually he released the child.

Such examples demonstrate how church leaders who wield moral authority influence gang decisions. Some pastors appear to thrive in this role. Again, such pastors tend to be those who are older and who have achieved status in the community. One such pastor told me, "As a church we have been serious and we do not allow ourselves to be intimidated." For other pastors, attempting to engage in such negotiations is not easy. One NGO leader explained that "It is terrifying for them too. But they feel it is their responsibility." And although evangelical leaders can save lives by influencing the sentences gangs meet out, gang leaders do not always listen. They sometimes elect to carry out their originally intended punishments.

On those occasions when gang leaders do listen to pastors, they may feel like they are doing the pastor "a favor" by commuting or lessening a sentence. When this is the case, systems of exchange, not unlike Mauss's (1990 [1950]) gift theory, can emerge. A seasoned NGO leader with decades of experience in the region said that "when you ask for a favor, you get asked for favors back. It is kind of a basic human relationship." A second NGO leader from another organization confirmed that this often occurs.

The dilemma for pastors, then, is whether they can or should enter into patterns of exchange with gang members. By not doing so, they may miss out on the opportunity to reduce violence; by doing so, unhealthy linkages with gangs can quickly materialize. The aforementioned NGO leader stated unequivocally that "there are pastors who have maintained their integrity doing that," but then added that "I am sure there are some stories that would be really hard to hear about where pastors have compromised themselves." Johnson (2016) gathered some evidence to this effect. He reported that gang members in Brazilian prisons convinced some pastors to give them access to their bank accounts. In my research I (not surprisingly) never heard direct confessions, but I did hear numerous allusions to pastors in communities who had lost their way. The ethical decisions that emerge in these tricky and often dangerous contexts are highly complex; it is easy to see how evangelical entanglements of this nature can veer in directions that make them complicit with illicit activity.

Produce and Distribute Public Goods

Producing and distributing public goods is the fourth core function of governing entities. Transportation, education, and health infrastructure are among the most common and basic public goods. In Las Palmas, the state provides such infrastructure. But the state's provisions are either not available for everyone or are of very low quality. I did not find any evidence in my research that gangs provided the communities in this study with public goods.[3] Evangelicals, on the other hand, offered a broad array of services that filled the gaps of failing local state institutions. This increased the amount of soft power evangelicals had with community members and with gangs.

Churches and evangelical non-profit organizations in Las Palmas offer training in computer literacy, disaster relief, children's education, children's summer camps, spiritual guidance, and even transportation services, as pickup trucks can be seen with churchgoers crowding in the back in the evenings and on Sundays as they go to church. Less regularly, Las Palmas's evangelical transnational connections provide medical and dental clinics as local churches host short term medical mission teams. Such public services, taken collectively, move the needle in terms of the well-being of Las Palmas's residents.

Education and care for children is a particular focus for evangelicals in Las Palmas. Near the entrance of one of Las Palmas's lower-class neighborhoods, just a few doors down from the local jail, there is a Seventh Day Adventist school. The founder, Mirabel, was born in Las Palmas and was raised in one of Las Palmas's nicer neighborhoods. Mirabel said that when she was twenty-two years old, she recognized that most of Las Palmas's children were not receiving a quality education, and God put it on her heart to start a school. Part of the school's curriculum is thus dedicated to helping children come to know God more fully.

Mirabel started small, offering classes only for kindergarteners and first graders. But she added a grade each year, and now students can complete their primary and secondary education at the school. When I interviewed Mirabel, 216 students were enrolled; she hoped she could eventually increase enrollment to 300 students.

The Adventist School is a private school, and thus not accessible to the entire community. Mirabel has to charge students a tuition fee of about $25 per month to keep the school open. Pastor Enzo, for example, lives just around the corner from the school. He thinks Mirabel's students are very disciplined and receive a good education, but he feels the cost puts it out of reach for his family.

Still, the school is positively viewed in the community. It is a source of local employment for teachers and staff. According to Mirabel, some of her graduates have gone on to universities and technical schools. They have studied to become doctors, nurses and teachers. "They are people that contribute to society," said Mirabel proudly. The education the Adventist church provides is perceived to be significantly better than that of the public school system.

Other evangelical initiatives target the poorest in the community. The child enrichment center at Pastor Nicolas's church is one such program. Over 300 public school students participate. Each child is sponsored by a well-known international NGO, and local program staff reinforce their classroom exercises and also attend to other needs the child might have. The program is discussed more fully in Chapter 7.

Pastor Vincente's church supports and enriches public school education in ways that are different from the program at Pastor Nicolas's church. Perhaps the most significant public good that Pastot Vincente's church provided during my research was access to its building and grounds. The local public elementary school was being torn down in order to be replaced by a new building. During construction, Vincente allowed the school to have classes in the church building. Vincente's church also works with an international NGO (a different NGO than the one partnering with Pastor Nicolas's church) to implement enrichment programs that run for twelve weeks. Each child in the program is presented with a gift box that usually includes a toy, articles of clothing, and personal care items. The pastor guides the children through the twelve-week curriculum that is based on biblical stories. At the end of the twelve weeks, the church throws a party for the graduates. Vincente said that they reached 862 students in two schools, and the program was popular with the students.

It is important to keep in mind that in all of the public goods produced by evangelicals just mentioned, either people who are connected to gangs or gang members themselves benefit from such programs. As Pastor Nicolas explained, "The love of God is for everyone," so, although the law prohibiting organizations from helping gangs sometimes creates problems, most pastors do not try to exclude gang members or their affiliates from their ministries. Pastor Vincente concurred with Pastor Nicolas's statement, saying "I know [the local gang members], . . . I speak to them about Christ and they respect me. Whenever they see me, they say, 'Brother, Pastor, God bless you and I wish you well.' I always invite them here." Vincente comfortably talked about the ex-gang members who were members of his church and noted that one ex-gang member had been very helpful in starting a daughter church in an adjacent community. Gang presence in churches and ministries will be further explained in Chapter 7; I mention it here because it is important to remember that the public goods evangelicals provide often benefit all residents, including gang members.

Conclusion

I have argued that evangelicals and gangs collaborate to fulfill the basic functions of government in lower-class Salvadoran communities. Leaders of both groups act as internal stakeholders who are helping to order their own community. Along the way, I have suggested that another layer of analysis is needed to explain how evangelical pastors, whose ranks are often targets of gang violence and who view gangs to be under the influence of Satan, become willing dialogue and governance partners with gangs. I offer moral logics, which are asserted, resisted, and accepted at different times by both groups, a potential key to unlocking this puzzle. Here I provide concluding analysis of both arguments.

Collaborative Governance

The evidence presented in this chapter indicates the endless ways in which pastors and clique leaders pattern the discussions that determine community governance. The process involves the probing and negotiation of strength and type of authority that the two groups possess in a given community and at a given time. These dynamics are unstable and highly dependent on aptitudes and dispositions of specific actors. Sometimes local understandings of justice are violated. Gangs can manipulate pastors, who then find themselves in morally compromised positions. Even when their integrity is intact, pastors might fail to protect community members who depend on them. Government failure, in other words, is common.

Often, though, collaboration between evangelicals and gangs results in the best form of governance that is currently on offer for lower-class Salvadoran communities. The two groups collaborate across four key mandates of governments: protection and security, establishing and enforcing rules, judicial services, and the production and distribution of public goods. Failed or failing state government entities are absent to different degrees in all of these sectors; evangelicals and gangs fill in for the state's inadequacies and, in some cases, push the state further to the side.

Gangs exercise hard power; evangelicals exercise soft power. Hard power gives gangs a stronger hand than evangelicals in the areas of providing security, establishing and enforcing laws, and (although less so) in judicial services. Even though gangs may have more influence in such areas, evangelicals can benefit from gang policies and decisions, especially where gangs protect evangelicals and church properties, and where evangelical and gang rules align.

But evangelicals' soft power should not be discounted: it changes community dynamics and patterns of behavior. Of most direct relevance are two points: first, gang members sometimes need, urgently, the protection that evangelicals sometimes provide in the face of police raids. Second, public goods generated by evangelicals are a core part of the soft power they wield. Such goods put legs on evangelicals' moral authority and provide material evidence that evangelicals have a legitimate stake in determining events in the community. Evangelical pastors thus have real leverage in the evangelical/gang community governance partnership.

Evangelicals often use such leverage to reduce various forms of gang violence. This is consistent with roles that religious actors often play in conflict zones around the world. Religious actors utilize "moral and spiritual resources that emphasize shared identities and experiences, common moral and spiritual values" to resolve problems in society (Kadayifci in Birdsall 2021). In the case of El Salvador, evangelical leaders use their unusual ability to dialogue with, and even confront, gang leaders who are considering violent or oppressive strategies to pursue their own goals.

It is important to remember that not all evangelical pastors and leaders are able to engage gang leaders in this way. While most pastors are the *caciques* of their own congregations, fewer rise to the status of being a *cacique* at the community level. Those who fall in the latter category are those most likely to create productive relationships with gang leaders in the context of community governance.

Moral Logics

There are many potential obstacles to evangelical co-governance with gangs. A central one is the aforementioned belief of evangelicals that gangs are under the influence of Satan. The behavior patterns of the two groups also vary widely, and divergent interests within communities can pit the groups against each other. These and other realities break down trust, especially evangelical trust of gangs. In the face of such tensions, what makes the co-governance that I have empirically observed possible? I suggest that one key to this puzzle are the moral logics that circulate in lower-class Salvadoran communities.

Evangelicals and gangs both introduce moral logics, or assertions of how things ought to be, into community discourse. These logics often do not match behavior, but consistent messaging of how things ought to be none-theless allows values to be shared and mutually understood. It helps that at the abstract level, evangelical and gang morality overlaps—a fact that is connected to their shared cosmology, as discussed in Chapter 2. But even when moral assertions are not shared by the conversation partners, their articulations help to build greater understanding. In this way, evangelicals and gangs begin to have a set of shared expectations. Along with overlapping family and patrimonial networks, such discursive work helps to establish grounds for collaboration.

Moral assertions often color relations between evangelicals and gangs with strands of respect and, within specific relational constellations, cariño, or affection. The latter is perhaps best exemplified by Pastor Daniel's relationship with younger gang members in his community. Even where such affection does not exist, moral logics often give both sets of actors a sense that although they stand in different positions of the community's cosmology, they understand how the world should work in similar ways. Pastor Nicolas can thus confidently state that gangs don't shoot up a pastor's car, even after this precise event occurred. It turned out that Pastor Nicolas's belief that gang members should not do such a thing was validated by a gang leader. When moral logics have the consensus of evangelicals and gangs, even if they are often violated in everyday life, they create greater trust between evangelicals and gangs within the communities they share.

It needs to be emphasized that moral logics have social power in spite of the fact that patterns of behavior often do not align with moral assertions. Gang assertions uncovered in this study included orders to a community member to stop beating his wife, even while gang members themselves are frequently guilty of abusing or even killing their domestic partners (Martínez 2016). Regardless, it was a moral logic that resonated with Pastor Nicolas and established a common moral ground between the actors. Likewise, when a gang leader stopped by to tell Pastor Enzo that he ordered kids to stay off the church roof, Enzo naturally agreed that kids should not be destroying church property. Such assertions send signals to evangelicals that gang members share at least some elements of their basic understanding of right and wrong.

Other logics put forth by gangs are more complicated. Gangs communicate, for example, that violent punishment is sometimes justified and even needed in the community. Pastors in this study consistently rejected the use of violence as a deterrent to negative behavior. But sometimes they agreed that there should be a deterrent to such behaviors, and at least one pastor admitted that a gang leader was right—violence might be the most effective deterrent—even if the pastor argued against its use. Pastors' ability to understand why gangs use violence, and when to expect violence, established an important base line for evangelical communication to gangs in several cases discussed in this study. In some of them, pastors worked within this logic to successfully advocate for alternative, less violent approaches to community governance.

Moral logics can also be proposed by evangelicals. Pastor Jose, for example, asserted that a youth who was a member of his church could not be jumped into a gang. A gang leader accepted this logic and kept a church-going youth from joining his clique. Multiple pastors, Erik among them, told gang members to let little children in the community come to church so they didn't "end up like them." This made sense to the gang members: they wanted a different life for their younger siblings, at least in theory, and the gang members believed the church could help to put the younger children on a different life trajectory. Here again, a shared understanding of a moral, edifying life, facilitated by public goods that evangelicals produce, reinforced trust and communication between the two groups.

Some evangelical moral logics are resisted by gang members. Gang members do not, for example, live by evangelicalism's ascetic codes. Still, gang members validate asceticism by understanding it as part of the moral fabric of the community. This is the underlying assumption of the Brenneman/Wolseth thesis. In specific instances, such as when gang members are near church grounds, some gang members conform to these ideas of morality.

Such validation, along with isolated instances of conformity, provides more layers of trust between the two groups.

In sum, evangelicals and gangs are unexpected partners in community governance. The traditional, patrimonial power structures discussed in the previous chapter, coupled with a failing modern state, create the conditions in which evangelicals and gangs often hold the most authority at the local level. Moral logics, in addition to overlapping family and patrimonial ties, create enough trust for leaders of the two groups to collaborate. The situation is imperfect and "government failures" occur with this arrangement. But, as the ample empirical evidence presented in this chapter shows, evangelicals and gangs still provide community leadership across the most fundamental categories of local governance.

6

Economic Engagements

The role of economic activities in the identity of gangs in El Salvador is a subject of debate. Many assume that a primary goal of gang activities is financial gain. Steven Dudley, however, argues that MS-13 is primarily a social rather than economic organization: what "drives them is their social cohesion, and their bonds with one another, and their relationships with one another" (in Williamson 2021). Dudley points out that many of the murders and other crimes MS-13 commits do not lead to financial gain, and their tattoos and other forms of creating identity make many members too visible to be good at sophisticated crimes. In one example, Dudley shows gang members as being so unmotivated by finances that, instead of selling marijuana a clique receives from a bulk vendor, they just smoke it (Dudley 2020). In short, gangs' primary activities are geared not toward getting rich, but rather about finding a place to belong.

Dudley's position on the primary *raison d'être* of gangs resonates with my own research, but (and as Dudley acknowledges) a narrow focus on this reality ignores the significant and growing economic power gangs possess. Some 500,000 people in El Salvador are directly dependent on gang activities for part or all of their livelihoods (Bargent 2013). Not only are millions of dollars already flowing through MS-13, but some elements of the gang are "graduating" to the more sophisticated activities of major cartels (Williamson 2021). Farah and Babineau talk of the "gang's growing, visible, financial fortune," and of a government operation that uncovered 157 gang related businesses in El Salvador, among them "bus and taxi companies, luxury car lots, brothels, motels, restaurants, and crack houses" (2017, 61). In some communities, gangs have a stake in the sale of most basic goods, including gasoline, bread, drinking water, public transport, and auto parts (Martinez D'Aubuisson 2022). All of these financial activities exist on top of gangs' extortion practices, which remain the most common and ubiquitous form of gang income. Such realities point to the fact that even if gangs in El Salvador are primarily social organizations, and it bears repeating that they

Blood Entanglements. Stephen Offutt, Oxford University Press. © Oxford University Press 2023.
DOI: 10.1093/oso/9780197587300.003.0007

are, especially at the neighborhood level, there is an undeniable and growing financial element to their existence.

Evangelicals are also, in part, economic beings. Much of the literature on evangelicals and Pentecostals has noted their entrepreneurial orientation (see, among others, Gooren 1999; Martin 1990; Offutt 2015). Evangelicals start churches, non-profits, media outlets, and other types of businesses. Even for evangelicals who are not entrepreneurially inclined, some form of economic activity is necessary for basic survival. There have been glimpses of what this looks like in previous chapters, including maid service, working at grocery stores, fishing, and subsistence farming. Such work is not glorious, but it helps lower-class evangelicals maintain basic levels of shelter and nourishment.

It is thus that evangelicals and gangs both, inevitably, participate in local economies. This creates yet another dimension of entanglement between the two groups. In this chapter I ask: what kinds of economic interactions exist between evangelicals and gangs, and how do they shape the relationship between the two groups?

Four Types of Economic Relationships Connecting Evangelicals and Gangs

I argue that there are four broad types of economic relations between evangelicals and gangs. They include, in order of frequency: 1) impersonal transactions, 2) gang exploitation of evangelicals, 3) "win-win" arrangements between evangelicals and gangs, and 4) economic activities by both groups that are intended to empower, or at least to avoid harming, the other party. As shown in Figure 6.1, the four types contrast sharply, painting different impressions of relations between the two groups. To get a full understanding of what is happening in lower-class communities, all four must be taken into account.

The four types also vary in the level of relational intimacy and in the intensity with which they impact the daily lives, meaning systems, and well-being of evangelicals. Selling a popsicle to a fourteen-year-old who also happens to be in a gang, for example, does not require the same level of relational investment and moral processing as, say, responding to an extortion demand. The nature of a congregation's response to the latter may create the possibility of retaliatory gang violence; it may also help to define a congregation's

FOUR TYPES OF ECONOMIC RELATIONSHIPS CONNECTING EVANGELICALS AND GANGS

IMPERSONAL TRANSACTIONS

The economies of gangs and evangelicals are so overlapping that everyday transactions happen without anyone giving special notice.

ECONOMIC EXPLOITATION

Gangs often extort evangelicals who own local businesses; they occasionally extort churches. Pastors sometimes use their soft power to ward off extortion efforts, but this can be dangerous.

WIN-WIN ECONOMIC ARRANGEMENTS

Because they are in the same locations, gangs and churches sometimes hire members of the other group for their activities. Partnerships of convenience can spring up in local marketplaces between evangelicals and gang members when both benefit from such arrangements.

EMPOWERING AND AVOIDING HARM

Evangelicals and gangs sometimes use economic activity to show goodwill. Many churches are exempt from gang extortion practices. Non-profits and churches sometimes hire gang members when they engage in community development projects.

Figure 6.1 Four types of economic relationship connecting evangelicals and gangs (created by Thomas Hampton).

local identity. Still, while less controversial, impersonal transactions can have a more important, if subtle, impact than the actors involved perceive. I begin with these.

Impersonal Transactions

Simple, impersonal transactions between evangelicals and gangs occur perhaps thousands of times a day in lower-class communities across El Salvador. Evangelicals with snack shops in their windows sell not just popsicles and potato chips to children, but also phone cards with minutes for cell phones used in gang surveillance. Evangelicals who run *pupuserias* out of their house sell pupusas, the national Salvadoran food, to anyone who passes by; this likely sometimes includes gang members on their way home from committing a crime. An evangelical employee in a fast-food restaurant might sell family size orders of fried chicken and Cokes, which are then eaten during a meeting of the local clique. Such economic transactions between evangelicals and gangs are as organic to local economies as they are ubiquitous.

The proximity of the homes of Pastor Enzo and his father-in-law to the local jail provides an opportunity for an ethnographic look at how dynamics of impersonal economic transactions play out. I arrived at Pastor Enzo's house around 10:00 in the morning with Ronaldo, my friend and fellow researcher. Pastor Enzo had agreed to visit some communities in Las Palmas with us, which would take us most of the day. Raquel, Enzo's seventeen-year-old daughter, waved cheerfully as we entered the patio. She was busy washing dishes in the *pila*, which was located on the far side of the patio and up against the outside wall of the local jail. The front of the jail is located on a main street, but a side street runs along the side of the jail, with four small lots between the side street and the jail. Pastor Elias lives in the fourth and final lot that is adjacent to the jail.

As Raquel turned back to her work, she said, "I saw two trucks full of prisoners this morning. I think one was the army and one was the police." She guessed they were transferring prisoners from other locations. Ronaldo mentioned he heard something about overcrowding in a nearby prison.

Our conversation shifted to the activities of the day. As we talked, I could hear the rise and fall of voices through the thin walls of the jail. Enzo soon emerged from his house, ready to go. We said our farewells to Raquel and walked the seventy-five feet or so to the main street from his house. There we ambled up onto the porch of Don Ignacio, who is Enzo's father-in-law.

As we turned the corner a policeman was opening the bed of his pickup truck and taking a youth by the arm. He looked young and scared. As he hopped out of the truck and turned sideways, I saw that his hands were cuffed behind his back. He stared at the ground as he was led into the jail. I wondered if he knew he was about to enter a facility that had absorbed two other truckloads of prisoners earlier that morning.

Don Ignacio has more entrepreneurial energy than most. He grew up in a highly impoverished, rural community and has hustled his way to lower-class urban respectability. His porch is evidence of an entrepreneurial life. In addition to the typical snack store that is found in the front windows of so many Salvadoran homes, Don Ignacio's family sells used clothes, which they display on twine that runs between the poles that hold up the porch awning. Some of Don Ignacio's family take such wares door-to-door in nearby neighborhoods: even Pastor Enzo, when money gets tight, has made the rounds.

Don Ignacio's bestselling items on the porch are new, rather than used, clothing items: white t-shirts, white shorts, and white croc-type sandals. This is the dress code for prisoners in the jail next door. That morning we witnessed why such merchandise moves so quickly. We had not been there long when a young woman who was not from the community approached the jail. She had makeup on and was dressed sharply. She talked to the police at the gate for a few minutes, and then made her way over to Don Ignacio's porch, examining the croc sandals. Enzo's nephew began to talk to her about the price. Her eyes were red and moist with tears. She bought a t-shirt, shorts, and a pair of crocs (all two dollars each) and headed back to the jail.

Before long, five more women showed up, all examining the white t-shirts, shorts, and white crocs. They made their selections and lined up on the porch to pay for the clothing. All of the women were dressed neatly and, although somber, looked like they were ready for church. Some had the head coverings worn by the most conservative (and often the poorest and most rural) Pentecostal denominations. Some appeared to be mothers, others sisters, or girlfriends. A few pre-adolescent boys accompanied them. I gathered myself to see if I might gently engage one of the women in conversation. But Enzo, normally extroverted and friendly with strangers, stopped me. He explained that we don't have any "confianza," or trust, with them. Knowing what brought the ladies here, and not wishing to do anything that might draw unwanted attention to Don Ignacio or Enzo, I sat back down in my chair.

As we got in our car, a man was walking in our direction from the jail. He wore a jacket and pants suitable for an uptown nightclub and carried the swagger and appearance of wealth. He seemed out of place in our humble surroundings. "Who's that?" I asked. "That's probably a lawyer," said Enzo. Then we left to visit another neighborhood.

Three hours later, we returned. The store's entire clothing inventory had been wiped out. Enzo's wife had gone to the open-air market in San Salvador to purchase more. Enzo tended to some quick chores and we were about to leave again when several police guided eight to ten prisoners, all clad in their white attire that presumably had been purchased from Don Ignacio hours earlier, out of the jail and into the back of a pickup. Off they and their new clothes went, likely to be processed at another prison facility.

Although relationships were not formed, such impersonal transactions helped to shape the social reality of the evangelicals that were involved. Don Ignacio and his family provided needed supplies for inmates and their families. They did so respectfully, discretely, gently, and carefully. The conservative women with their heads covered were able to provide some form of comfort and care for the inmates to whom they were relationally attached through the purchases they made. The sales also allowed Don Ignacio to put a bit more distance between himself and abject poverty. While such transactions were not embedded in personal relationships, they were part of how people navigated difficult moments and made sense of their lives in that little corner of Las Palmas.

Economic Exploitation

A second prominent strand of economic engagements between evangelicals and gangs is that gangs exploit and disempower evangelicals. Gangs have more financial power than evangelicals and are more directly interested in dominating sectors of local economies and accruing wealth. The imbalance in power and financial motivation means that gangs often take what they want from evangelicals. But they do so within the context of a broader set of interactions. This means that some form of moral logic is often (but not always) proffered for the exploitation that occurs. It also means that evangelicals are able to use soft power to defend themselves in some instances. In this section I look briefly at how this works within the context of gangs' extortion practices, local drug economies, and other more diffuse effects of economic power imbalances between the two groups.

Extortion

I explained in Chapter 1 that cliques generate most of their income through extortion or "rent," and that rent collection is often fairly businesslike. Levels of efficiency and professionalism vary widely from clique to clique, but there are general procedures in many communities, and local businesses, on the whole, know what to expect.

Gangs use a moral logic to justify extortion in their communities. The logic is simple: they control the territory and they protect citizens and businesses within the territory. Such governance and protection services come with a fee, especially for those entities which accrue an income. Gangs use force to collect the fees that are due to them.

As will be touched on later in the chapter, there is an important exception to this logic. Non-profits and congregations are often, but not always, exempt from making monthly extortion payments even if they are still sometimes approached for irregular and unplanned requests for money or goods. Exemption policies for churches vary from clique to clique and are constantly evolving.

For the most part, however, evangelicals who live in gang-controlled communities must decide how to respond to the gang logic and practice of extortion. They take both theological and practical considerations into account, as well as how gangs might respond to the position they choose. The latter varies from community to community, depending on the disposition of cliques toward evangelicals and the level of community control or repression they exercise. Given such complexities, it is not surprising that evangelicals report diverse ways of thinking about and responding to gangs' extortion demands. The most common of these are explained in the following pages and summarized in Figure 6.2.

Theological Responses to Extortion

Evangelicals have different theological points of view when it comes to paying extortion. Some believe that the Bible encourages them to pay extortion. Early in my research, Pastor Nicolas reported telling his members to

Theological argument for paying extortion:	Theological argument for rejecting extortion:
• Gangs are the local authority, and the Bible says, "Give unto Caesar what is Caesar's".	• Gangs do not qualify for the "Give unto Caesar" mandate.
Pragmatic reasons to pay extortion:	Pragmatic reasons to reject extortion:
• Extortion payments are necessary for NGOs/churches to complete community projects • If evangelicals play by the gang's rules, they can ask gang leaders for protection.	• Extortion payments put churches under gang power. • Payments or gang use of church property may create problems for the churches with the state.

Figure 6.2 How evangelicals think about extortion.

willingly pay the "rent" money that gangs charge. He justified this by saying that such an arrangement is biblical. In the New Testament book of Matthew, he said, we are told to "give unto Caesar what is Caesar's." I was struck by this use of biblical logic, so I asked several pastors in following interviews if they held a similar view. Some did. Pastor Diego, one of two pastors I interviewed with a college degree, for example, argued that the parallel made some sense: "while this power exists, you have to respect it," he argued.

Other pastors, however, believed that paying extortion was against Christian teaching. Most who took this position were community level *caciques*, and perhaps felt they had enough sway in the community to resist gangs' extortion efforts. Pastor Jose, for example, rejected Pastor Nicolas's assertion that the New Testament calls for evangelicals to pay extortion money to gangs. In doing so, Pastor Jose did not reject the idea that gangs have authority: "We know that they have control of the community," he said. "But we don't share the opinion of giving Caesar what is Caesar's." For Pastor Jose, the state remains the government authority the Matthew passage is referencing. "Taxes must be given to the government," he said. As for the gangs, Pastor Jose said, "We respect them and they respect us . . . other churches pay the rent because of fear . . . but we have never given them anything." The rebuke of Pastor Nicolas's way of thinking was clear.

Pastor Jose and other *caciques* were nonetheless careful in how they articulated their rejection of extortion demands to the gang members themselves. Pastor Jose reported telling gang members who come to the church asking for rent that "things in the church are not ours, but God's. Therefore, we cannot give them." Other pastors made similar statements, including Erik, the American missionary. Because of Erik's status in the community, the gang framed its approach a bit differently: they asked Erik to pay a "collaboration fee" in order to convey more of a cooperative agreement between entities that are both invested in the community. Erik, however, reported telling the gang representative he would not financially collaborate. Like Pastor Jose, Erik told the gang he could not pay the fee even if he wanted to because the money that comes to the church is God's money. Typically, as Pastor Jaime explained in the previous chapter, once a request for money is issued by the gang, it is very difficult for the gang to walk that request back. But Pastor Jose and Pastor Erik's *cacique* status, ability to wield spiritual (soft) power, and, in these two cases, good working relationships with local cliques made it possible for them to diplomatically fend off such requests.

Pragmatic Responses to Extortion

Evangelicals see the pragmatic costs and benefits of paying extortion differently. For many, and particularly for evangelical NGOs, paying gang extortion is a simple and necessary requirement for doing community outreach. An employee at one evangelical NGO reported that extortion payments are simply part of the reality of gang-controlled communities. His NGO allows churches located in such neighborhoods to include a line item for the "rent" in proposals they submit for community projects. A well-traveled employee at a different evangelical NGO noted that entities other than gangs also extort people in similar contexts. "I see people, like Americans, react terribly," he said.

> [They say] "How can you [pay money to gangs]?" . . . But I've been extorted when I have been stopped by police or soldiers in places where you have to give them something to keep going. Did I do something morally wrong [when I gave those groups money]? I know businesses [in El Salvador], *of course* they are paying taxes to gangs, [and those are] middle class people. That's the governance reality—just like you paid to a king in the Middle Ages. That is the working reality of the poor.

Again, such responses were based on pragmatism more than scriptural reference, but they reflect acceptance of the gangs' moral logic at least at the operational level, and, arguably, an implicit acceptance of the biblical logic asserted by Pastor Nicolas.

For Pastor Nicolas, evangelicals have recourse when they work within the gang's moral order. He said that when unauthorized threats or demands for payments occur, evangelicals who have played by the gang's rules have the right to complain to the clique's leader. There are times when this is helpful. In one instance, a clique leader responded to a complaint he received from an evangelical by talking to the offending member of his clique. According to Nicolas, the clique leader said, " 'Look, we assigned you to take care of our people, and the [evangelical] brother always helps us. Why did you threaten him?' Then [the clique leader] went to the store owner and said: 'Look brother, it will not happen again, I apologize.' And he apologized to the [store owner's] pastor too." Such accounts indicate a financial element to the governance arrangements discussed in the previous chapter. It also shows how gangs are able to show good faith to those within the community who submit to their extortion demands.

But Pastor Jose sees significant downsides for churches that pay extortion money or that give gang members access to other church resources. Doing so can create or enhance a power dynamic between the two entities that further disempowers churches. It can also create problems for churches with the state, especially when gangs utilize a church's physical, visible resources. Churches, for example, sometimes own vans or minibuses that they use to pick up parishioners for services or to take youth groups on excursions. Gangs often view vans or minibuses, especially those that are not owned by the gang, as useful vehicles for "missions." Pastor Jose said that,

> One night, a gang member with a gun in his hand asked us for the minibus. He wanted it to transport gang members. We told him that we couldn't give it to him because the minibus serves us for the "bread and chocolate" ministry. We left the community as quickly as possible; thank God nothing happened to us. In church we have agreed to say "no" when we are asked for something that is not right. So we took the risk, and we didn't give him the vehicle. We also don't carry a gang member in our vehicles. It's not convenient. In church we have learned to say no, even if we put life at risk.

Pastor Nicolas and Pastor Jose represent two different forms of evangelical thinking on how to handle extortion demands from gangs. Both ways of thinking marshal biblical and theological material to support their views. Both also weigh the risks of conforming or not conforming to gang demands. A pastor's position in this debate may not, however, be what determines his actions. A pastor may be conceptually against paying extortion to the gang but would prefer to pay the extortion and keep his life and the lives of his family and his congregation.

Variation in Extortion Outcomes

This points to the fact that there are variations in the outcomes of evangelical decisions with respect to extortions. Some who follow Pastor Nicolas's model find trouble with the police. For example, according to Pastor Jose, in a neighborhood close to his church, another pastor decided to accede to gang demands to transport gang members in his pick-up. But this strategy of compliance to gang requests ended badly for the pastor, as the police apprehended the pastor and linked him to the gang. "Those are the risks that are run," Pastor Jose said. "We have to understand that we cannot have the link with them."

But there are also risks to following Pastor Jose's approach. A church lay leader (not a pastor) who lived in a neighborhood not far from Pastor Nicolas's church refused to cooperate with gang demands. He did not want to pay rent on the vehicle he used to transport a U.S. missionary, and he did not cooperate with other gang requests. As a result, he was physically assaulted by the gang and forced to flee the country. This is an all-too-common outcome.

Everyday evangelicals (evangelicals who are not pastors or leaders) who run small, informal businesses out of their homes cannot seriously contemplate the idea of refusing to pay extortion. They know the repercussions would be too severe. Yet, paying extortion still does not always bring benefits. One of Don Ignacio's sons, for example, has a bread delivery business and owns several small motorbikes that employees use for bread delivery. When the gang increased the amount of money they required on each of the motor bikes, Don Ignacio's son was forced to pass this cost on to the consumers. But the new price of bread turned out to be too high for most of his customers, and his sales fell sharply.

There are also indirect costs that evangelicals feel because of gangs' extortion practices. Camilo, a typical community member in Las Palmas, feels the pinch from a cost of living that he believes has been increased because businesses have to pay gangs. "Everything is more expensive," he said. The extortion demands have reduced profits for the stores, so they are charging their customers more. Over the last five years, reckons Camilo, this has played a part in his worsening economic situation.

Finally, gang members who convert to evangelicalism also face financial consequences. In addition to losing income, in many communities, gang members who are allowed to leave the gang must continue to pay a monthly fee to the gang. As Pastor Nicolas noted, this is often a life-time financial commitment.[1]

Drug Economy

Gang recruitment provides a window into the economic interfaces between evangelicals and gangs that are supported by, or occur within, the drug sector of local economies. Access to alcohol, marijuana, cocaine, ecstasy and other drugs for Salvadoran residents does not greatly differentiate El Salvador from other Latin American countries (Organization of American States 2015). MS-13 and the 18th Street gang in El Salvador have easy and direct access to cocaine and other drugs, as they are (increasingly) involved in trafficking routes from Nicaragua (InSight Crime 2021). Most of these drugs pass through El Salvador to larger markets in the north, but gangs ensure that there is enough product in the country to meet local demand.

This provides employment opportunities for interested youths. Drug sales net high incomes for youths in poor neighborhoods. Santiago, a former inmate who grew up as an evangelical, recalled when he sold drugs as a teenager. "On the street, making money was so fast," he said. It was also dangerous, which made Santiago stop for a while. But then money got tight, so Santiago "decided to go back to the streets [to sell drugs], and with more involvement this time." Not surprisingly, his income spiked again.

Profits from drug sales provide gangs with one of the "carrots" they have to entice children and youths. Pastor Enzo, for example, has seen gang members waiting for kids outside of school and then giving them small sums of money. This is a signal for the recipients that greater resources could be accessed if they begin to relate to the gang. For children who experience resource scarcity on a daily basis, the reason such an offer might be enticing is obvious.

I talked to gang members and former gang members who experienced this aspect of recruitment. Julian, an inmate, explained that while he was growing up, he would "get together with friends who were on the street and were lost, and they told me lies, they told me I was going to have everything, money, clothes, and everything I could need." Sebastian referenced a similar experience: he said that when he was growing up, he "met some people who started talking to me about the gang and everything, saying that you would have everything you need, you would always be supported, and all of that." Such messages are powerful for impoverished youths who feel that part of growing into manhood is gaining the ability to provide for oneself and for loved ones.

But such comments from gang members and former gang members were almost always accompanied by references to drugs. Juan, an inmate, explained that "the gang distributes drugs in the neighborhoods, they distribute them and you begin with the drugs that the gang distributes, and then you go further, little by little, getting from the drugs to the gangs. And then you are already in the gang." Sebastian, quoted in the paragraph above, concurred: "And so it goes, as the other brother said, it's due to the drugs that you become more involved."

Gangs' claims of increased economic resources are largely believed to be legitimate: current and former gang members and pastors alike agreed that youths in gangs have, on average, more money than their non-gang peers. Youths growing up in evangelical homes can see the financial reality of their neighborhoods. Some choose what appears to be a fairly obvious path to more money and less poverty as they come of age.

Gangs' Financial Power and Evangelicals

The financial power of gangs creates other constraints on evangelicals' economic well-being. Such constraints are diffuse and diverse. Finances, for example, can complicate pathways out of gangs for members wishing to convert to evangelicalism. More commonly, impoverished evangelicals just trying to scratch out a living can be thwarted by expressions of gang power over economic activity.

Gangs' finances are highly guarded secrets. Within the gang, only senior leaders and their accountants have a good picture of a gang's national and transnational earnings and assets. But people with such knowledge, it is widely believed, cannot leave the gang. Pastor Diego explained that "leaders like this cannot actually leave. They have status. They also put their families at risk if they leave." This logic filters down to people with financial responsibilities within cliques. The stakes are lower at the neighborhood level because the sums of money are less. But financial information is still closely guarded, and there are financial linkages between cliques and the national gang leadership.

It is thus the case that even at the clique level, members with financial responsibilities find it more difficult to leave the gang. Arturo, for example, was in charge of getting the rent from a fairly large marketplace in San Salvador. "That place's rent [accrued] thousands of dollars a month," Arturo told Pastor Adrian after he was arrested and sent to prison. "I have a team of other young people who go to the stores to go pick up everything, then

I am the administrator of that rent. I am in prison but I continue to be in charge . . . there is a second in charge left outside, but he reports to me because I still report to my leader, the one who is in a higher rank than me." The rent for an open-air market is a significant amount of income at the clique level, and presumably large enough for program or national gang leaders to remain attentive.[2]

In prison, Arturo began participating in Pastor Adrian's Bible studies, and became interested in converting to the evangelical faith. But Arturo's position in the inner circle of trust within his clique made it less likely that he could leave the gang. Arturo told Pastor Adrian that he wanted to become an evangelical, but that it would take time. "Look pastor, I need to work things out with the gang, they will let me out but I have some things to work on, I have to put everything in order." During the time of this research Arturo was not successful in creating the necessary conditions for his departure from the gang.

Other elements of gang power negatively impact evangelicals' economic well-being. Gang boundaries, the governance aspect of which was alluded to in the previous chapter, may be foremost among these. Boundaries serve as barriers to local job markets for evangelicals. Pastor Lucas mentioned several young men in his congregation that lost their jobs because gang members would not let them cross their boundaries. Boundaries also impeded evangelicals from education and training that might help youths obtain jobs. Pastor Benjamin noted that several young people in his church had to stop going to school for the same reason. Such issues are common for evangelicals and others who live in gang-controlled territories.

Bullying, for lack of a better term, by gangs within the territories they control also has negative economic impacts for evangelicals. Alba is a twenty-four-year-old resident of Las Palmas. Until recently, she sold handicrafts near the entrance of the dock in Las Palmas. The dock is a busy place: fishermen sell their catch there and it is a weekend tourist destination for middle class Salvadorans seeking sun, surf, and fresh seafood. Alba could make a modest profit in that location. Unfortunately, some gang members unilaterally decided that she was no longer allowed on or near the dock. Alba was not particularly friendly with the gang members, but she was also not able to report a specific incident or reason they would turn against her. Regardless, Alba was forced to give up her business. At the time of my research, she was simply staying home and pondering her next steps.

Win-Win Economically Motivated Arrangements

Mutually profitable economic partnerships between evangelicals and gang members are often embedded in pre-existing relationships. Such relationships create trust between actors in part because they offer different forms of recourse if people do not act in good faith. Family relationships are perhaps the most common ties that undergird mutually beneficial economic activities between members of the two groups. As seen in the examples in this section, family ties support the provision of employment opportunities across groups, as well as standard economic arrangements that that many deem necessary to carry on in El Salvador's local economies.

Cross-Group Employment Opportunities

Gangs and evangelicals sometimes find themselves hiring members of opposing groups. On these occasions, both parties believe that it is in their best interest to engage in an employer/employee relationship. The motivations are often economic, but because they are embedded within broader relationships, other types of motivations may also exist.

Nancy's experience provides an opportunity to explore the nature of cross-group employment. Nancy, who was introduced in Chapter 3, grew up attending an evangelical church with her mother. But she also grew up in close proximity to gang life, as her older brother was a leader in the local MS-13 clique and held clique meetings in their house. Nancy did not join the clique, but as mentioned in Chapter 3, she became a "gang girlfriend." More relevant here are her financial activities: she sold drugs and collected extortion money for the gang. During this time of her life, she did not identify as an active evangelical.

As Nancy got older and was raising three children of her own, she began to rethink her relationship with God. Nancy started going to church again. She rededicated her life to the Lord and renewed her evangelical identity. Nancy also stopped selling drugs for the gang, but she continued to collect the "rent" from local businesses for the gang. This was partly because she needed the money—it is a good job that allows her to earn up to $50/week— and partly because she feared damaging her relationship with gang members by refusing to work for them.

It is somewhat common for evangelical women in impoverished communities to collect extortion money for gangs. This is a widely known fact in lower-class El Salvador and sometimes a source of consternation for pastors. "Evangelical women collect rent from businesses," Pastor Diego confirmed flatly. He did not comment further, but it was not something he reported with pleasure. Numerous other pastors concurred. Such employment for evangelical women is one of several dynamics that led an international evangelical NGO worker to admit that "it is probably true that some evangelicals benefit economically from gang activity." There is some danger to women in talking to a researcher about working for gangs; Nancy was the only woman I interviewed who openly admitted doing so. But my ethnographic research and interviews show that Nancy is far from the only evangelical woman with such life experiences.

Gangs also hire children who are in evangelical churches. This can be part of gang recruitment efforts, but even if the children do not become gang members, gangs need to employ people to serve as runners or to watch what is happening in the community. According to Pastor Benjamin, the gangs often choose "nine- or ten-year-old children. These children are already working with the gangs." I saw a child not much older than that just sitting at a community entrance with a cell phone, evidently texting someone in the community whenever a person of interest entered or exited. These kinds of jobs provide the sources of income that, according to Pastor Jose, some evangelical parents want their children to procure.

For those children who appear to be tracking toward gang membership, money is not the only form of payment. Drugs, as seen earlier, are distributed to young children, along with other forms of contraband. Ramon, an inmate, said that before he joined the gang, a gang member gave him a gun. "They wanted me to trust them more, they wanted me to show them I trusted them. That's the way it was," said Ramon. But money remains an important currency, and doing work for gangs provides children, evangelicals among them, with a feeling of empowerment in impoverished environments.

Evangelical-owned businesses also hire gang members. This can be intentional, but evangelicals may also be unaware that youths they hire are gang members. Emilio, for example, grew up in a strong evangelical home, with both parents very involved in church activities and siblings who were very involved in a youth group. Emilio, though, stopped going to church as a teenager and got involved in questionable activities.

Although rebellious, Emilio remained well-meaning and enterprising. He decided to open up a bakery. Emilio's business quickly grew, and he hired four or five younger men he knew in the community. At the time he hired them, Emilio said, "I thought they were not gang members, but while already working for me they told me they were members of a gang. But I did not care about that and continued working with them." Originally, Emilio said he wanted to have a positive influence on these friends/employees. He was a few years older than they were, and he felt they really wanted to learn. But Emilio began to be drawn into the other elements of their lives: "I was curious about some of the things they talked about, like some felonies they had committed," he said. Emilio started driving them to the locations where they committed felonies, and he soon entered the gang himself.

Eventually Emilio ended up in prison. His parents remained committed both to him and to their church. There was an economic strand to this relationship: his parents sent him money while he was in jail. "And I would spend it on drugs," said Emilio. "I was buying and selling drugs and cigarettes. I would leave some of [those products] to my personal use." This pattern continued for over a year until, for reasons that were not economic, Emilio began a personal journey back to the church. The point here, however, is that Emilio, a person with a strong evangelical background, provided employment to gang members. Then Emilio's evangelical parents provided Emilio, now a gang member, with the capital he needed for his black-market economic activities within the jail.

Evangelical/Gang Economic Partnerships

The second element of Emilio's story points more to evangelical/gang economic partnerships than to cross-group employment opportunities. Partnerships occur within neighborhoods and are almost always part of the informal economy. They seldom include large sums of money, but they do facilitate economic activities that, for evangelicals, can help cover meager cost of living expenses.

The story of Eva and her sister, Blanca, provides a window into how such partnerships work. They run a booth near the entrance of Las Palmas's open-air market. The two sisters sell fresh produce two or three days a week. The other days are dedicated to household chores and procuring the goods they sell. Eva and Blanca enjoy the hustle and bustle of marketplace life.

I met the two sisters when I accompanied Pastor Enzo to a birthday party for Luis, Eva's six-year-old son. Eva and Luis attend Pastor Enzo's church. Blanca does not attend, but cheerfully greeted Pastor Enzo when we arrived. Both sisters are friends of Ana, Nancy's cousin, whose story was told in Chapter 3.

The two sisters married a pair of brothers, one of whom was at one time a full gang member, the other a gang sympathizer. When I met Eva, her husband, Tristan, had recently become a *calmado*, or had mostly stopped his active gang activities. Neither of the men attended Pastor Enzo's church, and neither were at Luis' birthday party.

Both, however, help Eva and Blanca maintain their booth in the open-air market. The street that runs through the formal market serves as the primary boundary between the two gangs. MS-13 controls the booths that run along the north side of the street; the 18th Street gang controls the booths along the south side of the street. Both gangs charge $1/day to those who wish to rent the booths. Booths situated right on the road, such as the one Eva and Blanca have (see Photo 6.1), receive the most foot traffic. They are thus the most coveted. It helps to know someone in the gang to get those booths.

Evangelicals find themselves paying gangs for spaces in open air markets throughout El Salvador. This is not always seen as onerous: an employee of an evangelical NGO asserted that some sellers even see positive results of a gang presence in open air markets. They view gangs as a deterrent to outside competition that might bring inferior products into the community at lower prices.

For now, things are going well for Eva and Blanca. Their produce sells well and they make enough that paying the rent money is not a problem. But other vendors might like to be in the booth the sisters are using. Because Tristan has become a *calmado*, his influence in the gang will likely recede. That may mean that the booth will eventually go to a different vendor.

Activities Intended to Empower or at Least to Avoid Harm

The final category of economic engagements between evangelicals and gangs is comprised of those that are intended to support, protect, or empower members of the other group. Such good intentions run both ways. Outreach to gang members by evangelical non-profits and churches can include job opportunities for youths in gangs, which also serve to get gang members

Photo 6.1 Evangelicals renting a booth in a gang-controlled marketplace (photo: David Torres Ayala).

involved in projects that improve their community. Gangs, for their part, provide exemptions from extortion for many evangelical churches. In neighborhoods where such economic engagements are present, they do much to set the relational tone between the two groups.

Hiring of Gang Members by Churches and Non-Profits

Churches and NGOs sometimes hire people for community development projects. A common belief in government and NGO circles is that if youths have better employment options, they are both more likely to leave a gang and less likely to join a gang in the first place. Many evangelical ministries subscribe to this way of thinking and incorporate job opportunities into their community and gang outreach strategies.

Community improvement projects, particularly construction projects, are well-suited to such an approach. An example of this was referenced in Chapter 3, when Erik hired Carlos and other gang members to help build houses in their neighborhood. By doing so, Erik was able to forge a relationship with the gang members, provide them with short term jobs, and invest in their families through the provision of a new house. It was an effective strategy in that it increased the standard of living for Carlos's family and established trust between Erik and Carlos's family. Carlos and his friends, however, remained in the gang.

Pastor Daniel also provides employment opportunities for youths who are in the gang. He has partnered with an evangelical NGO to do multiple community projects such as repairing the road, building a retention wall where soil erosion was endangering the neighborhood, and creating community gardens. Like Erik, Pastor Daniel believes that community empowerment and gang prevention efforts must include employment opportunities. He has therefore incorporated (usually younger) gang members to work in these projects. Pastor Daniel regrets that because the work is on a project basis, it is only temporary. But he believes he is providing a viable short-term opportunity that could change the way a given gang member thinks about his future.

Not all hires of gang members by evangelical ministries are intentional. During my research, a local evangelical NGO (different from the one with which Pastor Daniel partners) built a new church building in a community. Hannah, the NGO's director, hired community members to serve as brick masons and perform other jobs. Shortly after construction began, Hannah learned that one of the brick masons she had hired was a gang member. So she consulted the other construction workers to see what they thought should be done. The consensus, she reported, was that hiring the gang member was a positive development for the project; having him there ensured that the workers and the materials would be safe until the project's completion. Hannah took the advice of the workers and kept the gang member on the project. The workers' predictions proved correct: there were no security problems during the life of the project, and the gang member was happy to have the job.

Exemption of Many Churches from Extortion Payments

The most obvious way in which gangs choose not to harm evangelicals in a financial sense is the exemption they provide most churches from extortion. Of the more than forty church leaders I interviewed, talked to informally, or who participated in a focus group, none reported needing to pay regular extortion. It is possible that fear or other motivations kept them from divulging this information, but even the pastors with whom I developed fairly close relations with over the course of the project believed that only a small (but gradually growing) minority of churches in El Salvador were forced to pay regular rent installments to gangs.

Why would gangs make exceptions for churches? The answer is complicated, but different threads can be found in previous chapters. An important thread is the common belief system described in Chapter 2. Gang members overwhelmingly believe in the Judeo-Christian God. They also believe that local churches, by and large, try to do God's work in the community. Extorting churches would, by extension, be akin to extorting God. Many gang members do not have an appetite for inciting God in that way.

Another thread, found in Chapter 3, is that many gang members have family relations who benefit from church services and programs. Indeed, gang members themselves sometimes benefit from such ministries. Following Mauss's (1990 [1950]) logic of gift giving, reciprocity in such relationships is natural. Exemption from extortion is an easy way for such reciprocity to occur.

More generally, gangs believe churches are pro-community organizations. Keeping in mind that gangs also present themselves as pro-community organizations, gangs assume that churches are giving to the communities rather than taking from the communities. Part of this distinction is that churches are non-profit rather than for-profit entities. Churches' motivation to serve God and to help humble people in the communities, rather than to make money, seems to be important to gangs when they establish extortion policies.

Some churches, it must be noted, do pay extortion to gangs. Many pastors I talked to could reference other churches in this predicament. And their numbers appear to be growing. According to a recent U.S. Department of State (2018) report, "A missionary stated that MS-13 and 18th Street gang members, whom gang leaders had previously forbidden from extorting the religious community, had recently begun demanding extortion payments from churches and religious groups. An NGO source said that this may be localized as determined by each clique." Pastors in my research also believed that gangs were subtly and slowly changing their thinking on extorting churches.

Pastors indicated two primary reasons some churches have to pay rent. First, hostilities can grow between specific cliques and specific churches. One of the points of leverage cliques can use in such situations is to force churches to pay them rent. Second, many pastors believe that wealthier churches are more likely to be extorted. As Pastor Enzo noted, "the *postres* come to church. They hear the announcement about how much they get in tithes. So they begin to charge rent for the church." This is partly because, believe some pastors, gangs perceive that such churches can afford to be extorted and partly because gangs may think such churches are as interested in gaining wealth for themselves as they are in helping communities.

Even churches that are protected from regular, monthly payments can be approached for occasional, sometimes impulsive requests for goods or services. Numerous pastors I talked to, and who report that they do not make monthly extortion payments, said they had experienced such requests. Some examples of such requests appeared earlier in the chapter.

Such irregular extortion efforts are not always in the form of money. For example, Pastor Jose related an incident in which a youth came to him on behalf of a local clique leader and requested a new pair of Nike shoes for each member of the clique. Pastor Jose told the young man that he could not use the church's money for such a request. He would use his own money, but only had enough money to purchase much cheaper shoes at Par Dos, a local Salvadoran shoe outlet. Pastor Jose said that the young man "went to speak to his leader, and then returned. 'He says to forget that we asked for it.' And they didn't ask for more." Such a one-off request may have been generated by the clique leader noticing a Nike commercial or feeling like his own shoes were a little worn. It may also be true that there is more room for negotiation for such requests than there is for regular, monthly installments.

Such haphazard motivations for requests do not establish enduring patterns of interaction between specific cliques and congregations. They happen often enough, in general, though, that they are part of the relational dynamic between the two groups.

Conclusion

Sharing neighborhoods means sharing local economies—this is an unavoidable reality. From the daily impersonal transactions to the intentional economic engagements, evangelicals and gangs are woven into the larger set of community relationships and transactions. There may be different perceptions of such activities and different approaches to marketplace behavior but engaging in local economies is a necessary part of basic survival. The idea that evangelicals and gangs meet each other within local economies and have economic relationships should not be surprising.

The question is thus not *if* evangelicals and gangs have economic relationships, but *how* the two groups conduct themselves within such relationships. As this chapter has shown, the groups exhibit a range of strategies, including manipulation, cooperation, and well-intentioned efforts to empower members of the other group. Any analysis that does not take this range of behaviors and attitudes into account will likely present a distorted view of the complex sets of economic relationships that tie evangelical and gangs together in local communities.

What conclusions can thus be drawn when we look at the four types of economic interactions covered in this chapter?

First, people often feel a sense of community collaboration, including across evangelical and gang loyalties, in marketplace or storefront activities. This could be seen in the interactions on Don Ignacio's porch and in Las Palmas's open-air market. Even when transactions are not embedded in established personal relationships in Las Palmas, they are often conducted between people who know they are experiencing a shared social reality. The sharp contrast between the wealthy lawyer and the humble surroundings he entered into as he sauntered toward the jail had the effect of highlighting the shared, humble traits of Don Ignacio's family and those who shopped for simple goods on his porch. Such actors may have consciously or unconsciously recognized their shared ways of dress, speech, comportment, and general understanding of how the world works. Such affinities led to a collaborative atmosphere in which people who did not know each other shared in their efforts to address the realities of incarceration, gang membership, and scarce resources. The actual financial transactions in Don Ignacio's store were part of such efforts and were embedded in these larger social realities.

Second, as in Chapter 4, contested moral logics emerged from gangs and evangelicals to justify the imposition of certain relational patterns. This was perhaps most explicit in the area of extortion. The gang asserted a moral logic justifying extortion. Pastors chose to either accept or challenge gang logic. Those who challenged the logic countered with a different script about how the relationship between the two groups ought to be patterned, and why gangs could not be given money from the church. Those who accepted gangs' logic presented the idea that by doing so, they were not making trouble in the community. On the contrary, they were both doing the right thing and creating protection for themselves. Such responses reflect the frequency and variety of requests churches and pastors receive from gangs. They also reveal the diversity in opinions among evangelicals about how to engage gangs on this issue.

Finally, the opportunities for employment by gangs of evangelicals and by evangelicals of gangs points not just to cross-group financial transactions, but also to the presence of gangs and evangelicals within the same organizations. Such arrangements present difficult questions about how to understand the impact of organizational identity on personal identity, and vice versa, of gang members and evangelicals alike. These are the themes, topics, and questions I seek to explore in the following chapter.

7

Infiltrated Organizations

Are evangelicals and gangs entangled within their respective organizations? If so, how? And what might be the implications?

To answer such questions, I present three case studies: those of an evangelical non-government organization (NGO), an evangelical church, and an evangelical ministry to prisoners. I argue that low barriers to entry and entangled social networks allow for a gang presence within evangelical entities, and an evangelical presence within spaces dominated by gangs.

The impact of such entanglement within organizations varies and can be analyzed from multiple perspectives. Culture, resources, and power are all negotiated by evangelicals and gangs within and beyond organizations in unexpected ways. The following case studies tease out some of the dynamics that emerge within such contexts.

An Evangelical NGO: Infiltrated and Infiltrating

Evangelical NGOs and other non-profit ministries often have high levels of exposure to gangs in El Salvador. They sometimes welcome gang members into their ministries, sometimes are infiltrated by gangs, and sometimes penetrate gang members' intimate spaces.

An international evangelical NGO, which I call Children First, provides insights into such realities. I have made reference to Children First in previous chapters, but a fuller picture of the organization can elucidate certain elements of the entanglement thesis, particularly the way in which low barriers to entry and social networks create porous organizational boundaries.

Children First has a strong evangelical North American donor base. Children First promotional materials can be seen on church bulletin boards across the United States; advertisements appear in Christian magazines and other public venues. Potential donors can visit Children First's website, which offers an opportunity to view photos of children and select a child from any

Blood Entanglements. Stephen Offutt, Oxford University Press. © Oxford University Press 2023.
DOI: 10.1093/oso/9780197587300.003.0008

one of a number of countries around the world. The sponsorship costs about $40/month. Children First hopes that the selection of a child is the beginning of a personal relationship that will last for a decade or more.

The child/sponsor relationship is an important part of Children First's approach. The child, or beneficiary, is required to send at least two letters a year to the sponsor, and the sponsor is encouraged to write back. Marcela, Children First's national director in El Salvador, explained that "there is a Donor and Sponsor Team that is in charge of sending the letters of every single child and sponsor." The team in El Salvador is staffed by sharp, friendly, bi-lingual young people, some of whom were Children First beneficiaries as they grew up. The team translates letters from English-writing donors and Spanish-writing beneficiaries. They also act as hosts for U.S. sponsors who come to El Salvador to visit their beneficiaries. Children First believes that such relationships are good for the children; they also believe the approach attracts additional donors. Children First thus invests significant resources to build organizational capacity in this area.

Children First always partners with churches in poor communities. The organization views church partnership as the most foundational and non-negotiable element of its approach. The partnership revolves around a child development center which Children First finances and local churches run. Children First provides training for pastors and church leaders so that they know how to run the center. They also provide the church with most or all of the resources needed (churches are free to seek other donors or add to program components with their own resources), including salaries for center employees. Partly because of this, the centers are quite popular among poor churches in El Salvador and other countries. Church leaders are invited to send an application to Children First if they think such a partnership would be a good fit for their congregation.

Children First's child development centers follow a basic template, with room for some variance. The template requires all centers to address the cognitive, nutritional, socio-emotional, and spiritual development of their children. The variation comes in how centers approach these central tasks. A center run by a larger church in an urban neighborhood, for example, has a small computer lab, sewing machines, a kitchen where students receive culinary training, and a music band for their students. None of these are unique: in fact, Children First students come together from across El Salvador to put on a music concert in one of the country's most prominent music halls each year. But a development center in a different part of the country, with a smaller and institutionally weaker church partner, did not have any sewing machines or a computer lab. Still, they had (more modest) pedagogical tools that they used to pursue each educational area in Children First's basic template.

The commitment to church partnerships ensures that Children First's centers are embedded within communities and managed by local leaders. Pastors and center staff are the face of Children First's projects in the community. This approach is consistent with the literature on best practices of community development (whether or not such efforts are faith-based), which strongly urges local ownership (Pouligny 2009). Scholars and practitioners find that projects can be more sustainable and can result in more effective human empowerment under local leaders.

But running efficient community development programs under local leadership is not easy. Pastors and other leaders in poor communities often only have a grade school education, yet they must navigate complex administrative tasks. Children First attaches significant amounts of paperwork to every student in the program. Lines of communication from every beneficiary to every donor, as well as lines of communication with local public school administrators and teachers, can be taxing. Further paperwork is generated by Children First's monitoring and evaluation efforts. If local leaders are not well educated in the first place, no amount of training from Children First will fully equip them to handle such responsibilities, and organizational foibles emerge.

More to the point of this book, neighborhood programming under local leadership also means that Children First is embedded in local networks. In El Salvador this often and inevitably includes networks of gang members and gang sympathizers. The story of Esteban provides one perspective of how such networks affect their programs.

Esteban's Story

Esteban is a nineteen-year-old who lives in Las Palmas. He is the oldest of three half-brothers and a half-sister, each of whom has a different father. Melisa, his mother, works in a local eatery to pay the bills. Esteban's father emigrated to the United States when he was very small. Over a ten-year period, Melisa lived with the fathers of her other two boys at different times, and then with her Aunt. Eventually she had a falling out with her Aunt, which left her and her three boys homeless. Pastor Enzo happened to be looking for a security guard for the church, and he invited her to come and live there. Toward the end of my research Melisa married and had a baby girl. The new husband now lives with Melisa and the children in the church. Melisa and her baby are pictured in the church foyer in Photo 7.1.

Esteban and his siblings are the demographic that Children First wants to help. They are also the demographic that is most susceptible to gang activities and relationships. In Esteban's case, Children First was the first and more formative influence on his life. He began attending one of Children First's child development centers when he was five years old. He "received Christ" when he was eight years old.

Through the first three times his family moved, Esteban continued to attend the child development center. He made friends, gained literacy in computer programs, received help with his public school homework, and studied the Bible. Esteban also learned life skills, including culinary lessons like how to make *horchata*, a traditional drink made of rice. Children First's program provided stability and consistent educational reinforcement for Esteban in the midst of years of instability, volatility, and poverty at home.

Photo 7.1 Mother of youth that gangs expelled from evangelical education program (photo: David Torres Ayala).

The family's move to the church, however, cut Esteban off from Children First's program. They had crossed gang boundaries even as they remained within easy walking distance of the child development center. The neighborhood in which Children First is located is controlled by the 18th Street gang. Esteban explained that, "when we moved [to Pastor Enzo's church], this is where MS runs things. So I kept going [to the child development center] for a little while. But then a gang member told me I should not go any more. So I stopped going." Esteban thus became one of over 150 Salvadoran youths who involuntarily left Children First's program due to violence during that fiscal year.

The 18th Street gang's participation in the program likely played a role in its decision to tell Esteban to stop attending. Esteban stated that a youth in the program was an active gang member. The pastor of Children First's church partner confirmed that children of gang members were also in the Children First program. These realities were not, from Esteban's perspective, good things. They were part of the social reality that made it impossible for him to graduate from the program.

Gang Members Enrolled in Children First's Programs

Beneficiaries of Children First who join a gang create a significant conundrum for the organization. Children First clearly does not want gang members compromising its initiatives. But Children First is also reluctant to cast aside children in whom donors, partners, and staff have spent years investing.

Children First's response is further complicated by its decentralized structure. Children First's international office gives national offices considerable latitude to make their own decisions; national offices recognize the independence of the local congregations that partner with them. Actors at each level respond to different contextual realities, which is why issues as delicate as gang-related policies must be considered in different ways across the organization.

Children First's international office does not have a policy that bans gang members from participation in their programs. Rather, there is a recognition that as youths grow up in impoverished conditions, they make life decisions that are not always the best ones, but which also do not exclude them from God's love. Matthew, speaking from Children First's international office, confirmed that just as it is true that some of their beneficiaries experience teenage pregnancies and other issues that negatively impact youths, some of their beneficiaries become gang members. Matthew explained that gang membership may sometimes results in expulsion from the program, but taking such a step is not always best for the child and is not required by the international office.

Children First's El Salvador leadership must take its national context into account. The *Ley de proscripcion de maras, pandillas, agrupaciones, asociaciones, y organizaciones de naturaleza criminal* that was passed by El Salvador's National Assembly in 2010 restricts all organizations in their interactions with gangs and gang members. This law was reinforced with additional legislation in 2022 (El Faro English 2022b). As mentioned in previous chapters, evangelical leaders are frustrated that the law sometimes inhibits their ministry efforts. Children First is just as aware as other ministries that continued engagement with a youth who has just joined a gang can help the youth reverse course. It is also aware of what might occur if Children First is perceived as being out of step with national law.

Finally, Children First's church partners, operating in neighborhoods, are looking at a third set of social and relational realities. Pastors and other staff are with children in their programs for years. They build relationships with them, watch them grow up, and pour much energy into trying to help them succeed. Just as their own children may make bad life decisions, sometimes children in their program decide to join a gang. Within such a relational context, Marcela stated that "pastors have the space to support [youths who enter gangs] but they are careful. They don't want the police to know about this because police might then associate them with the gang. It is a serious matter." Partnering pastors that I talked to for this study did, carefully, engage youths in gangs in different ways.

Children First believes that there are relatively few gang members in their programs, and those who are enrolled are low-level gang members. Fabio, also speaking from Children First's national office, stated that "we have a low rate [in proportion to the national percentage] when it comes to teenagers joining gangs. There are isolated cases." Matthew observed that gang members who are in the program tend to be those who are "a little more peripheral in the gang system . . . in the early stages of gang membership." My community research supported this claim: the gang member Esteban referenced, for example, appears to fit such a description.

Still, the decisive empirical reality is, as Esteban and others at the grassroots level verified, that gang members are enrolled in Children First programs. Children First must grapple with how to address such cases at all three levels of the organization. Although no one associated with the organization stated this, it may also be the case that in some neighborhoods, gang members are in the program either without the consent or without the knowledge of Children First or its church partners.

Children of Gang Members Enrolled in Children First

Children First enrolls children of gang members in their program far more frequently than they enroll active gang members. The presence of such children is fairly ubiquitous and less controversial within the organization. Children First staff and church partners were happy to confirm this practice, even to the point of volunteering this information without being asked.

Accepting children of gang members into the program can build trust in the community. Gang members or their wives or girlfriends come by the church multiple times a week to drop off and pick up their children. They interface directly and consistently with staff at the center. Gang members' children build relationships with other children in the program. It is easy to imagine that children want to continue such relationships by playing at each other's homes in the evenings. Like all children's educational facilities, the center serves as a focal point for building relationships in neighborhoods: gang members and their families are embedded in this mix.

But significant challenges come with opening the organization to children of gang members. Such youths sometimes use violence within child development centers. Tomas, a third representative from Children First's national office, explained that children of gang members are often exposed to intrafamily violence at home. They imitate such behavior in the child development centers, even at very young ages. So, Matthew explained, children of gang members "are more likely to fight," and sometimes they "threaten classmates and even staff." When such threats come from gang-affiliated individuals (Matthew stated that threats to staff also come from non-affiliated children who are regularly exposed to violence), Children First staff must carefully sort through which threats might be actionable.

Children First is aware that children of gang members sometimes serve as gang informants. Such children, once in the program, can provide gangs with intimate knowledge of Children First's human, physical, and financial resources, at least within a given child development center. Active gang members in the program heighten such exposure. This, according to Matthew, creates fear among staff in some child development centers.

Gang members and children of gang members can also engage in illicit activities in Children First's child development centers. Although my research did not uncover examples of this, it is not difficult to imagine gang members bringing drugs and other contraband to the center and giving or selling such merchandise to other students. This would be consistent with gang members' activities in public schools and other public spaces.

In spite of such challenges and risks, Children First decision makers believe that including gang members' children and, occasionally, gang members themselves, in child development centers is consistent with the goals of the organization's ministry and with biblical principles. They believe they are staying true to their mission of reaching the most vulnerable, and to the logic that every child, regardless of his or her background, should be given a chance to experience God's love.

Returning to Esteban's Perspective

Esteban, however, does not see it this way. He liked being in the Children First program. He wanted to stay until he graduated. But violating a directive from the 18th Street gang to stop attending would be dangerous. The presence of an 18th Street gang member in the program and other members of the 18th Street gang dropping their children off and picking them up each day ensured that Esteban could not slip in unnoticed.

To Esteban it was clear: the 18th Street gang controlled, at least in part, who got to participate in the child development center. Children First had gang members and children of gang members in their program. Gang members excluded him from the Children First program.

Montes (2021) studied a cohort of youths that, much like Esteban, lived in gang-controlled territories in El Salvador but were not in gangs. Montes' subjects described gang members as people who inflict violence on others, rob them of opportunities, take advantage of the hard work of others in the community by forcing them to pay rent and through other manipulative mechanisms, eliminate the opportunity to study by telling other youths they are not allowed to attend the public school any more, and don't allow other youths to enjoy simple social activities like recreating in the park or in other social spaces. Youths suffering such indignities are desperate for social spaces, or havens, in which they can escape gang control and breathe freely for a time.

Esteban, and others like him, would like Children First to be such a haven. Esteban articulated only positive feelings of his Children First experience except when it came to the gang member in the program. Esteban would have been in favor of an institutional context that excluded the gang member and allowed him to remain enrolled. ·

But another of Esteban's observations is likely correct: Children First and its local partners do not completely control their own enrollment. Over the years, gangs have created hundreds of forced departures from Children First's programs. They do this by giving directives such as the one Esteban received and, as Matthew pointed out, by forcing families of beneficiaries to leave their community, often by way of emigration. Gang members and children of gang members are, unless there is a rift within the gang, not likely to be among those whom gangs force out of the program.

These empirical realities exist alongside the empirical reality that Children First's child development centers are often still able to approximate gang-free havens, even when children of gang members are enrolled. As I mention in Chapter 3, many gang members get their children involved in evangelical organizations as part of a strategy to keep their children out of the gang. Such gang members are thus essentially asking for child development centers to be a sanctuary from gang control—at least for their own children. The child development centers I visited had the characteristics of a gang-free environment: the children were enthusiastically engaged in various learning activities, and Children First has documented evidence of many students from gang-controlled territories who have gone on to study at colleges and universities and are now enjoying professional careers.

Esteban reaped many of the program's benefits because his forced departure from the program did not come until he was seventeen. He was only a year or two away from graduation. When I interviewed Esteban at the age of nineteen, he had not yet found employment, but, like another friend in the program, he had decided to get educational training beyond high school, which is unusual in Esteban's neighborhood. Esteban wanted "to become a missionary or a pastor." Pastor Enzo was mentoring him, and he was about to start taking classes at a local Bible college.

Esteban's brothers were not as fortunate. His middle half-brother, Rodrigo, never enrolled in Children First's program. Although bright and very attentive at church—as a child Rodrigo unexpectedly handed me notes he had carefully taken during a sermon—he chose not to finish ninth grade. His mother explained that virtual video games had become more interesting to him than school. Esteban's youngest half-brother, Caspar, enrolled in the child development center before the family moved to the church. Melisa indicated that the gang still allowed Caspar to attend the center after they informed Esteban he should no longer attend. This might be because, unlike Esteban, Caspar still had a father living in the 18th Street gang-controlled neighborhood, and because Caspar was only six years old: he did not pose a threat. But Melisa said Caspar did not like the program as much as Esteban, and it was a hassle for Melisa to get him there, so she seldom took him. At the time of my conversation with Melisa, it did not seem likely Caspar would stay in the program much longer.

Children First Penetrating Gang Environments: Home Visits

In opening themselves to the presence of gang elements within their child development centers, Children First also creates opportunities to enter into gang members' domains. This is primarily done through home visits. "We would consider going out to the homes, knowing the family, understanding their problems, maybe helping in different ways as central to ministry," explained Matthew. Such a practice extends to children whose parents are gang members, which means that Children First, and its local church partners, ask for, and often (but not always) receive permission to enter into gang members' homes.

Gang members may be willing to host Children First personnel in their homes for the same reasons they want their children in the Children First program. They believe that Children First and its local church partner are truly interested in helping their children. Home visits under such a pretext can create poignant moments in which church workers share God's love with gang members and their families, many of whom are likely under duress in various dimensions of their lives. Such moments can build trust and goodwill, and open opportunities for empowerment. Sometimes, according to Children First staff, they even are able to convince fathers of children in their program to leave the gang through these interactions.

There are, however, cases in which gang members are not interested in allowing Children First personnel into their homes. Homes of gang members can be centers of gang activity. No outsiders may be allowed into certain homes, and attempting entrée can be dangerous. According to Matthew, in some instances "the risks are so high that home visits are not carried out."

Children First's commitment to child protection may be another reason its personnel are not always welcome in gang members' homes. As noted in Chapter 3, intra-family violence is a common experience in lower-class Salvadoran neighborhoods. Gloria, another Children First employee, stated that many "families are stressed out" in impoverished neighborhoods, which can manifest in violence within the home. Although reliable statistics are nearly impossible to collect on such themes, it is widely believed that intra-family violence within the homes of gang members is higher on average than in homes of non-gang members.

Children First policy states that staff must try to intervene if children in their program are suffering from abuse. "We actually sign off on a pledge to protect kids . . . . Everybody in these churches who works with the kids is actually trained in child protection," explained Matthew, who helped to write the organization's initial child protection policies. But such training does not make it easy. "Frankly [domestic abuse intervention] is scary anywhere. But in Central America . . . there are a lot of kids who get sponsored who have gang member parents . . . . So you risk a lot if you are trying to follow up on this," stated Matthew.

Those who take such risks can become gang victims. Because of this, multiple Children First staff stated that they believe there are cases of abuse that go unreported, just as cases of abuse go unreported in society more generally. But many cases are reported, and Children First employees make house calls that are efforts at intervention. "There are a lot of courageous people out there, I tell you—especially women," said Matthew. "There are women out there who really stand up to gangs . . . There are some amazing people. And plenty have died doing it too . . . . Workers in churches have absolutely been murdered." Matthew did not parse out a specific statistic of workers who had been killed. He did say, however, that one year in the early 2010s, a combined total of perhaps one hundred of the program's children, children's immediate family, and church workers were killed in El Salvador and Honduras.

Some of this number may also be from case workers attempting to help beneficiaries who are not affiliated with gangs but who are gang victims.

"We had a case of a girl that was being abused by a gang member," explained Fabio. "We have had parents that have been murdered, so the church has been comforting them . . . Sometimes since the family is afraid of the gangs, they withdraw their complaint. But we are always encouraging the church and community and most important the parents to denounce these issues."

Children First recognizes that people who take a stand against violence might as a result become targets of violence. This could include church leaders and Children First staff. "Gang members are always listening to the narratives that these churches have [about violence], because they know they are generators of that violence," explained Marcela. "So, how do you think that they are going to interpret that message? If . . . you talk about programs for the prevention of violence, that can turn us into enemies [of the gang]. And our local pastors and beneficiaries and tutors can be in danger." Children First thus tries to frame violence prevention efforts as a "development plan" and integrates it into other programming. Using such strategies allows Children First to work against violence without immediately drawing the gangs' ire.

Children First Summary

Children First's presence in lower-class Salvadoran neighborhoods makes them vulnerable to gang infiltration; it also allows them to infiltrate gang spaces. The relatively easy entrance of such spaces in both directions can be surprising. But it also makes sense. The topics of conversation are small children and youths. And the conversation is taking place between neighbors and family relations. Children First provides resources and a formal organizational structure, but it seeks to be part of the local community. The extent to which it is effective in empowering children lies at least in part in its willingness to be vulnerable.

A National Gang Leader Goes to Church

I met Diego[1] when I was living in El Salvador more than a decade before I began research for this project. We were both working for NGOs at the time. He often had insightful things to say, and I visited him on my trips to El Salvador after I returned to the United States.

In 2016 I visited Diego at his new job: he was now an assistant pastor at a church in San Salvador. It was by no means a megachurch, but it was well known and had many transnational connections. Diego previously worked in prison ministry; the stress of being in close contact with a violent population had taken its toll and was one of the reasons he decided to switch to a position with presumably less psychological stress. Eventually, though, I told him about my research and our conversation turned to the topic of gangs.

Diego got up and shut his office door. He sat back down and began talking more quietly. Diego noted that gangs were hard to escape. "Gangs are in the police, the army, the [local governments]. They are probably also even in churches," he said. Then he leaned in a little closer and said that during his years in gang ministry, he met an inmate who was a senior gang member. "Now that person comes to this church with his family." The gang member claimed to have converted to evangelicalism and to have left the gang. It was clear, however, that Diego was skeptical. Someone of his status, reckoned Diego, could never leave the gang. The situation was a source of extreme stress for Diego and the other pastors in the church.

I visited Diego again a year later, when he confirmed that the gang member attending his church was none other than Marvin Adaly Ramos Quintanilla, known as "El Piwa," and one of MS-13's most prominent national leaders. El Piwa was no longer going to the church because he had returned to prison. The stature of El Piwa within the gang, the conditions of his return to prison, and his dalliance with the evangelical community created a splash in national and international media.

El Piwa was born in 1980 and grew up in the less populated eastern side of the country. In 2000 he was convicted for attempted aggravated homicide and sentenced to fifteen years in prison (Aleman 2016a). He served twelve years in Zacatecoluca's maximum security prison, colloquially referred to as "Zacatraz." Over time he became MS-13's treasurer and a member of the *ranfla historica*, or gang's senior national leadership within El Salvador. This allowed him to take on the role of being among MS-13's most prominent spokesmen within the country (Lemus 2016; Martínez & Valencia 2017).

In 2012 President Mario Funes' administration brokered a truce between MS-13 and Barrio 18.[2] El Piwa was a primary negotiator for MS-13 (Dudley 2020; Rauda Zablah 2016). During the negotiations he had "a close relationship with Salvadoran Defense Minister David Munguía Payes" (Farah & Babineau 2017). One of the accessions the government made was to transfer some gang leadership to less secure penal centers. The idea was to allow them more communication with gang members outside the prison so that they could better facilitate the truce. Consequently, in March 2012 El Piwa was transferred to the less fortified Ciudad Barrios prison.

A number of evangelical organizations have prison ministries. A group called the Red Nacional de Pastores Torre Fuerte (RNP)—the literal translation of which is National Network of Pastors Strong Tower—was working in Ciudad Barrios at the time El Piwa was transferred. The RNP describes itself on its Facebook page as an organization of pastors and chaplains that serves God and El Salvador. Representatives of the RNP met El Piwa and began to cultivate a relationship with him (Rauda Zablah 2016). While still in prison and within the context of these relationships, El Piwa claimed that he had left the gang to become an evangelical.

El Piwa was released from prison in 2013 to participate in a program designed to reinsert former gang members back into society. He was given a job with the municipality of Ilopongo working under the mayor, an ARENA politician named Salvador Ruano (Silva Avelos & Avelar 2016). Under Ruano, El Piwa directed the Temporary Income Support Program, financed through the United States Agency for International Development (USAID). The program channeled assistance to female-headed households and youths in the urban areas of the country (Aleman 2016b). Munguía Payes even issued a gun permit for El Piwa, "who legally acquired numerous weapons" during this time (Farah & Babineau 2017).

El Piwa also deepened his ties with the evangelical community. He started going to church with his wife and family at Diego's church. His wife, a bilingual Christian school teacher (Aleman 2016a), had been going to the church on her own for years. El Piwa also stayed close to the RNP. Although he attended church with his wife, he considered Nelson Valdez, a pastor and the executive president of the RNP, to be his pastor (Rauda Zablah 2016).

El Piwa even entered a training program to become a pastor through the RNP. According to Valdez, he completed a degree in theology that included 1,252 hours of class time, graduating as "an ordained and accredited pastor" in November 2015. El Piwa obtained a license as a prison chaplain and occasionally appeared on local television stations to preach. He was a charismatic leader and his neat, clean-shaven look allowed him to fit the profile (Rauda Zablah 2016). Everything seemed to be going well.

Then the government dropped a bombshell. It had run a massive investigation beginning in 2015, but which built on information gathered as early as 2013, on MS-13s finances. The results of "Operation Check" (as in checkmate) were released in July 2016, when the police issued 120 arrest warrants and made 157 raids on gang-linked businesses and properties (Silva Avalos & Avelar 2016). El Piwa, they argued, had not only remained in the gang (Lemus 2016), but was, along with a leader named Malvado, the head of "the Federation," which was MS-13's governing body outside of the prison (Dudley 2020). El Piwa was perhaps the most prominent gang member arrested as a result of Operation Check.

Investigators were certain of El Piwa's continued gang leadership during his time as an evangelical pastor. "Piwa handled the gang's car businesses and managed the money, according to a government indictment" (Dudley 2020, 239). While he was a pastor, El Piwa "orchestrated MS 13's financial growth, primarily through the sale of cocaine and crack from secret pozos controlled by the ranfla histórica" (Farah & Babineau 2017).

There was also major conflict within MS-13 at this time. A member of the Fulton clique named Chory accused the *ranfla histórica*, or the national gang leadership, of having received $25 million from the government during the truce negotiations and of keeping it to themselves (Silva Avalos & Avelar 2016). El Piwa was at the center of the intra gang conflict because he had helped to negotiate the terms of the truce. Chory thus targeted El Piwa by burning one of his car dealerships to the ground. In response, and as part of a larger effort to enforce loyalty to the gang's original leadership structures, El Piwa gave the order for Chory to be assassinated. The order was successfully carried out on January 6, 2016 (Dudley 2020), less than two months after El Piwa was ordained as a pastor.

None of this surprised Diego. But it did have a significantly negative impact on the church he was serving. Because El Piwa was a nationally recognized figure he generated tremendous fear. Many people left the church in the midst of these events. Mercifully, the church did not come into the cross hairs of the police investigation. The police talked to neighborhood residents about the church (Aleman 2016a), but they placed much more focus El Piwa's relationship with the RNP, to the point that they confiscated hard drives and files from the RNP's central office as part of Operation Check (Barrera 2016). No public statements ever implicated any RNP employee for involvement with, or facilitation of, gang activities.

Valdez served as the RNP's spokesman during this time. He affirmed in an in-depth interview with Nelson Rauda Zablah, an *El Faro* reporter, that El Piwa appeared to be authentic in his conversion and diligent in his studies. "I have seen much Christianity in his behavior," he said. Valdez also used the interview to continue to promote government and civil society dialogue with the gangs, as he believed such dialogue could reduce conflict and violence. He also affirmed the idea that gang members can be reintegrated into society, arguing that Jesus did not come for the good people in society, but for the lost. Followers of Jesus, then, must also work with such people. The one concession that Valdez made was that admission policies into the RNP's theological studies program might need to be revisited (Rauda Zablah 2016).

The differences in the response to El Piwa between Diego and Valdez are stark. Years of working in prison contexts and close interface with gang members made Diego wary of El Piwa from the beginning. Empirically speaking, he correctly anticipated the way that events played out. Valdez also has extensive experience with gangs. While he claimed to be surprised by El Piwa's recalcitrance, Valdez's underlying philosophy—more dialogue with gang members is always better—and his lack of fear of the gangs perhaps more decisively distinguishes him from Diego. Both pastors would agree with Valdez's assertion that Christ came to save the lost and would want all gang members to have the opportunity for a conversion experience. But the two differ on how to realistically think about gangs and their response to Christ's invitation. This may again be due in part to their social standing: Valdez, at least before these events, simply seemed to carry more authority, which might be one reason that El Piwa considered him his pastor rather than any of the pastors at his wife's church. Regardless, the two perspectives represented by Diego and Valdez can be found in pastors around the country.

El Piwa is a high-profile example of something that happens with some regularity: gang members penetrate churches. At the grassroots level, I heard reports in one neighborhood that a family of gang members had decided to attend a specific church. They remained active gang members and had no intention of converting. The pastor of that congregation felt powerless; he could not get them to leave the church and he could not get them to reform their ways. They simply decided to make that church their own.

The importance of El Piwa is that such a high-profile case changed the church's image, even with gangs. El Piwa may have inspired copycats: rank-and-file gang members may be more likely to use the façade of evangelical leader. But even before El Piwa's arrest reports of such cases appeared in the media. In one case, MS-13 members pretended they were pastors conducting open air services in central San Salvador. This allowed them to receive "offerings" that were in reality extortion payments (Diario1.com 2015). Even without El Piwa, gang infiltration was and continues to be part of El Salvador's empirical reality.

Evangelicals Go to Prison

Evangelicals infiltrate gang-controlled spheres of society, including El Salvador's prisons. Formal ministries, such as Transformation—the ministry this case study examines—come into prisons where a grassroots evangelical presence already exists. Many inmates grew up in evangelical homes and maintain an evangelical identity. Many evangelical and non-evangelical inmates have evangelical relatives who provide religious support such as prayer, Bible references, and even words of prophecy. Most inmates thus know and understand the ethos of the evangelical organizations that populate prison spaces.

Evangelical ministries permeate prison culture in various ways. I visited Cliffside, a youth detention center, in the middle of a typical weekday. A pastor from a local church was preaching in Cliffside's small chapel. Some inmates were helping with the service; several more had taken up seats inside the chapel. They sang emotively, prayed, and listened to the sermon. Adrian, the Transformation pastor I accompanied, noted that a number of pastors in the area sign up for time slots to preach at Cliffside. After observing the service, we moved on to meet some inmates in Cliffside's small library. Bibles vastly outnumbered any other book, or even genre of books, on the library shelves. There was also material from a different evangelical prison ministry on one of the shelves. All of this appeared to be part of the taken for granted reality of prison culture for the inmates we met.

Transformation is largely the creation of Erik, the missionary referenced in earlier chapters. Relationships with gang members in neighborhoods near his church led him to get involved in the prison system. As relationships deepened and he and his pastoral staff got more involved, Erik decided to create a non-profit and establish a more systematic approach. The outreach efforts quickly expanded to include Bible studies and preaching engagements in prisons, collaborations with other prison ministries, networking with prison administrators, relevant police personnel, and other government and multilateral organizations, a recently constructed transition center or halfway house, and outreach to family members of prisoners in the communities. I do not cover all of those activities here. Rather, I focus on Transformation's work at Cliffside and its transition center.

Cliffside

Cliffside's inmates committed serious crimes as minors, including police assassinations and other homicides. Most are 18th Street gang members (coming from both of the 18th Street factions, the *revolucionarios* and the *surenos*). Sentences that begin when inmates are minors often keep them there until their early to mid-twenties. The feel of the detention center is thus less that of one for juveniles and more of one for young adults.

Transformation's strategy in prisons is to build relationships with the inmates. I had a sense of the vulnerability of this approach on my first visit to Cliffside with Adrian. We went into the prison yard, where perhaps forty inmates were passing time in different ways. Our entrance caught everyone's attention. The guards let us in, then locked the gate behind us and left. Immediately we were surrounded by inmates, some of whom seemed hopped up on drugs. I was keenly aware that I was at their mercy. But they energetically greeted Adrian. Some friendly banter ensued before Adrian told the inmates about Transformation's programming plans for the next couple of months, encouraging as many as possible to attend.

Transformation's Bible study at Cliffside employs a twelve-step program which takes three months to complete. It was developed by a U.S. based group called Living Free (https://livingfree.org/). Adrian explained that in going through the steps, he and his colleagues help gang members try to identify past traumas and discern if such experiences are connected to current addictions or "dangerous feelings" towards family members of other people in their lives. "We want to teach them how to overcome those feelings," said Adrian. "In each step . . . we try to recognize the issues and find solutions for them. We also make sure to focus on Jesus because he is the best opportunity they have to leave all of their problems behind." Adrian and Transformation hope the program will release inmates from addictions, create clear change in their behaviors and lifestyles, and help them leave the gang.

At the time of my first visit, Adrian had twenty-one inmates in the Living Free program, or roughly 7 percent of the inmates at the detention center. Some of these simply responded to Adrian's initial invitation. Others came because a cellmate encouraged them to attend. The Bible study was discussed by inmates even when Transformation staff were not at the facility. This was especially the case after some who attended claimed that, as a result of the program, they had chosen to leave the gang and join the church. In this respect, Transformation's efforts to infiltrate and impact Cliffside's population and culture was successful.

The Living Free program also serves as a filter for inmates who may be a fit for Transformation's transition center, which opened in 2021, the final year of my field research. Part of the center's grounds are pictured in Photo 7.2. Transformation hopes to move inmates who have done well in the twelve-step program out of Cliffside and into the transition center. But they can only qualify after they have completed more than 50 percent of their sentence. The Transformation staff takes case files of potential fits to a judge. Adrian explained that "I tell the judge: 'I want to have these [inmates]. I know them. They have received the discipleship program and study, they also graduated. I think they are ready to move into our center.' Then the judge will evaluate them." The judge can accept or reject Transformation's proposal, thus determining the number of inmates the transition center will house. In 2021, the judge granted only six of the eighteen cases Transformation proposed. Because one subsequently dropped out (explained below), the transition center, which was built to comfortably house eighty inmates, operated at less than 10 percent capacity. In a country with a massively overcrowded prison system, this was a rarity.

Transition Center

The transition center nonetheless provided the full range of programming to its first cohort of inmates. This included vocational training. There is a small agricultural plot on the premises, and inmates are taught how to cultivate various types of crops. Inmates help with livestock; they constructed cages for the animals and received classes on how to breed rabbits. Transformation also involves inmates in daily food preparation. In addition to gaining culinary skills that are personally useful, inmates learn how to make sausage and other items that could result in employment opportunities upon their release.

Transformation's programming also addresses inmates' psycho-social and spiritual well-being. Its staffing reflects its psycho-social emphasis: one of the

Photo 7.2 Evangelical rehabilitation center for incarcerated gang members (photo: David Torres Ayala).

four full-time staff members is a psychologist. Daily events show the level of spiritual engagement: inmates agree to come to the center knowing, according to Erik, that "they have to go to the chapel every night. They have to read the bible in the morning . . . they have two hours of Teen Challenge discipleship every afternoon . . . They also go to church every Sunday." Inmates are not required to become Christians—Transformation could not house inmates in the national prison system if this were a requirement. But Transformation staff are explicit that they hope inmates leave the gang and join the church.

Such an environment does not work for everyone. Wilfredo, an inmate, asked to return to Cliffside within two weeks of arriving at the transition center. Wilfredo explained to Erik that he worshiped Santa Muerte, or "Saint Death." Chesnut notes that "there is no denying [Santa Muerte's] special appeal to those who live, work, and die in the criminal underworld" (2012, 19). Within prisons, "Lines of cocaine, prison moonshine . . . cigarettes, and marijuana joints figure among the common offerings at her altars" (2012, 15). Wilfredo, Erik reported, felt comfortable going to Bible studies at Cliffside because it was a small part of the day, and he could engage in other religious activities outside of that. But life at the transition center brought his religious activities into sharper conflict with each other. So, although the transition center provided vastly better resources and treatment, Wilfredo returned to Cliffside.

Wilfredo's experience highlights the extent to which the transition center allows Transformation to bring gang members onto their "turf." In pulling inmates out of gang-controlled prisons and into a church-like environment, they follow the haven thesis model. For Wilfredo, life in the haven that Transformation created did not work. But the other five inmates all voiced strong appreciation for the transition center and a desire to stay. Three of the five gang members in the transition center had left the gang and become Christians, either while still at Cliffside or in the transition center. The haven approach can still help evangelicals accomplish their goals in social engagement.

But the intermingling of gang and evangelical beliefs and worldviews is still evident at the transition center. This is visually evident in Photo 7.3, where an inmate at Transformation is holding a Bible with one hand and making a gang sign with the other. Felipe, who became a Christian through the Living Free program at Cliffside, continued to deepen his faith at the transition center. He also maintained good relationships with the gang members there and advocated for better treatment of gang members by prison guards and police. "The police abuse that is in this country is too much," he said. "In the prisons they don't give us food, sometimes they even withhold water,

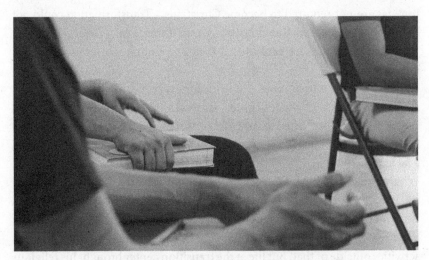

Photo 7.3 Inmate with one hand on Bible, one hand making gang sign (photo: David Torres Ayala).

they don't let us leave the cell," Felipe said emotionally. He sees the same dynamics in the communities, where "the police are only there to mistreat us.
Even for a youth that is not in the gang, the police will just hit him for the fun
of it. They do not see the hate this sews in the country." Such perspectives, be
they gang-friendly or empirically accurate or both, exist alongside Felipe's
powerful testimony about the Holy Spirit saving him and the work of the
church in the community. "[Other] people think [youths in gangs] are crazy,
but the church sees something in the youths that God can change. They believe in the things that God can do," said Felipe.

Transformation also works with family members of inmates. Erik invites
those who live close enough to his church, which is where I met Felipe's
mother, Marta. Marta's own life has been difficult. Her mother died when she
was very little, and she did not finish high school. Marta has had five children
with multiple partners. She said that she did not know Felipe had joined the
gang because at that time, she had to leave for work nearly every day and although he was still quite young, she admitted she neglected him. Years later,
Marta attended church for the first time when she came to see Felipe's baptism. (Transformation received permission to bring, heavily guarded, some
of the inmates at Cliffside to Erik's church for a baptismal service.) Marta is
grateful for the changes she sees in Felipe's life and she regularly attended
Erik's church at the time of my interview. The church staff was providing her
with love and support. The church, like the transition center, is a safe place in
which Transformation can conduct its ministry.

Not all of Transformation's family outreach takes place in the church.
As part of its effort to reduce recidivism, Transformation goes into gang-
controlled neighborhoods to meet with family members, some of whom
are also part of the gang. Erik mentioned, for example, that Felipe's younger
brother appears to be active in the gang. Erik is aware that building
relationships with gang members and operating in gang-controlled
environments, especially as a person who is trying to bring former members
out of the gang, carries with it some risk. "There is danger," he said. "There
are so many unknowns. We are walking blind." He noted that some members
of his staff have small children, which implies added vulnerability. But so far,
they have faced no repercussions: "Since we started [the transition center],
no [gang member] has come here, no one has said anything. Sometimes we
are waiting for the other shoe to fall." Such risk is an unavoidable element of
circulating in gang spaces and gang culture.

Conclusion

Previous chapters have shown that social networks, beliefs, and attitudes of evangelicals and gangs intermingle in public spaces. This chapter shows that entanglement occurs even within evangelical organizations and in gang-controlled social spaces.

Gangs have demonstrated the ability to penetrate evangelical churches and non-profits. Seen most positively, gangs can seek to benefit from evangelical ministries that are in part intended for them. In other words, gang members can be the intended beneficiaries of evangelical programs, including the use of evangelical ministries to put their own children on a different life trajectory. But more darkly, gangs can control who gets into evangelical programs. Gang members can be "wolves in sheep's clothing," using the cover of being churchgoers in order to carry on with gang business. They can threaten and manipulate evangelicals from within churches and ministries. Such dynamics pose significant problems for pastors and other church leaders.

Conversely, evangelicals can penetrate gang organizations. I wasn't able to attend meetings of a gang clique, so the parallel isn't perfect. But prisons are gang-controlled areas, and homes of gang members are intimate places. Children First and Transformation staff regularly inhabit such spaces. They are able to introduce culture change at the micro level and change the outcomes of gang members and their family members. Gangs, it seems, have come to expect some level of evangelical presence in such spaces.

Conclusion

I return to the questions that motivated this book and which were posed in the Introduction. First, how do evangelicals and gangs interact? Different components of interaction have emerged as the book's chapters have unfolded. The tasks in this concluding chapter are to paint a composite picture of evangelical/gang interaction, lay out policy recommendations that follow from such observations, and highlight what the study tells us about the second question that motivated this book: What does this tell us about how evangelicals interact with society and social problems generally?

A Composite Picture

I use the entanglement thesis, explained more fully in the Introduction, to frame the composite picture of how evangelicals interact with gangs. The thesis's three main components are as follows: first, an entanglement approach privileges the geographic and physical proximity to social problems over the cultural distance that evangelical churches might try to create; second, an entanglement approach recognizes the implications of low barriers to entry on evangelical identity and community in impoverished places; and third, an entanglement approach pays attention to the social networks that connect church leaders and members to the rest of the community. Each of these components will be utilized in turn.

Component (1) of the Entanglement Thesis

Evangelicals' geographic and physical proximity to social problems (in this case, gangs) are best understood through community studies. The community studies that comprise part of this research illuminated the places, institutions, and experiences that evangelicals and gangs share. The two groups, for example, are afflicted by the same poor water and sanitation

Blood Entanglements. Stephen Offutt, Oxford University Press. © Oxford University Press 2023.
DOI: 10.1093/oso/9780197587300.003.0009

systems, health and education systems, and national and global political and economic realities. Their shared lower-class social status means they are afflicted by many of the same forms of social exclusion. A baseline of common experiences thus exists between evangelicals and gangs.

Within such contexts, three spheres of evangelical/gang interaction can be unveiled through community-level analysis: shared cosmologies, community governance, and local economies.

Evangelicals and gangs share a cosmology in which both groups believe in God, Satan, angels, and demons. The two groups agree that it is possible to communicate with such beings through prayer and witchcraft. They also believe in miracles and the power of curses. Finally, evangelicals and gangs understand and find meaning in the same set of symbols and rituals. Such commonalities have wide ranging implications for how the two groups relate to each other.

The shared cosmology, for example, provides pathways for youths to travel back and forth between evangelical and gang identities. As youths explore affiliation with one group or the other, or perhaps both groups simultaneously, they may switch allegiances to the forces of good or the forces of evil, but their understanding of such forces remains largely the same. They also do not necessarily "lose touch" with beings in the cosmology. Youths in many cases continue to communicate with God, for example, when they are in the gang; they also know the Beast is real and active when they are in the church. How youths and young adults think about such entities has a multidirectional causal relationship with their group affiliation and the decisions and actions that they take.

The second area of interaction between evangelicals and gangs that a community-level analysis unveils is local governance. In the presence of broken state and municipal governments, evangelicals and gangs often, in ad hoc ways, collectively decide how communities will be run. These arrangements can have cross-group benefits. Evangelicals, for example, benefit from, and sometimes seek out, protection provided by gangs. Conversely, evangelicals sometimes hide youths who are in gangs from the police or from other gangs. Evangelical pastors can also influence gang decisions: they sometimes successfully advocate for community members who violated gang rules, and thus are targets of gang "punishment." Community development projects are a third area that can generate mutual areas of evangelical/gang involvement. How a Christian NGO, for example, constructs a water project, and how it will be maintained once it is constructed, may need church and gang input and buy-in. Such decisions are the stuff of local governance, and often engage evangelicals and gangs in collaborative decision-making processes.

Significant limitations exist to the efficacy of evangelical/gang governance. Neither gangs nor evangelicals want to assume all the responsibilities of a good local government. Relations are never perfect between the two groups: gangs do not listen to all pastors in communities; evangelicals are often victimized, rather than protected by, gangs. Both groups engage in activities that are neither sanctioned nor supported by the opposing group. Such realities exist alongside the occasions in which evangelicals and gangs collectively fill the void of broken or absent municipal governance.

The third main area of interaction between evangelicals and gangs that a community-level analysis unveils is the participation of each in local economies. Members of both groups must earn money and buy basic goods while living in the same communities. Sometimes such activities create unexpected relationships. Evangelical non-profits, for example, sometimes hire gang members to work on church and community construction projects. Evangelicals hope that providing alternative income sources makes it possible for youths to leave a gang; they also know that a gang presence provides increased protection for their project. Conversely, local gang leaders hire evangelicals (often women) to collect extortion payments for them. Sometimes they collect extortion money from other evangelicals: those with small businesses are routinely charged "rent." Churches fall into a different category for gangs and are often spared monthly fees. But many churches are nonetheless confronted with sporadic requests for a "collaboration fee." Such dynamics create interesting ethical and theological dilemmas.

Moral Logics in Evangelical/Gang Discourse

Evangelicals and gangs seek to resolve such dilemmas through moral reasoning that is inspired by shared cosmologies and articulated in governance and economic spheres. Moral logics embody or seek to leverage commonly understood ideas of good and evil. Even when such logics are contested, they make sense to both groups.

References to examples that appeared in earlier chapters may be helpful. In the governance sphere, a gang member might explain to a pastor that gangs are victims of excessive police violence and that pastors should thus not dialogue with police. Or the gang member might explain to a pastor that a youth who stole from the gang must be punished, and that the punishment will be death. In the economic sphere, the gang member might justify extortion demands by saying that gangs help churches and the community by protecting it, and that this service comes with a fee. He might further explain that paying the fee can also facilitate good community relations. Use of such logic is a regular part of gang discourse with evangelicals.

Pastors accept, reject, or seek to modify such logics with moral logics of their own. Pastors may, for example, acquiesce to extortion demands and tell their congregants to do the same because, they say, the Bible says to "Give unto Caesar what is Caesar's," and gangs play the role of Caesar, controlling the community. Other pastors, though, may reject such extortion requests because gangs are asking for God's money, which cannot be given to the gang under any circumstances. Finally, pastors may seek to modify gang logic. They might argue that death is too severe a punishment for youths who steal from gangs. They might also argue that pastors need to interact and respect police because police are made in the image of God, even as they hasten to validate gangs' protests against police abuse.

Local gang leaders sometimes allow the decisions they make to be influenced by such counter logics. They do so in part because the logics fit within the moral and cosmological context to which evangelicals and gangs both belong.

Component (2) of the Entanglement Thesis

The second component of the entanglement thesis, to recognize the implications of low barriers to entry on evangelical identity and community, is a call to analyze social problems and other social influences within evangelical organizations. Accordingly, this study analyzes how low barriers to entry allow for a gang presence within evangelical congregations and ministries.

The case of Children First (a pseudonym), an NGO, was presented in the previous chapter. Children First empowers local churches in El Salvador to run child development centers in poor communities. Children First's programs lead to many positive child development indicators, but sometimes gang members are enrolled in their programs. This can happen when a child already in the program becomes a gang member or when a gang member enrolls in the program.

The resulting evangelical/gang entanglements run in multiple directions. Children First raises money in the United States through child sponsorships; all children in the program in El Salvador, including gang members, are required to write and often receive multiple letters from their sponsors each year. Such communication can create long distance relationships between gang members and suburban families in the United States. More pressing, a gang presence within the child development programs creates risks and challenges. Gangs can collect information on program resources as well as on staff and other students. Gangs can play a part in determining which youths are allowed to participate in Children First programs. A gang member told a youth in my study, for example, to stop attending the Children First program because his family had moved into a nearby community controlled by a different gang. This is just one reason gangs remove youths from the Children First program: more than 150 Salvadoran youths involuntarily left Children First's program due to violence in one recent fiscal year.

Antipathy does not always characterize Children First's relationship with gangs. Children First, for example, seeks to incorporate children of gangs. They believe every child, regardless of his or her background, should be given a chance to experience God's love. Gang members, for their part, are often pleased with this philosophy: they trust Children First to help pave their child's way to a future that does not look like their own. But there are risks: children of gang members are more violent on average than non-affiliated youth, and more likely to threaten staff and other students. Children First thus must navigate such ministry opportunities carefully.

The unwanted presence of gang members and the desired presence of gang members' children in Children First's programs reflects a more general pattern within evangelical organizations. Sometimes gang members come uninvited into evangelical organizations. When this occurs, evangelical congregants and/or staff respond with angst and fear. El Piwa, for example, was a national leader of MS-13. He converted to evangelicalism while in prison. He then claimed he left the gang and was released from prison through a government rehabilitation program. It was, however, a ruse. Members of the evangelical church he attended suspected this to the case, and many fled the church. After ordering at least one assassination while attending the church and occasionally preaching on local television, El Piwa was recaptured and sent back to prison.

A church that partners with a prison ministry exemplifies efforts to bring gang members to church. Pastors and church staff build relationships with youths in gangs and their families through community outreach. Such youths sometimes accept the invitation to come to church. The pastor also invites ex-prisoners who are still on probation to do their social hours at his church, even if they have not left the gang. Congregants who are not affiliated with the gang do not appear to view such visits as a threat, and often help in various ways with the ministries. The examples of Children First, El Piwa, and the prison ministry are explored more fully in Chapter 7.

The net effect of such dynamics is that evangelical congregations, whether they wish to be or not, often either have a gang presence in the church or are vulnerable to gang members who may at any time wish to enter the church. The prevalence of this reality creates a very different image of how evangelical organizations function in society than the image created by the haven thesis.

Component (3) of the Entanglement Thesis

The third component of the entanglement thesis pays attention to the social networks that connect church leaders and members to the rest of the community. This book, and Chapters 3 and 4 in particular, has paid special attention to how evangelicals and gangs are entangled in the same families and in the same patrimonial social networks.

It is common for evangelicals and gang members to populate the same families in lower-class El Salvador. This can lead to relational loyalties across evangelical and gang identities. Jorge is an evangelical youth who claimed that his brother, a gang member, was his hero: his father stopped beating his mother the day his brother joined the gang. Evangelical/gang family ties can also lead to conflict. Ana is a middle-aged evangelical who angered family members who were in a gang. She suffered abuse and fear until the problem was resolved. Family relationships knit communities together; they also create intimate vulnerabilities.

Family connections between evangelicals and gangs impact children's life trajectories. Children of evangelicals are often raised in the church. But they may also have close family ties to gangs and are in this way drawn into the gang. This even occurs to children of pastors. Conversely, children of gang members often have evangelical relatives and end up eschewing the gang for the church. The causal connection between family relationships of children to their future religious and gang affiliation is strong, but sometimes unpredictable.

Evangelicals and gangs both utilize patrimonies to organize their communities. Patrimonies are family networks that are extended through imaginary kinships. Congregations create imaginary kinships by, among other things, referring to one another as brother and sister. Cliques do the same through rituals that affirm a strong sense of belonging. But for both groups, patrimonies extend beyond formal members of congregations and cliques. It is in such a context that most community members are connected with people who are part of evangelical and gang patrimonies, and who may even be simultaneously affiliated with both.

Leaders of evangelical and gang patrimonies collaborate but also compete. Collaboration is possible because their forms of power are different: pastors use soft power tools such as moral authority; leaders of local cliques use hard power tools such as violence. Many of the goals of the two groups also differ: evangelicals want to introduce people to God and impact community culture; gangs want to control territory. But the groups ultimately have different visions for what the community should look like. Such differences can bring the patrimonies into serious conflict: multiple pastors were killed in El Salvador during the course of this research.

Conclusion

Using the three components of the entanglement thesis, a clearer vision of the evangelical/gang relationship comes into view. It is one which is spiritually dynamic and lived out in the public squares of economic and government life, both by collaborating for the common good and by competing for local influence and power. But entanglements are not only in the public square: they often infiltrate congregations and cliques. Finally, perhaps the most intimate space in which evangelical/gang relations are built is between family members. The evangelical/gang relationship is thus far ranging and pervasive. It is a prominent part, and sometimes a defining characteristic, of the everyday reality of those who live in lower-class Salvadoran communities.

Policy Implications

Evangelicals are organically part of efforts to solve El Salvador's "gang problem." What their role is, and how they can be more effective, is thus important. Below I situate evangelicals in the broader field of actors in gang prevention efforts. Then, based on the findings of this study, I make recommendations for how evangelicals can be more effective in reducing gang prevalence and violence in lower-class El Salvador.

The Field of Actors in Gang Prevention Efforts

There is a crowded field of actors involved in gang prevention efforts in El Salvador. Multilateral organizations, national governments, and human-itarian organizations are all seeking, and willing to fund, solutions. The Net Official Development Assistance El Salvador received in 2019, for example, was over $300 million (World Bank Data 2021b). Much (but not all) of such funding attempts to solve problems that are either causes or consequences of street gangs. Note the last two planks of the United States' Strategy for Engagement in Central America, which "was designed to pro-mote economic prosperity, strengthen governance, and improve secu-rity throughout the region" (Congressional Research Service 2020, 17). Congress appropriated roughly $411 million for El Salvador from FY2016 to FY2020 to pursue those goals (Congressional Research Service 2020).[1] El Salvador also received U.S. funding through the Central America Regional Security Initiative (CARSI), which was intended "to support justice sector reform, including support for the attorney general's office, police unit vet-ting, border and port security, anti-gang efforts, drug interdiction, human rights monitoring and protection efforts, and violence prevention programs" (Congressional Research Service 2020, 18). In FY 2016 and FY2017, CARSI funds to El Salvador totaled over $70 million each year. These are just two pieces of the total aid picture for El Salvador: over the course of this research project (2013–2021) El Salvador received well over $1 billion in foreign aid (World Bank Data 2021b).

Some such aid is geared toward reform of the economic, political, and so-cial structures that underly El Salvador. The European Union, for example, stated that the "transversal axis" of its €149 million Multiannual Indicative Programme, running from 2014–2020, was "job creation and formaliza-tion of employment" (European Commission 2021). The second compact of the Millennium Challenge Corporation, a $365 million U.S./Salvadoran government initiative running from 2015–2020, sought to increase El

Salvador's transportation infrastructure, regulatory environment, and education system, including a revamped national education curriculum and the construction of thirty-two new schools (Millennium Challenge Corporation 2020).

While such initiatives are not specifically geared toward the reduction of gang violence and prevalence, some government officials believe that changing the structural conditions of society is the most powerful way to create a flourishing economy and good governance, which in turn should remove the perceived need for gangs and thus the local support for, and interest in joining, gangs. Such logic is in many ways compelling. The problem is that gangs have risen in the midst of international efforts to improve El Salvador's political economy; aid for such programs has been flowing since at least the 1960s. This approach may thus be necessary but not sufficient to resolving gang violence in El Salvador.

Some international aid more specifically targets security issues. Such aid funds two main strategies. *Mano dura* (hard hand) policies are episodically instituted by Salvadoran governments (Holland 2013; Dudley 2020). These utilize aggressive, often militarized measures to crack down on gangs. Tactics include targeted home invasions, community sweeps, and filling prisons with gang members (Jutersonke, Muggah, & Rodgers 2009). They also include extra-judicial killings. Rigorous scholarship has, however, repeatedly demonstrated the ineffective nature of such policies (two examples: Holland 2013; Wolf 2017).

Community-based prevention programs, sometimes referred to as *mano amiga* (friendly hand) and *mano extendida* (extended hand), embody a different approach. They hope to address direct causes (causes more immediately connected to crime than the underlying structural causes mentioned above) of crime. Community-based prevention programs are often relational in orientation and seek voluntary gang participation and collaboration in solving social problems. Other community-level actors are also often included, including churches.

Like *mano dura* policies, community-based prevention programs have a decades-long history. In 2002, the Inter-American Development Bank provided El Salvador with a $27.9 million loan for the Support for the Social Peace Program, which was intended to "promote community-based social organizations, upgrade recreational facilities such as sports fields and meeting halls, establish employment and job training programs . . . support

interventions in schools . . . prevent and treat domestic violence, and rehabilitate young offenders" (IDB 2002, 68). Other major donors have funded
"urban programs such as 'Municipalities Without Weapons'; [and] public
and private population health programs targeting risk factors for violence"
(Jutersonke, Muggah,. & Rodgers 2009, 389). More recent *mano extendida*
programs include direct talks between gang leadership and non-government
and government actors, as well as efforts by Salvadoran NGOs to pressure the Salvadoran government to favor relational rather than militarized
approaches (Wolf 2017). The results of such gang prevention approaches are
mixed, with some communities experiencing decreases in violence during
the life of a program (Berk-Seligson et al. 2014). However, it is less clear that
community-based prevention programs create sustainable and long term
decreases in violence (Jutersonke, Muggah, & Rodgers 2009; Wolf 2017).
Fluctuations in national homicide indices, for example, do not appear to be
connected in any significant way to localized community-based prevention
efforts. There is also little evidence that such approaches reduce gang control
of specific communities.

Street Gangs in the Context of Global Crime

Why are street gangs so impervious to the hundreds of millions of dollars of
aid intended to reduce their prevalence? The answers are complicated and
run in multiple directions. But they include the fact that in the larger picture, the local youths that appear in this study are pawns in a constellation
of illicit actors that stretches far beyond El Salvador's poor neighborhoods.
Most believe that national gang leadership has connections with actors at
the highest levels of Central American public and private sectors, who in
turn are connected to shadowy figures in the United States and throughout
the western hemisphere. Hard data is difficult to gather and dependable re-
porting is dangerous to publish on such topics. In 2022, for example, Juan
Martínez, a journalist who has done extensive gang related investigative re-
porting, was forced to flee El Salvador because he feared reprisal from national government leaders (El Faro English 2022c). His work, as well as the
work of his brother Oscar (see, for example, Martínez 2016) and that of a
few other journalists give us glimpses into how this world works and what it
looks like.

Prospects of Success for Gang Prevention

Given such realities, knowledgeable people do not think that eliminating gangs from El Salvador is a realistic goal. This was true of a security expert I interviewed at the U.S. Embassy in El Salvador. Others I talked to in positions of influence expressed similar skepticism. Leading gang experts agree. Steven Dudley, founder of *InSight Crime*, is on record as saying that MS-13 is learning sophisticated ways to become more powerful (Williamson 2021). Dudley voiced the possibility that rather than developing strategies to remove gangs from society, the best way forward might be to incorporate gangs into mainstream public life. Other options have not worked, and are not likely to work in the coming decade.

While this book was going to press, Bukele embarked on the most significant *mano dura* initiative in El Salvador's history. His truce with the gangs fell through in March 2022. The gangs responded by going on a killing spree, recording sixty-two murders in a day: the highest number of violent casualties in a single day since El Salvador's civil war ended in 1992 (Renteria 2022). Bukele responded by declaring a state of emergency. By September 2022 the government claimed it had arrested over 52,000 people (Ministerio de Seguridad 2022). The scale of the initiative has made El Salvador's incarceration rate per capita, at least temporarily, the highest in the world.

This initiative could have cross-cutting consequences. It has at least temporarily changed the gang dynamic in lower-class communities. In August 2022 I was able to enter some communities that gang control previously made inaccessible. Community members testified to less gang surveillance and interference in their everyday lives. However, human rights advocates have decried such efforts, noting that innocent people are being arrested and physical abuse is being endured by the newly incarcerated (Renteria 2022). To this point in El Salvador's history, gangs have not been weakened when high numbers have been sent to prisons. Bukele has also not bowed to pressure from the U.S. administration to extradite gang leaders, indicating that while he is incarcerating the gangs' foot soldiers, some semblance of an understanding with the gangs may still be in place. At the time of this writing, it is not clear what the long-term strategy of the Bukele administration might be.

For now, some of the dynamics discussed in this book have been moved inside the walls of the prisons. Thousands, and likely tens of thousands, of the recently incarcerated identify with the evangelical faith. I heard numerous reports of pastors also being incarcerated for suspected ties to gangs in their community. El Salvador's Vice President, Felix Ulloa, startled many in the evangelical community, including evangelicals who support Bukele, when he proclaimed to a French media outlet that "80% of pastors are part of gang structures" (El Mundo 2022). How Ulloa arrived at this statistic and what the political motivation was to make such a claim was difficult to discern. Meanwhile, many faith-based gang ministries to gang members have been shut down, and numerous gang members who had left the gang by converting to the evangelical faith have also been arrested. Although Bukele's approval rating in El Salvador remains incredibly high, including among evangelicals, such developments are pushing some evangelicals into closer relationships with gangs.

The recent moves of the Bukele administration notwithstanding, the opinions of Dudley and U.S. officials are telling. It is one thing for victimized and relatively powerless community members to throw their hands up in hopelessness. It is quite another for representatives of the world's most powerful government and one of the foremost experts on hemispheric security issues to essentially do the same.[2]

Evangelicals

This, then, is the context in which poor evangelicals in impoverished communities are being asked to help reduce gang influence and violence. Most of the evangelical churches I visited in this study have incomes of less than $250/week. It is empirically not true, as has been insinuated elsewhere (O'Neill 2015), that evangelicals are awash in the millions of dollars of state and multilateral funding just described. They are, with very rare exceptions,[3] simply not part of that world (Brenneman 2016b). None of the organizations and none of the churches that appeared in my research received funds from any government or multilateral organizations. Two NGOs that I studied are well resourced through private donors, but their budgets remain miniscule compared to the financial flows outlined above.

Evangelicals are nonetheless among the most effective entities in engaging gangs (Brenneman 2012; Cruz et al. 2017; Johnson 2017; Williamson 2021; Wolseth 2011). Because of the dynamics described in this book, evangelicals are able to operate in spaces and have conversations that others simply cannot. As one evangelical leader commented to me, "the gangs chose us" to be the group with whom they are most willing to dialogue. The body of evidence suggests that he is right. A USAID evaluation, for example, noted that "churches play an especially important role in crime and violence prevention [by] . . . getting youths involved in positive social activities, reaching out to youths who are already in gangs, and serving as mediators between warring gangs" (Berk-Seligson et al. 2014, 15).

Evangelicals do not have a master strategy for engaging gangs. Their engagements with gangs arise naturally, almost impulsively, out of relationships in local contexts. "Solving" the national gang problem is not an evangelical ambition. They would, in any event, fail.

Policy Recommendations for Evangelicals

But evangelicals can do more to limit the impact of gangs in their neighborhoods. I present recommendations for how they can do so. The recommendations are grounded in the empirical realities this book has described. They are not flashy and they do not represent a silver bullet. They also take into account that other entities are more capable and have more resources to pursue structural and program related alternatives. My recommendations are intended to start conversations that may lead to altered life trajectories at the community level.

They are as follows:

Work within the communities' shared cosmologies. Local churches and evangelical non-profits should operate out of their religious identities. They should not be turned into secular entities, shorn of the spiritual elements that play a significant role in providing the unique influence and relationship that they have with gangs.

Strengthen networks with non-evangelical institutions. While evangelicals should remain religious, they should also *carefully* construct stronger ties with non-evangelical institutions. There are risks: some international actors may seek to use evangelicals instrumentally to achieve their own program goals. Gangs will likely see through such a relationship, which will limit evangelical impact. National and local governments may be corrupt. Fahlberg (2018) studied a Brazilian community in which members (not evangelicals) tried to subvert gang control by establishing semi-secret arrangements with local state administrators. They were subsequently killed: the state administrators, it turned out, were in league with drug traffickers. Evidence exists of similar problems with Salvadoran government personnel.

Evangelicals nonetheless have trustworthy potential partners. Public school systems might be one. Gangs control student populations of many schools and may be able to leverage their influence to manipulate teachers on occasion. But I did not hear any reports of gangs infiltrating the ranks of teachers in my research—incentives for gangs to do so are not immediately obvious. Teachers are in positions to do good in communities: they have relationships with their students, some of whom are in gangs and some of whom are non-affiliated. Many teachers in lower-class El Salvador also attend evangelical churches. Synergy between churches and schools thus seems within reach. Evangelicals might also build stronger networks with nonsectarian NGOs. Evangelicals might be able to help youths they care about by funneling them into NGO programs in health, job training, and other technical areas. Even if they have been infiltrated at the grassroots, the motives of such entities are not likely to be viewed with great suspicion by gang members, and thus maybe safe partners.

Continue to extract youths from gangs. The morgue rule exception, or the unique proviso that allows youths to leave gangs through conversion to evangelicalism, is what first drew the attention of religious scholars to the relationship between evangelicals and gangs in Central America (Wolseth 2011; Brenneman 2012).

There were signs in my research that the morgue rule exception was eroding in some communities. Evangelicals should do the relational work needed to ensure that local gang leaders continue to honor it, as its loss would fundamentally change community dynamics. Those most obviously affected would be youths who leave the gang through the morgue rule exception. Parents who seek the help of pastors to extract their children from gangs would have no other recourse. And many gang members who never attempt to leave are comforted by simply knowing there is a way out. Finally, it may negatively impact the overall nature of the evangelical/gang relationship. Much, then, is at stake.

Strengthen and proliferate efforts to rehabilitate youths who exit gangs. Youths who leave the gang all too often later return to the gang. Evangelicals can reduce such recidivism with deeper, more consistent mentorship and rehabilitation programs. They should use religious symbols, ideas, and language as they do so. Preparation for baptism, a highly meaningful symbol for evangelicals and gangs alike, should include strategies that free youths from addictions, facilitate spiritual or psychosomatic healing and maturity,[4] and place youths in conditions where success is more likely. Such processes will help them undergo real and lasting change and prepare them for integration into society.[5]

Cognitive behavioral therapy (CBT), or efforts to alter distorted thinking among gang members, is a concept that overlaps significantly with what I am proposing. Organizations in the U.S. have had success with this approach, and positive gains have been made through efforts to modify these concepts and apply them in Central American contexts. Catholic Relief Services, for example, has run programs in Central America that provide participants with tools to manage their thoughts and feelings, and in so doing, reduce the use of violence in their interpersonal interactions (Gardner, Kim, & Wolley 2021). Such programs sometimes include an explicitly spiritual component even in some mainstream and North American applications of CBT; appropriately contextualized efforts to provide lower-class Salvadoran pastors with some of the skills needed to provide CBT to youths who are exiting gangs could be effective.

To become productive, engaged members of society, youths need to either return to school or receive job training and job opportunities. Pastors could direct former gang members to NGOs that run job training or micro enterprise programs. More organically, members of the church could teach such youths a trade or allow them to work in the open-air market with them. Such opportunities send positive signals about how human flourishing can work at the local level.

Create systems to identify and remove pastors who are gang members. El Piwa's decision to serve as a pastor while being in a gang, detailed in the previous chapter, is not unique. Less prominent gang members have also assumed this disguise (Choco 2022; Diario1.com 2015[6]). Denominations and community networks of pastors should develop sensitivity to this gang strategy. They should have a plan for what to do when it occurs. It is possible that negotiations with gangs will be necessary to remove such pastors from their posts.

Increase the ethical and theological capacity of pastors and other evangelical leaders. Pastors are often called on to make complicated ethical decisions. (Should pastors hide gang members during police raids? Should evangelicals collaborate with gangs in community empowerment projects? Etc.) Many pastors know the Bible and their communities well but have only a grade school education. This sometimes contributes to unpredictable and even contradictory decisions and moral logics.

A grassroots, relational option could be more effective than enrolling pastors in university programs for which they are not academically prepared. Local and denominational networks could serve as a venue for seminars or other learning spaces. A feeling of community among leaders who are facing the same pressures could be fostered. Academics could act as facilitators and provide books, videos, or other resources. The end goal would be to provide pastors and other leaders with the relational, ethical, and theological toolkits needed to make decisions and to create moral logics that are ethically and theologically sound.[7]

Increase training for pastors and other evangelical leaders to provide trauma counseling. Perpetrators and victims of violence alike seek out pastors and other evangelical leaders as they deal with psychological trauma that comes from such experiences. Most pastors have not received any significant training in how to address such needs. Pastors would be more effective in this role if training were made available.

Find more ways for pastors and other evangelical leaders to leverage soft power. The moral authority pastors, especially *caciques*, have may be underutilized. Daring moves, such as running a drive for gang members to hand in their firearms, are rarely, if ever, attempted. Pastors must be careful not to overplay their hand, but they might find success if they paired such efforts with, for example, campaigns against police violence. The key may be to demonstrate a commitment to a community ideal (in this case peace) that is consistent with biblical teaching and makes sense for everyone rather than endorsing a single tactic that may be perceived as benefiting one set of actors over another.[8]

Frame gang intervention and outreach efforts through the lens of family. In a culture where family relations, although complicated, remain the building blocks of society, and where patrimonies are how authority is exercised, it makes sense for evangelicals to use family roles to reach at-risk youths. This study found evidence, for example, of the continued centrality of the mother figure in lower-class Salvadoran family and culture. It also found evidence that not all mothers live up to the archetype.

Within this context, some evangelical women, particularly those of motherly or grandmotherly age, play a role in the lives of gang members. That is, such women have demonstrated the will and ability to, as church representatives, gain access to intimate gang spaces, confront gang members about the way they treat their own children, and create modest behavior change in lifestyles of gang members. Such efforts do not always have the desired effect and can be dangerous: women have lost their lives in such endeavors. Evangelicals should elevate and enable the women who do this type of outreach; they should also find ways to lower the risks involved.

This study also found evidence that older pastors are often trusted by younger gang members. A corresponding finding was that the vast majority of gang members I talked to either did not know their father or had a dysfunctional relationship with him. Older pastors, operating in both patrimonial and familial systems, can default to a fatherly role in the lives of younger gang members. Such relational approaches should not be forced. But if older pastors were to view younger gang members as youths in need of a father figure (as some already do), relationships that facilitate gang prevention efforts could result.

Provide education on parenting and physical/sexual abuse. Most education and NGO professionals I talked to believe that absent parents and/or poor parenting are major contributors to gang growth in El Salvador. Even the mother of a gang member referred to her neglect of her own son as a causal factor in his decision to join the gang.

Evangelical churches should provide parents, or those raising children, with multiple and repeated parenting enrichment opportunities. Because many gang members come from evangelical homes, churches could reach much of the target population if they were to work within their own congregations on this issue (community wide seminars would be helpful, but less likely to be achieved). Parenting seminars are also a natural fit for evangelical teachings. It would likely not be hard to convince pastors to place greater emphasis on such themes.

It might be more difficult to convince evangelicals to provide educational opportunities about physical and sexual abuse in churches, but these are much needed. Arlen, a man in his late forties, showed me various spots on his body where his mother intentionally burned him when he was a child. Arlen reported that his mother also sexually abused him and his brother. Arlen later benefited from an evangelical ministry and joined a church community in which he has experienced love and support. But he never felt emotionally healthy enough to marry and have his own family; he remains single. Arlen's brother joined a gang and was killed in a shootout with police. Arlen believes he would have ended up like his brother were it not for the love he found at church. But Arlen also strongly believes that education about sexual abuse should be provided within church contexts. His experience is that the issue is almost never broached in sermons or other church venues. In the church services I attended in El Salvador, I also never heard the issue raised.

Affluent Salvadoran and U.S. evangelicals should engage in political advocacy. Community members are the primary actors in the recommendations to this point. Affluent Salvadoran and U.S. evangelicals can also be involved through political advocacy. Policy decisions regarding Salvadoran and U.S. approaches to the gang problem are not always, and perhaps not often, made in the best interests of lower-class community members.

Affluent Salvadoran and U.S. evangelicals could seek policy change in multiple ways. Religious actors in the public sphere are often best served by basing recommendations on moral principles (Reynolds 2015). Evangelicals could articulate the principles that are relevant for residents in gang-controlled communities. They could then find ways to hold governments responsible for creating technical solutions that uphold such principles. A second option might be for well-equipped evangelicals to develop and champion well-researched policy strategies that have high likelihoods of success. In either approach effective political advocacy is not easy. But the social change it creates can be profound.

Create more support for churches inside prisons. If the Salvadoran government intends to maintain the highest prison population per capital in the world for a sustained period of time, evangelical churches in prisons will likely proliferate. Evangelicals outside of the prison system should find ways to support such congregations.

A New Image of Latin American Evangelicalism

What does the study of evangelicals and gangs tell us about the character of Latin American evangelicalism?

In a previous study (Offutt 2015), I looked at evangelicals in leadership positions and noted that global and local religious social forces are constantly creating change in Latin American and African evangelicalism. Global religious social forces include transnational networks that penetrate national evangelical communities and the religious symbols and resources that flow through them. Local religious social forces include evangelicalism's entrepreneurial spirit. These forces continue to reshape a religious movement that, during the second half of the twentieth century, was characterized by ascetic practices and social withdrawal.

Today, national evangelical communities in the Global South are much larger and more socioeconomically diverse than they were during the Cold War period. Evangelicals, especially those in the middle and upper classes, are more likely to be engaged in social issues and more willing to participate in party politics or other aspects of the political system. On balance, such developments are viewed as positive: civil and political participation is needed to help make democracy work. El Salvador is no exception to these larger trends.

In this book I look more exclusively at poor evangelicals in poor communities. The findings nonetheless corroborate many of the findings from my earlier research. Evangelical growth in poor communities has, for example, met and usually exceeded evangelical growth in higher socio-economic strata. Poor evangelicals remain entrepreneurial: they are busily starting new churches and little businesses out of their houses. Finally, poor evangelicals are integrating themselves into various dimensions of community life in ways that simply were not the case three or four decades ago.

Poor communities are not, however, the same as middle- and upper-class communities. Participation in civil society and democratic institutions in communities where things more or less function as one might hope[9] is very different than political participation in gang-controlled communities. Rather than running for local office with noble aspirations of making the community a better place, poor evangelicals are faced with grim decisions on how to engage with power holders that use violence and do not necessarily have the best interests of society in mind.

Poor evangelicals nonetheless enter into public spheres and forge relationships with community actors. Sometimes evangelicals do so intentionally, such as when they seek to develop working relationships with gang leaders in communities. Sometimes evangelicals do so unintentionally, such as when their siblings are in a gang. The results of increased exposure to society and social problems have been mixed—evangelicals are more likely to save someone's life or reduce the negative impact of gangs. Evangelicals are also more likely to be incarcerated, and surprising numbers of gang members have grown up in evangelical homes. Both for better and for worse, evangelicals are, in many ways, increasingly part of the fabric of mainstream society.

An anonymous reviewer of this book provided some theological reflections on what has been described here. He noted that

> Martin Luther once described a Christian as *Simul Justus et Peccator*, a saint and sinner entangled within the same personality. Theologians have always claimed that the church is both righteous and sinful. It will always be entangled with the world in complex ways until the end of time.

Such observations should shape both historical and contemporary analyses of Latin American evangelicalism. Historically, Latin American evangelicals have always had entanglements and "sin" in their congregations. This has been true alongside their tendencies toward social withdrawal. In contemporary Latin America, the "sin" in their congregations continues to exist. What is different is that, as evangelicals become more prominent in public spaces, they contribute more to their communities, but they also find themselves in compromised positions outside their congregations more frequently. It is thus the social location and the increased diversity in types of entanglements that is different for evangelicals today.

It bears repeating that much of the literature that supports the haven thesis remains valid. Faithful evangelicals, more so than the newer category of cultural evangelicals, still reflect much of their evangelical heritage. Data collected in this study supports many of the claims that have been made in support of the haven thesis. In fact, much of the evangelical/gang relationship in communities is predicated on evangelicals having characteristics that the haven thesis highlights. I am not seeking to replace the haven thesis with the entanglement approach.

I am, though, seeking to provide a competing perspective. This is important because the haven thesis never captured the full realities of the evangelical experience. Nor can it capture newer dimensions of this ever-changing religious movement. No single perspective ever could.

The entanglement thesis helps in this regard. It seeks to follow the movement into the new social spaces it inhabits. It also hopes to place emphases on parts of the movement that have traditionally been underemphasized. This study has shown the entanglement approach's utility in illuminating heretofore undocumented elements of interactions between evangelicals and gangs. It is likely to be helpful in analyzing other aspects of evangelicalism's interaction with society and social problems.

Methodology

The data for this book is drawn from the Religion, Global Poverty, and International Development Project (RPD). The RPD's primary intent is to analyze religion's intersection with poverty and development before, during, and after a major state development project. The project under analysis is a $365 million joint initiative of the U.S./Salvadoran governments.[1] A pilot project for the RPD was conducted in 2012–2013. The formal research project was launched in 2014 and is ongoing.[2]

Although the study of evangelicals and gangs was not the catalyst for the RPD, the pilot project revealed that insecurity is the most pressing element of poverty in the communities under study. The UNDP's multi-dimensional poverty index, the primary metric I utilize to measure poverty, does not cover insecurity. I thus modified the research design to include data collection on gangs and intra-family violence. As I conducted ethnographic research in 2014–2015 and built trust in communities, I gained an even clearer view of the extent to which gangs and violence both drive and define poverty. I thus made more concentrated and careful efforts to gain data on the interface between gangs and religious actors.

These efforts were integrated into the formal research design, which includes ethnographic research, interviews, focus groups, and a baseline survey. As part of the ethnographic research I visited twenty-four churches. I engaged in deeper participant observation in one congregation and visited three other churches regularly. I also visited the U.S. Embassy, Salvadoran government departments, offices of five NGOs, two youth detention centers, four local schools, a community health clinic, transportation posts, and several sites of employment and local entertainment. I spent time in the homes of people in the neighborhoods and met them and their families at local eateries. Finally, I followed the social and religious networks of people in these neighborhoods to other locations in El Salvador and conducted supplemental research in these other locations.

I conducted the baseline survey in 2014. The survey asked questions based on the UNDP's multi-dimensional poverty index. It also asked questions about religious identification, religious practices, and religious networks. We canvassed six neighborhoods, going door-to-door in each neighborhood.

The RPD interviews and focus groups fall into three categories: local religious or community leaders, community members, and representatives of state actors and NGOs. Some key respondents were interviewed more than once. From 2014 to 2021 I conducted 143 total interviews with 118 different people, although not all of these addressed the topic of gangs. These can be broken down into forty-one interviews with thirty-eight community members, forty-four interviews with twenty-seven pastors or church leaders, and fifty-eight interviews with fifty-three individuals who are engaged in development in some way. Not counted in the interviews are the countless informal conversations I had in churches and neighborhoods along the way. A small research team and I also conducted sixteen focus groups; eight of these were explicitly intended to find out more about intra-family violence and gang activity. I conducted three such focus groups in youth prisons or detention centers with a total of sixteen focus group participants.

Ethnographic research was critical to this study. I recorded seventy-four different ethnographic activities from 2014 to 2021, ranging from participation in prayer meetings to attending soccer games. Such events provided a better sense of how local actors view their reality and how different community-based organizations, including churches and gang cliques, are socially located. As I became known in the neighborhoods, I occasionally met gang members when I accompanied pastors or members of local congregations. Outside of prisons and detention centers I did not, however, conduct any formal focus groups or interviews with active gang members. This research is intended to shed light on how evangelicals interact with gang members. It does not provide an in-depth look at gangs themselves.

When appropriate, I recorded interviews and focus groups and had them transcribed. In more sensitive situations I took notes during the interview and refined them after the interview. I loaded interview and focus group transcriptions as well as ethnographic notes into Atlas.ti and coded them.

Notes

Introduction

1. O'Neill (2015) did not focus on the morgue rule exception and does not use the lens of the haven thesis (described later in this chapter). However, my methods, analysis, and conclusions all vary from those of O'Neill.

2. The Waldensians were formed by Peter Waldo in Lyon in the twelfth century. They were an ascetic movement within the Catholic Church before the Reformation. They were declared heretical by the Catholic Church and faced intense persecution. When Waldo and his followers were driven away from Lyon, they settled in the Italian Alps (Piedmont) and in Luberon. The movement spread to South America through Italian immigration. Beginning in the 1500s, the Waldensians forged formal relationships with different Protestant groups, perhaps most notably the Calvinist and (later) the Methodist traditions. This was the case in Uruguay at the time of Penzotti's conversion (Geymonat 1994).

3. In 1887 Penzotti was named the American Bible Society's representative on South America's Pacific Coast. Penzotti became known was the Founder of Peruvian Methodism during this time and was thrown into a Peruvian prison in 1890 by order of a Catholic priest. Eight months later, after his case garnered the attention of the international press, Penzotti was released (Bravo 2015; House 2019).

4. Scholars have used other terms to describe the haven tendency, such as a "walk-out" from society (Martin 1990) or "life-worlds" that exist apart from mainstream culture (Lindhart 2014). Regardless of the term that is used, six decades of scholarship are mostly in agreement that separation from society and a place of refuge are defining characteristics of Latin American evangelicals.

5. "Mara" came into the Salvadoran lexicon via a 1954 movie, *The Naked Jungle* (starring Charlton Heston), which was a cinematic reproduction of Carl Stephenson's 1938 short story, "Leiningen versus the Ants." The protagonist battles fictitious "marabunta ants" in the movie, a name perhaps inspired by a wasp in British Guiana. Marabunta ants captured the imagination of the movie's global audience, and the term "mara" seeped into the lexicon of South and Central American countries. In 1960s El Salvador, the name came to mean groups of children or youths who formed at church or school and who began to spend time together.

6. Ward cites MSS activity dating possibly as far back as 1975; Dudley asserts that the MSS was founded in 1983.

7. In 2005 the 18th Street gang split into two factions in El Salvador: the "Revolucionaros" and the "Surenos." It is thus now more correct to say that there are three main gangs in El Salvador (InSight Crime 2018).

Chapter 2

1. Parts of the previous four paragraphs were reprinted by permission from Springer Nature Switzerland AG. They appeared in: Offutt, Stephen. (2019). "El Salvador." In: Gooren, H. (eds) *Encyclopedia of Latin American Religions. Religions of the World.* Springer, Cham.

2. Chesnut (2018) does not deny the possibility of a connection to Aztecan deities but highlights Santa Muerte's ties to the grim reaper and other figures in medieval Spanish Catholicism.

3. In El Salvador such discussions often carry references to "the Beast," a term that has multiple meanings. Sometimes it is another name for Satan; sometimes it is a personification or spiritualization of acts of violence, particularly homicide. Sebastian, another inmate, said that "Many [gang members] worry, 'how will God will take care of me if I'm killing [other people]?' And they say 'No, the Beast, the Beast is with me,' and they cling to some relationship with the Beast, which is the Devil, as protection . . . they cling to the [idea] that 'no, the Beast is with us,' 'the Beast has taken care of us,' 'the Beast, we must entrust things to the Beast.'" This psychological and spiritual dependence on the Beast is often worked out through formal rituals.

4. The reference to hardened hearts is a biblical one. It is a phrase used in the Old and New Testaments to refer to people who reject God's message.

5. This will be explained more fully in the following chapter. Here I simply reinforce how common this is by mentioning that multiple sources estimated that 40–70 percent of all gang members grew up in evangelical households.

6. The theologically informed reader will note that many evangelicals believe in a "once saved always saved" doctrine, which would hold that individuals who make a faith commitment are always Christians. This doctrine has Reformed roots. Santiago, Miguel, and Leonardo, like most gang members in El Salvador, have been taught Pentecostal doctrine, which holds that one can lose one's salvation, thereby moving from a status of being a Christian to being a non-Christian.

7. Brenneman (2012) explains in more depth the role of emotion within these complicated social dynamics.

8. Gangs carry some syncretic religious ideas, as they are influenced by, for example, Santeria. But Santeria was already a hybrid religion with Christianity.

Chapter 3

1. Families act upon society, but they are also acted upon. El Salvador's economic, political, and social history have shaped family structure in lower-class neighborhoods. Contributing factors can be traced as far back as the radical land reform laws that allowed for the forced removal of local populations so that *Ladinos* (Central Americans of European descent) could establish coffee plantations in the late nineteenth century (Williams 1994). The authoritarian military government that served El Salvador's landed elite by maintaining oppressive control of the peasants up into the second half

of the twentieth century maintained rigid class distinctions (Wood 2000). The impact on the family of this arrangement was similar to that which occurred throughout much of Latin America: upper-class family systems tended to experience greater stability and was established through formal nuptials, whereas cohabitation and temporary unions, created without legally binding contracts, were standard features of family structures among the lower-classes (Ulmann, Maldonado, & Nieves 2014). El Salvador's bloody civil war (1980–1992) further devastated family systems through death and violence, and it led to massive internal and external migration, which spatially distends and often weakens family ties (Menjívar 2000, 2007). These more recent dynamics, in tandem with broader shifts in the global political economy have caused further decreases in marital stability and formalization throughout the region since the 1980s (Cerruti & Binstock 2009).

2. The Families Code Group consists of twenty-five separate codes consisting of 300 quotations (266 co-occurrences). The quotations were created from interviews, focus groups, and ethnographic notes that were taken with community members and community leaders, including evangelicals and gang members. In almost all cases, questions about specific types of family members were not asked. Rather, references to family members emerged from narratives of life experiences.

3. An enormous literature exists that explores such issues (see, for example, Giddens 2000; Jelen & Diaz-Munoz 2003; Kibria 2006; Seccombe 2012; Walsh & Menjívar 2016). My interest here is not to do a review of this literature, but rather to show how local institutions perceive and seek to interact with these problems.

4. Gender issues are closely intertwined with family issues; for the sake of simplicity I am using the frame of family to capture all of these concerns.

Chapter 4

1. Bueno traces *caciquismo*'s use and evolution through the centuries. The *cacique* system existed outside of, and parallel to, imposed colonial structures. In the rural areas, this approach created local shadow governments in the mid-nineteenth century. They thrived under, and helped give birth to, military dictatorships in the latter part of the nineteenth century and into the twentieth. The form continued to thrive under the shallow and somewhat artificially democratic governments in the mid- to late twentieth century.

2. The phrase is a nod to Christian Smith's (1998) book with that subtitle. Here I refer to related dynamics but within a very different context that has a different set of actors.

3. In the pre-Bukele era, both the FMLN and ARENA also negotiated with the gangs for votes (Dudley 2020).

4. I have not focused on the contestation of authority or influence between or within gang cliques or between or within evangelical congregations. Or, for that matter, between evangelicals and Catholics. All such competition is grist for interesting analysis, but it would take away from my primary interest in the competition between evangelicals, gangs, and police.

Chapter 5

1. Weaver, Rock, and Kusterer (1997) present multiple lists of things that governments in contemporary societies should do. I have consolidated these lists, which include the following: 1) establish and enforce policies, laws, and regulations; 2) produce routine regulatory actions; 3) issue licenses and permits; 4) monitor compliance of companies and individuals; 5) intervene to stop activities that do not meet regulatory standards; 6) allocate access to government resources and subsidies; 7) produce public goods (roads, schools, clinics); 8) distribute access to governmental goods and services according to its own criteria of need and program eligibility; 9) arbitrate disputes; 10) provide a safety net; 11) provide for the "common defense"; and 12) collect taxes. It is from this longer list that I established the four basic functions of government that I explore in this chapter.
2. After pastors and NGO leaders brought this law to my attention, I inquired about it during my conversations with a senior level official in El Salvador's National Civil Police (PNC) and with a security analyst at the U.S. Embassy. Both acknowledged that pastors involved in gang ministry might encounter this law, but neither would say that there were problems with the law. Rather, they pointed out that some pastors had been arrested because they were in fact helping gangs. They acknowledged that, more often than not, pastors who assisted gangs in illicit activities did so under threats to themselves or their family by gangs.
3. Some authors classify security as a public good; I have made security a different category.

Chapter 6

1. Remittance money, or money that is sent from Salvadorans living and working outside the country to family and friends back home, did not figure prominently in the interactions I heard about between evangelicals and gangs. But because remittances are so crucial to El Salvador's economy, it would be remiss to omit them from a chapter on local economies.

   El Salvador received almost $6 billion in remittances in 2020. This accounted for 23 percent of El Salvador's GDP and benefited roughly 360,000 households (Associated Press 2021). Seventy-nine percent of recipient households can be classified as poor or at risk of falling into poverty. Ninety-four percent of all recipient households report using remittances to cover daily consumption expenses (Keller & Rouse 2016). These statistics strongly indicate that many households within the poor neighborhoods focused on in this study benefited from remittance money.

   Pastors are very aware of the remittance money flowing into their communities. Pastor Gustavo, for example, estimated that 40 percent of the households in his neighborhood receive remittances and could point to specific homes in his neighborhood that he knew were receiving remittance money. Pastor Enzo and Pastor Luis both reported that 30–50 percent of the friends they grew up with in Las Palmas now live in the United States. Both are convinced that most who left continue to send remittances to their families.

I mention remittances in this section because I heard occasional references to gangs requiring households to pay the gang a percentage of the remittance money they received. Some pastors teach their congregants that remittances are a form of personal income, and so should be tithed, as with all income. Neither tithing nor charging rent on remittance money appeared to be common practice, but both ideas occasionally appeared within community discourse.

2. Gang control of open-air markets is well documented. Just one example of the literature touching on this theme is Farah and Babineau (2017), who included a quote from *La Prensa Grafica* (2016) of a merchant who had been working for thirteen years in an open-air market that was controlled by MS-13. The merchant described MS-13 in the following way:

They are the maximum authority. They extort, kill and walk around armed through the market with total impunity ... The gang member who comes by to collect the extortion every Saturday morning comes well-dressed. It is surprising to see now the boys are wearing dress shirts, dress pants and nice shoes .... They know how much each stall should pay because the quotas are different depending on what the owner is selling and the size of the business. For example, a fruit vendor will be charged less than those selling clothes and shoes. They know who owes how much from the previous week; they know how much a person's accumulated debt is. We are never late with our payments. It would cost us our lives.

Chapter 7

1. I maintain Diego's anonymity in this account, which is consistent with how I treat all subjects I interviewed for this project. However, because these events are publicly documented, I use real names for other actors and organizations in this section as they appear in national and international media.

2. The truce created a dramatic drop in homicide statistics nearly overnight and drew initial wide acclaim. However, it eventually unraveled and homicide statistics spiked even higher than they had been in the post-truce period. The government was heavily criticized for giving into gang's demands for the truce and making the gang situation in El Salvador worse (Farah & Babineau 2017).

Conclusion

1. In 2019 and 2020 the Trump administration allowed only a fraction of the allocated monies to be distributed, as it sought to put pressure on Central American governments to curb migration. However, the numbers provided by the Congressional Resource

Service do not take into account other U.S. funding streams to El Salvador, the most significant of which was the $277 million Millennium Challenge Corporation project being implemented during those years. Its primary goals were less directly related to curbing gang violence, but some elements of its projects, perhaps most directly the improvement to the national education system, were hoped to have an indirect bearing on gang recruitment.

2. It should thus be noted that the interviews I conducted and the quotes I referenced in the paragraph above took place before Bukele took such measures. It may be that those comments did not take into consideration the possibility of El Salvador coming under an authoritarian regime.

3. World Vision is the only evangelical organization I know of that received USAID or other government funds for work in El Salvador during the course of my research. World Vision was not working in the communities that I studied, but in communities where they were active some local churches partnered with them in USAID-funded programs.

4. A study done in El Salvador showed that "elevated levels of religiosity and spirituality are associated with less anti-social bonding, which in turn, is associated with lower levels of violent behavior among high-risk and gang-involved Salvadoran youth" (Salas-Wright et al. 2013, 183).

5. Authentic personal change, especially a transfer of loyalty away from the gang, is critical to social integration. Religious experiences and symbols are particularly helpful in effecting and signifying such change. Pressure exists in government and other circles to integrate (supposedly) ex-gang members into society who have not undergone authentic change. This is paramount to an invitation for more gang infiltration of society.

6. The first citation is a cartoon that appeared in a Salvadoran paper. It is not meant as evidence of a case of gang members serving as pastors. Rather it shows the idea is part of the public imagination in El Salvador.

7. This idea emerged in conversations with David Bueno (2021).

8. Reynolds (2015) explains how a articulating a commitment to relevant ethical and biblical values, as opposed to explicitly choosing sides in public debates, helped guide Costa Rican Catholic Bishops in their public engagement efforts.

9. The idea that El Salvador's political system is a properly functioning democracy, even for middle- and upper-class communities, is a very contentious claim, and unfortunately the country's political climate is making it ever more contentious. My claim is defensible in that I am talking about degrees of functionality.

Appendix

1. This is a Millennium Challenge Corporation initiative.

2. From 2014–2021 I made thirteen trips to El Salvador. Most of these were about a week in duration. Some were longer, including a five-week stay in July/August 2015. A small research team in El Salvador carried on some of the research while I was not in-country.

References

Albaladejo, Angelika. 2018. "El Salvador Convicts First Mayor for Ties to Gangs." *InSight Crime*, February 2, 2018. Accessed July 9, 2019. https://www.insightcrime.org/news/analysis/elsalvador-convicts-mayor-ties-gangs/.

Aleman, Marcos. 2016a. "En El Salvador, pandillero operaba con fachada de pastor." *AP News*, August 25, 2015. Accessed August 15, 2021. https://apnews.com/article/a4bdf66d8e3147948af8ebaf73b4e262.

Aleman, Marcos. 2016b. "El Salvador Strikes Blow against Powerful Street Gang." *AP News*, July 28, 2016. Accessed August 6, 2021. https://apnews.com/article/89251b1f23714d8b8c0a7f5dfee610f8.

Alonso, Luis. "El Salvador Police Resigning: Seeking Asylum Abroad." *InSight Crime*, October 25, 2016. Accessed December 12, 2022. http://www.insightcrime.org/news-briefs/el-salvador-police-resigning-seeking-asylum-abroad.

Ammerman, Nancy, Jackson Carroll, Carl Dudley, and William McKinley (eds.). 1997. *Studying Congregations: A New Handbook*. Nashville, TN: Abingdon Press.

Anderson, John Lee. 2016. "Foreword." In *A History of Violence: Living and Dying in Central America*, Oscar Martinez, pp. xi–xv. New York: Verso.

Ardalan, Sabrineh and Thomas Boerman. 2016. "Dynamics Between Gangs and the Church: An Overlooked Dimension of Central American Asylum Claims." *Immigration Briefings*, 16-07: 1–16.

Asmann, Parker. 2019. "El Salvador to Omit Key Data from Official Homicide Tally." *InSight Crime*, July 18, 2019. Accessed June 26, 2020. https://www.insightcrime.org/news/brief/el-salvador-omit-key-data-homicides/.

Associated Press. 2021. "Remittances to El Salvador Rebound after Early Pandemic Drop." *AP*, January 18, 2021. Accessed May 19, 2021. https://apnews.com/article/san-salvador-coronavirus-pandemic-el-salvador-1623416c0ddc7aa238911f8a422b6c8b#:~:text=SAN%20SALVADOR%2C%20El%20Salvador%20(AP,%245.92%20billion%2C%20authorities%20said%20Monday.

Bargent, James. 2013. "Nearly Half a Million Salvadorans Connected to Street Gangs: Study." *InSight Crime*, May 28, 2018. Accessed June 9, 2018. https://www.insightcrime.org/news/brief/nearly-half-a-million-salvadorans-connected-to-street-gangs-study/.

Barrera, Ezequiel. 2016. "Fiscalia investiga nexo del 'Piwa' con Red de Pastores." *La Prensa Grafica*. Published August 24, 2016. Accessed December 9, 2022. https://www.pressreader.com/el-salvador/la-prensa-grafica/20160824/281608124852262.

Bender, Robert H. 1905. "Salvador." *The Central American Bulletin* 11(4) (October 15): 14–15.

Berger, Brigitte (ed.). 1991. *The Culture of Entrepreneurship*. San Francisco: ICS Press.

Berger, Peter L. 1967. *The Sacred Canopy*. Garden City, NY: Anchor Doubleday.

Berk-Seligson, Susan, Diana Orces, Georgina Pizzolitto, Mitchell Seligson, and Carole J.Wilson. 2014. *Impact Evaluation of USAID's Community-Based Crime and Violence*

Prevention Approach in Central America: Regional Report for El Salvador, Guatemala, Honduras, and Panama. USAID and the Latin American Public Opinion Project (LAPOP), Vanderbilt University. Accessed October 12, 2021. https://www.vanderbilt. edu/lapop/carsi/Regional_Report_v12d_final_W_120814.pdf.

Birdsall, Judd. 2021. "USIP's New Religion and Mediation Action Guide: An Interview with Ayse Kadayifci." March 25, 2021. Accessed April 1, 2021. https://religionanddi plomacy.org/2021/03/25/usips-new-religion-and-mediation-action-guide-an-interv iew-with-ayse-kadayifci/.

Bravo, Jorge. 2015. *Cronologia de la Vida de Francisco Penzotti*. Accessed August 14, 2021. https://www.angelfire.com/pe/jorgebravo/penzotti.html.

Brenneman, Robert E. 2012. *Homies and Hermanos: God and Gangs in Central America*. New York: Oxford University Press.

Brenneman, Robert. 2016a. "Violence, Religion, and Institutional Legitimacy in Northern Central America." In *Religious Responses to Violence: Human Rights in Latin America Past and Present*, edited by Alexander Wilde, pp. 371–394. Notre Dame: University of Notre Dame Press.

Brenneman, Robert. 2016b. "Evangelicals and the "New Violence" in Central America." Presented at the Latin American Studies Association conference, May 11, 2016.

Brusco, Elizabeth. 1986. "Colombian Evangelicalism as a Strategic Form of Women's Collective Action." *Feminist Issues* 6(2): 3–13.

Bueno, David. 2001. "The Struggle for Social Space: How Salvadoran Pentecostals Build Communities in the Rural Sector." *Transformation* 18(3): 171–191.

Bueno, Ronald. 2019. "Community Engagement as a Contested Ritual: An Ethnographic Study of Five Pentecostal Denominations in El Salvador." PhD thesis. Oxford Center for Mission Studies.

Burkhart, Louise M. 1996. *Holy Wednesday: A Nahua Drama from Early Colonial Mexico*. Philadelphia: University of Pennsylvanian Press.

Byrnes, Timothy. 2021. "The Papacy Past and Present: Religious Soft Power and International Diplomacy." Presentation delivered for the Berkley Forum, Georgetown University, March 12, 2021.

Calderon, Beatriz con Hector Silva. 2016. "Capturan Exalcalde de Puerto el Triunfo por Apoyar a Pandillas en su Gestion." *La Prensa Grafica*, August 31, 2016. Accessed February 2, 2017. https://aps.com.sv/policia-captura-a-ex-alcalde-de-puerto-el-triu nfo-por-supuestos-nexos-con-pandillas/.

Carmack Robert, Janine Gasco, and Gary Gossen. 2007. *The Legacy of Mesoamerica: History and Culture of a Native American Civilization*, 2nd ed. Upper Saddle River, NJ: Pearson Prentice Hall.

Castillo, Vladimir. 2014. "A History of the Phenomenon of the Maras of El Salvador, 1971–1992." Master's thesis. University of North Texas. Accessed August 3, 2021. https://digi tal.library.unt.edu/ark:/67531/metadc799509/m2/1/high_res_d/thesis.pdf.

Central American Mission. 1897. "Fallen Asleep." *The Central American Bulletin* 3(4): 4–8. No date posted. Accessed December 13, 2022. https://www.caminoglobal. org/Files/Bulletins/1897/Central%20American%20Bulletin%20-%20Vol.%203%20-%20No.%204%20-%20October%201897.pdf.

Cerruti, Marcela and Georgina Binstock. 2009. *Familias latinoamericanas en transformación: desafíos y demandas para la acción pública*. Serie Políticas Sociales, no. 147. Santiago de Chile: Comisión Económica para América Latina y el Caribe. Accessed June 15, 2020. https://repositorio.cepal.org/bitstream/handle/11362/6153/1/ S0900608_es.pdf.

Chesnut, R. Andrew. 2012. *Devoted to Death: Santa Muerte the Skeleton Saint*, 1st ed. New York: Oxford University Press.

Chesnut, Andrew. 2016. "America's Top Two Santa Muerte Leaders Finally Meet." *Huffpost*, October 6, 2016. Accessed August 12, 2020. https://www.huffpost.com/entry/mexicos-top-two-santa-mue_b_8253318.

Chesnut, R. Andrew. 2018. *Devoted to Death: Santa Muerte the Skeleton Saint*, 2nd ed. New York: Oxford University Press.

Choco. 2022. "Pandilleros que simulan que son pastores." *Diaro El Salvador*, May 3, 2022. Accessed June 3, 2022. https://diarioelsalvador.com/pandilleros-que-simulan-que-son-pastores/222043/.

Coe, Michael. 1999. *The Maya*, 6th ed. New York: Thames and Hudson.

Coleman, Kenneth, Edwin Eloy Aguilar, Jose Miguel Sandoval, and Timothy Steigenga. 1993. "Protestantism in El Salvador: Conventional Wisdom versus the Survey Evidence." In *Rethinking Protestantism in Latin America*, edited by Virginia Garrard-Burnett and David Stoll, pp. 111–142. Philadelphia, PA: Temple University.

Collins, Randall. 2011. "Patrimonial Alliances and Failures of State Penetration: A Historical Dynamic of Crime, Corruption, Gangs, and Mafias." *Annals of the American Academy of Political and Social Science* 636: 16–31.

Congressional Research Service. 2020. *Background and U.S. Relations*, July 1, 2020. Accessed October 13, 2021. https://crsreports.congress.gov/product/pdf/R/R43616.

Cruz, José Miguel, Jonathan D. Rosen, Luis Enrique Amaya, and Yulia Vorobyeva. 2017. "The New Face of Street Gangs: The Gang Phenomenon in El Salvador." Report presented to the Bureau of International Narcotics and Law Enforcement Affairs (INL)—U.S. Department of State. Presented by Florida International University. Accessed April 30, 2018. https://lacc.fiu.edu/research/the-new-face-of-street-gangs_final-report_eng.pdf.

Danielson, Robert and Kelly Godoy Danielson. 2021. "Listening to Other Voices: Moving beyond Traditional Mission Histories—A Case Study from El Salvador." *The Asbury Theological Journal* 72(2): 400–441.

Diario1.com. 2015. "Pandilleros Fingían ser pastores y realizaban cultos para extorsionar en San Salvador." *Diario1.com*, October 27, 2015. Accessed June 3, 2022. http://diario1.com/nacionales/2015/10/pandilleros-fingian-ser-pastores-y-realizaban-cultos-para-extorsionar-en-san-salvador/#:~:text=Octubre%2027%2C%202015-,Pandilleros%20fing%C3%ADan%20ser%20pastores%20y%20realizaban%20cultos%20para%20exto rsionar%20en,el%20pago%20de%20la%20extorsi%C3%B3n.

Dudley Steven. 2020. *MS-13: The Making of America's Most Notorious Gang*. Toronto: Hanover Square Press.

Durkheim, Emile. 2008 [1915]. *Elementary Forms of Religious Life*. London: George Allen & Unwin, Ltd.

El Diario de Hoy. 1988. "Más de 40 mil ladrones fichados en la capital," *El Diario de Hoy*, July 11, 1988: 10, 33. In Castillo, Vladimir. 2014. "A History of the Phenomenon of the Maras of El Salvador, 1971–1992." Master's thesis. University of North Texas. Accessed August 3, 2021. https://digital.library.unt.edu/ark:/67531/metadc799509/m2/1/high_res_d/thesis.pdf.

El Diario de Hoy. 1990. "Terrorista revela nexus de 'Mara Gallo' con FMLN," *El Diario de Hoy*, January 15, 1990: 10, 47. In Castillo, Vladimir. 2014. "A History of the Phenomenon of the Maras of El Salvador, 1971–1992." Master's thesis. University of North Texas. Accessed August 3, 2021. https://digital.library.unt.edu/ark:/67531/metadc799509/m2/1/high_res_d/thesis.pdf.

El Faro English. 2022a. "Is Bukele's Gang Truce Unraveling?" *El Faro*, March 28, 2022. Accessed April 22, 2022. https://elfaro.net/en/202203/el_salvador/26100/Is-Bukele.

El Faro English. 2022b. "No New Ideas After El Salvador's Homicide Crisis." *El Faro*, March 31, 2022. Accessed April 21, 2022. https://elfaro.net/en/202203/el_salvador/26102/No-New-Ideas-after-El-Salvador%E2%80%99s-Homicide-Crisis.htm.

El Faro English. 2022c. "Gang Expert Flees El Salvador after Intimidation from Bukele." *El Faro*, April 15, 2022. Accessed April 21, 2022. https://elfaro.net/en/202204/el_salvador/26128/Gang-Expert-Flees-El-Salvador-after-Intimidation-from-Bukele.htm.

Ellis, Evan. 2021. *China and El Salvador: An Update.* Center for Strategic and International Studies, March 22, 2021. Accessed November 3, 2021. https://www.csis.org/analysis/china-and-el-salvador-update.

El Mundo. 2022. "Vicepresidente Ulloa: 80% de los pastores tienen nexo con pandillas." *El Mundo*, August 15, 2022. Accessed September 11, 2022. https://diario.elmundo.sv/politica/vicepresidente-ulloa-80-de-los-pastores-tienen-nexo-con-pandillas.

El Salvador Census. 2021. *Estimaciones y Proyecciones Municipales por Ano y Sexo.* Government of El Salvador. Accessed September 9, 2021. https://experience.arcgis.com/experience/57dc978cf0834d358f2730aeb2ffbd14/page/page_4/.

ElSalvador.com. 2016. "Allanan sede de iglesia relacionada con cabecilla de la MS." *ElSalvador.com*, August 23, 2016. Accessed August 6, 2021. https://historico.elsalvador.com/historico/323024/allanan-sede-de-iglesia-relacionada-con-cabecilla-de-la-ms.html.

Espinoza, Aaron. 1997. "GP Biography 2: Francisco Penzotti." *Ministerios Logoi.* Accessed August 15, 2021. https://logoi.org/resource/gp-biography-2-francisco-penzotti/.

European Commission. 2021. *International Partnerships: El Salvador.* Accessed October 20, 2021. https://ec.europa.eu/international-partnerships/where-we-work/el-salvador_en.

Fahlberg, Anjuli. 2018. "Rethinking Favela Governance: Nonviolent Politics in Rio de Janeiro's Gang Territories." *Politics & Society* 46(4): 455–484.

Farah, Douglas and Kathryn Babineau. 2017. "The Evolution of MS 13 in El Salvador and Honduras." *Prism* 7(1): 59–73.

Fazolla, Mark. 2020. "We're Deporting People Back to Gangs. What About Offering Refuge and Aid?" *The Philadelphia Inquirer*, January 12, 2020. Accessed June 27, 2020. https://www-inquirer-com.cdn.ampproject.org/v/s/www.inquirer.com/opinion/commentary/immigration-deportations-latin-america-el-salvador-violence-jobs-20200112.html?outputType=amp&usqp=mq331AQCKAE%3D&amp_js_v=0.1.

Flores, Edward Orozco. 2014. *God's Gangs: Barrio Ministry, Masculinity, and Gang Recovery.* New York: New York University Press.

Freston, Paul (ed.). 2001. *Evangelicals in Politics in Asia, Africa, and Latin America.* Cambridge: Cambridge University Press.

Friedrich, Paul. 1965. "A Mexican Cacicazgo." *Ethnology* 4(2): 190–209.

Garcia, Carlos. 2021. "'Blue': The Story of MS13's First 'Terrorist.'" *InSight Crime*, June 23, 2021. Accessed July 20, 2021. https://insightcrime.org/news/blue-story-ms13-first-terrorist/.

Garcia, Carlos. 2022. "Are MS Leaders Wanted for Extradition to US Free in El Salvador?" *InSight Crime*, March 31, 2022. Accessed April 21, 2022. https://insightcrime.org/news/ms13-leaders-extradition-us-free-el-salvador/.

Gardner, Alexia, Andrea Kim, and Allyson Woolley. 2021. "Can U.S. Anti-Violence Models Succeed in Mexico and the Northern Triangle?" Wilson Center/Latin

American Program, October 2021. Accessed April 28, 2022. https://www.wilsoncen ter.org/publication/can-us-anti-violence-models-succeed-mexico-and-northern-triangle.

Geymonat, Roger. 1994. *El templo y la escuela: Los valdenses en el Uruguay*. Montevideo: Cal y Canto.

Giddens, Anthony. 2000. *Runaway World: How Globalization Is Reshaping our Lives*. New York: Routledge.

Glader, Paul. 2015. "Christianity Is Growing Rapidly in El Salvador—Along with Gang Violence and Murder Rates." *Washington Post*, April 8, 2015. Accessed June 17, 2020. https://www.washingtonpost.com/news/acts-of-faith/wp/2015/04/08/christianity-is-growing-rapidly-in-el-salvador-along-with-gang-violence-and-murder-rates/.

Gooren, Henri. 1999. *Rich among the Poor: Church, Firm, and Household among Small-Scale Entrepreneurs in Guatemala City*. Amsterdam: Thela.

Hagopian, Frances. 2009. "Social Justice, Moral Values, or Institutional Interests?" In *Religious Pluralism, Democracy, and the Catholic Church in Latin America*, edited by Frances Hagopian, pp. 257–331. Notre Dame: University of Notre Dame Press.

Hall, David. 1997. *Lived Religion in America: Toward a History of Practice*. Princeton, NJ: Princeton University Press.

Hartman, Ann. 1995. "Diagrammatic Assessment of Family Relationships." *Families in Society: The Journal of Contemporary Social Sciences* 76(2): 111–122.

Holland, Alisha. 2013. "Right on Crime? Conservative Party Politics and Mano Dura Policies in El Salvador." *Latin American Research Review* 48(1): 44–67.

Holland, Clifton. 2008. *An Historical Profile of Religion in El Salvador*, September 17, 2008. Accessed August 12, 2021. http://www.prolades.com/cra/regions/cam/els/salva dor.html.

Holland, Clifton. 2011. *A Chronology of Protestant Origins in Guatemala, 1824–1980*, March 2011. Accessed August 14, 2021. http://www.prolades.com/encyclopedia/his torical/cam/guate_chron_1980.pdf.

House, Christie. 2019. "Penzotti, Francisco: Founder of Peruvian Methodism." Accessed August 14, 2021. https://methodistmission200.org/penzotti-francisco/.

Human Rights Watch. 2021. *World Report 2021*. Accessed April 21, 2021. https://www.hrw.org/world-report/2021/country-chapters/el-salvador#.

IDB. 2002. *Inter-American Development Bank Annual Report: 2002*. Accessed October 19, 2021. https://publications.iadb.org/publications/english/document/Inter-American-Development-Bank-Annual-Report-2002.pdf.

InSight Crime. 2011. "Barrio 18." *InSight Crime*, June 16, 2011. Accessed August 11, 2021. https://insightcrime.org/el-salvador-organized-crime-news/barrio-18-profile/.

InSight Crime 2018. "Barrio 18." *InSight Crime*. February 13, 2018. Accessed July 3, 2019. https://www.insightcrime.org/el-salvador-organized-crime-news/barrio-18-prof ile-2/.

InSight Crime. 2021. "Revived Drug Routes, Evolving Street Gangs in El Salvador." *InSight Crime*, March 24, 2021. Accessed May 7, 2021. https://insightcrime.org/news/drug-rou tes-gangs-elsalvador/.

InSight Crime and CLALS 2017. *MS13 in the Americas: How the World's Most Notorious Gang Defies Logic, Resists Destruction*. Washington, DC: American University.

Jelin, Elizabeth and Ana Rita Díaz-Muñoz. 2003. *Major Trends Affecting Families: South America in Perspective*. Report prepared for United Nations Department of Economic and Social Affairs Division for Social Policy and Development Programme on the Family. New York: United Nations.

Johnson, Andrew. 2016. "The Politics of Presence: Evangelical Ministry in Brazilian Prisons." In *Religious Responses to Violence: Human Rights in Latin America Past and Present*, edited by Alexander Wilde, pp. 395–416. Notre Dame, IN: University of Notre Dame Press.

Johnson, Andrew. 2017. *If I Give My Soul: Faith Behind Bars in Rio de Janeiro*. New York: Oxford University Press.

Jutersonke, Oliver, Robert Muggah, and Dennis Rodgers. 2009. "Gangs and Violence Reduction in Central America." *Security Dialogue* 40(4–5): 373–397.

Keller, Lukas and Rebecca Rouse. 2016. *Remittance Recipients in El Salvador: A Socioeconomic Profile*. Multilateral Investment Fund, the Inter-American Development Bank Group. https://publications.iadb.org/publications/english/document/Remitta nce-Recipients-in-El-Salvador-A-Socioeconomic-Profile.pdf.

Kennedy, Elizabeth. 2014. "No Childhood Here: Why Central American Children are Fleeing their Homes." *Perspectives*. Washington, DC: American Immigration Council.

Kibria, Nazli. 2006. "Globalization and the Family." *International Journal of Sociology of the Family* 32(2): 137–139.

Laguan, Jonathan. 2018. "Pastor Joven asesinado por pandillas tras recibir varias amenazas." *La Prensa Grafica*, July 16, 2018. Accessed April 19, 2021. https://www.lapr ensagrafica.com/elsalvador/Joven-pastor-evangelico-fue-asesinado-por-pandillas-tras-recibir-varias-amenazas-20180716-0025.html.

Lalive d'Epinay, Christian. 1969. *Haven of the Masses: A Study of the Pentecostal Movement in Chile*. London: Lutterworth Press.

La Prensa Cristiana. 2019. "Asesinan dentro del templo a joven miembro de Iglesia EDC Filadelfia AD en Santa Ana." *La Prensa Cristiana*, May 24, 2019. Accessed May 26, 2019. http://laprensacristiana.com/?p=5905.

La Prensa Grafica. 1988. "Banda de asaltantes se bate a líos con tropa," March 15, 1988. In Castillo, Vladimir. 2014. "A History of the Phenomenon of the Maras of El Salvador, 1971–1992." Master's thesis. University of North Texas. Accessed August 3, 2021. https://digital.library.unt.edu/ark:/67531/metadc799509/m2/1/high_res_d/thesis.pdf.

La Prensa Grafica. 2016. "Vendo en el Búnker de la MS en San Salvador." *La Prensa Gráfica*, December 14, 2016. In Farah, Douglas and Kathryn Babineau. 2017. "The Evolution of MS 13 in El Salvador and Honduras." *Prism* 7(1): 59–73.

Lemus, Efren. 2016. "Purgas en la cúpula de la MS-13 por dinero." *El Faro*, August 9, 2016. Accessed July 30, 2021. https://elfaro.net/es/201608/salanegra/19066/Purgas-en-la-c%C3%BApula-de-la-MS-13-por-dinero.htm.

Levine, Daniel. 2009. "The Future of Christianity in Latin America." *Journal of Latin American Studies* 41(1): 121–145.

Levitt, Peggy. 2001. *Transnational Villagers*. Berkeley and Los Angeles: University of California Press.

Lindhart, Martin 2014. *Power in Powerlessness: A Study of Pentecostal Life Worlds in Urban Chile*. Leiden: Brill.

Linthicum, Kate, Molly O'Toole, and Alexander Renderos. 2020. "In El Salvador, Gangs Are Enforcing the Coronavirus Lockdown with Baseball Bats." *Los Angeles Times*, April 7, 2020. Accessed March 19, 2021. https://www.latimes.com/world-nation/story/2020-04-07/el-salvador-coronavirus-homicides-bukele.

Malkin, Elisabeth. 2015. "El Salvador Cracks Down on Crime, but Gangs Remain Unbowed." *New York Times*, August 11, 2015. Accessed December 13, 2022. http://www.nytimes.com/2015/08/12/world/americas/el-salvador-cracks-down-on-crime-but-gangs-remain-unbowed.html?_r=0.

Martin, David. 1990. *Tongues of Fire: The Explosion of Protestantism in Latin America*. Oxford: Basil Blackwell.

Martin, David. 2002. *Pentecostalism: The World Their Parish*. Malden, MA: Blackwell Publishing.

Martínez, Carlos, Óscar Martínez, Sergio Arauz, and Efren Lemus. 2020. "Bukele Has Been Negotiating with MS-13 for a Reduction in Homicides and Electoral Support." *El Faro*, September 6, 2020. Accessed April 20, 2021. https://elfaro.net/en/202009/el_salvador/24785/Bukele-Spent-A-Year-Negotiating-with-MS-13-for-a-Reduction-in-Homicides-and-Electoral-Support.htm.

Martínez, Carlos and Roberto Valencia. 2017. "MS13 Seeks Dialogue with El Salvador Government." *InSight Crime*, January 11, 2017. Accessed December 13, 2022. https://insightcrime.org/news/analysis/ms13-seeks-dialogue-el-salvador-government/.

Martínez, Oscar. 2016. *A History of Violence: Living and Dying in Central America*. New York: Verso.

Martinez, Oscar and Efren Lemus. 2016. "The El Salvador Businessman Who Does Not Pay the Gangs." *InSight Crime*. Posted December 14, 2016. Accessed December 1, 2022. https://insightcrime.org/news/analysis/el-salvador-businessman-who-does-not-pay-gangs/.

Martínez, Oscar, Efren Lemus, and Deborah Sontag. 2016. "Killers on a Shoe String: Inside the Gangs of El Salvador." *New York Times*, November 20, 2016. Accessed November 2, 2018. https://www.nytimes.com/2016/11/21/world/americas/el-salvador-drugs-gang-ms-13.html.

Martínez, Oscar, Carlos Martínez, and Efren Lemus. 2020. "Gangs Threaten Anyone Who Doesn't Comply with El Salvador's Quarantine." *El Faro*, April 2, 2020. Accessed March 19, 2021. https://elfaro.net/en/202004/el_salvador/24225/gangs-threaten-anyone-who-doesn-t-comply-with-el-salvador-s-quarantine.htm.

Martínez, Oscar and Juan Jose Martinez. 2019. *The Hollywood Kid: The Violent Life and Violent Death of an Hollywood Hitman*. New York: Verso Books.

Martinez D'Aubuisson, Juan Jose. 2022. "The Omnipresent Business of the MS13 in El Salvador." *InSight Crime*, January 25, 2022. Accessed April 19, 2022. https://insightcrime.org/investigations/the-omnipresent-businesses-of-the-ms13/.

Mauss, Marcel. 1990 [1950]. *The Gift: The Form and Reason for Exchange in Archaic Societies*. Translated by W. D. Halls. New York, NY: W.W. Norton & Company.

Menjívar, Cecilia. 2000. *Fragmented Ties: Salvadoran Immigrant Networks in America*. Berkeley and Los Angeles: University of California Press.

Menjívar, Cecilia. 2007. "El Salvador." In *The New Americans: A Guide to Immigration Since 1965*, edited by Mary Waters and Reed Ueda, pp. 412–420. Cambridge, MA: Harvard University Press.

Menjívar, Cecilia and Andrea Gómez Cervantes. 2018. "El Salvador: Civil War, Natural Disasters, and Gang Violence Drive Migration." *Migration Information Source*, August 29, 2018. Accessed August 7, 2021. https://www.migrationpolicy.org/article/el-salvador-civil-war-natural-disasters-and-gang-violence-drive-migration.

Millennium Challenge Corporation. 2020. "MCC Marks Closeout of $277 Million El Salvador Investment Compact," September 9, 2020. Accessed October 29, 2021. https://www.mcc.gov/news-and-events/release/090920-mcc-marks-closeout-of-el-salvador-investment-compact.

Miller, Michael. 2017. "You Feel the Devil Is Helping You: MS-13's Satanic History." *Washington Post*, December 20, 2017. Accessed May 29, 2018. https://www.washing

tonpost.com/news/retropolis/wp/2017/12/20/you-feel-that-the-devil-is-helping-you-ms-13s-satanic-history/?utm_term=.8462e81c51a5.

Ministerio de Seguridad. 2022. "Más de 52 mil terroristas capturados en esta #GuerraContraPandillas. No nos vamos a detener hasta limpio por completo nuestro país." Ministerio de Seguridad Twitter Account. September 7, 2022. https://twitter.com/SeguridadSV/status/1567511244638142465.

Monroy, Daniel, Francisco Schmidt, Luis Gomez, and Julio Contreras. 1996. *Cien Anos de Presencia Evangelica en El Salvador*. San Salvador: CONESAL.

Montes, Esau. 2021. "Violencia de pandillas: Un obstáculo multidimensional para el Desarrollo Humano en Latinoamérica. El caso de las juventudes de la comunidad. San Jacinto, El Salvador (2016–2018)." Master's thesis. FLACSO, Argentina.

Moody, Kenton. 2018. "Dilemmas in Working With Gang Members in El Salvador." *WCIU Journal*, October 2, 2018. Accessed October 2, 2018. https://wciujournal.wciu.edu/area-studies/2019/9/30/reflection-dilemmas-in-working-with-gang-members-in-el-salvador.

Moody, Kenton. 2020. "Co-Existence of Opposing Powers: A Study of the Relationship Between the Evangelical Church and the Gangs in El Salvador." *WCIU Journal*, January 3, 2020. Accessed June 13, 2020. https://wciujournal.wciu.edu/area-studies/2020/1/3/co-existence-of-opposing-powers-a-study-of-the-relationship-between-the-evangelical-church-and-the-gangs-in-el-salvador.

Navarro, Mayra. 2012. "Honduras Prison Fire Kills more than 350 Inmates." *Reuters*, February 15, 2012. Accessed April 22, 2021. https://www.reuters.com/article/oukwd-uk-honduras-jail-fire-idAFTRE81E0R620120215.

Nelson, Wilton M. 1982. *El Protestantismo en Centro America*. Miami: Editorial Caribe.

Noe-Bustamente, Luis, Antonio Flores, and Sono Shah. 2019. *Facts on Hispanics of Salvadoran Origin in the United States, 2017*. Pew Research Center, September 16, 2019. Accessed October 18, 2022. https://www.pewresearch.org/hispanic/fact-sheet/u-s-hispanics-facts-on-salvadoran-origin-latinos/.

Nye, Joseph. 2004. *Soft Power: The Means to Success in World Politics*. New York: Public Affairs.

Offutt, Stephen. 2015. *New Centers of Global Evangelicalism in Latin America and Africa*. New York: Cambridge University Press.

Offutt, Stephen. 2019. "El Salvador." In *Encyclopedia of Latin American Religions: Religions of the World*, edited by H. Gooren. Cham: Springer. https://doi.org/10.1007/978-3-319-27078-4_349.

Offutt, Stephen. 2020. "Entangled: The Relationship between Evangelicals and Gangs in El Salvador." *Social Forces* 99(1): 424–445.

O'Neill. Kevin. 2015. *Secure the Soul: Christian Piety and Gang Prevention in Guatemala*. Berkeley and Los Angeles: University of California Press.

Organization of American States. 2015. *Report on Drug Use in the Americas 2015*. Washington DC: Organization of American States. http://www.cicad.oas.org/oid/pubs/druguseamericas_eng_web.pdf.

O'Toole, Molly. 2017. "Micro-extortion Is Costing El Salvador $4 Billion a Year, $10 at a Time." *International Women's Media Foundation*, June 17, 2017. Accessed October 18, 2022. https://www.iwmf.org/reporting/micro-extortion-by-gangs-is-costing-el-salvador-4-billion-a-year-10-at-a-time/.

O'Toole, Molly. 2018. "Can Megachurches Save El Salvador?" *The New Republic*, November 5, 2018. Accessed November 8, 2020. https://newrepublic.com/article/151877/can-megachurches-save-el-salvador.

Owen, Arron and Cecilia Suazo. 2014. "Sociodemographic and Cultural Factors of Adult Obesity in El Salvador: An Exploratory Cross-sectional Study." *The Journal of Global Health* 4(2): 7–10.

Papadovassilakis, Alex. 2020. "Are El Salvador's Gangs Behind Historic Murder Drop?" *InSight Crime*, January 20, 2020. Accessed June 26, 2020. https://www.insightcrime. org/news/analysis/gang-truce-behind-el-salvador-historic-murder-drop/.

Partlow, Joshua. 2016. "What We Have Now Is a civil war." *Washington Post*, October 28, 2016. Accessed December 13, 2022. http://www.washingtonpost.com/sf/world/2016/ 10/28/el-salvadors-conflict-with-gangs-is-beginning-to-look-like-a-war/.

Perlman, Janice. 2010. *Favela: Four Decades of Living on the Edge in Rio De Janeiro.* New York: Oxford University Press.

Pew Research Center. 2014. *Religion in Latin America: Widespread Change in a Historically Catholic Region.* November 14, 2014. Accessed August 28, 2019. https://www.pewfo rum.org/2014/11/13/religion-in-latin-america/.

Pouligny, Beatrice. 2009. *Supporting Local Ownership in Humanitarian Action.* Global Public Policy Institute and Center for Transatlantic Relations. https://citeseerx.ist.psu. edu/viewdoc/download?doi=10.1.1.599.7743&rep=rep1&type=pdf.

Ramsey, Geoffrey. 2012. "Tracing the Roots of El Salvador's Mara Salvatrucha." *InSight Crime*, August 31, 2012. Accessed August 9, 2021. https://insightcrime.org/news/analy sis/history-mara-salvatrucha-el-salvador/.

Rance, DeLonn. 2004. "The Empowered Call: The Activity of the Holy Spirit in Salvadoran Assemblies of God Missionaries." PhD thesis. Pasadena: Fuller Theological Seminary.

Rauda Zablah, Nelson. 2016. "Cualquiera puede tener hijos en las pandillas y no darse cuenta." *El Faro*, August 2, 2016. Accessed August 6, 2021. https://elfaro.net/es/201607/ el_salvador/19053/%E2%80%9CCualquiera-puede-tener-hijos-en-las-pandillas-y- no-darse-cuenta%E2%80%9D.htm.

Renteria, Nelson. 2022. "In El Salvador's Crackdown, Quotas Drive 'Arbitrary' Arrests of Innocents." *Reuters*, May 16, 2022. Accessed September 11, 2022. https://www.reuters. com/world/americas/el-salvadors-gang-crackdown-quotas-drive-arbitrary-arrests- innocents-2022-05-16/.

Reynolds, Amy. 2015. *Free Trade and Faithful Globalization.* New York: Cambridge University Press.

RFCatolica Radio Online. 2015. "Historia de la Llegada de la Patrona de El Salvador a San Miguel: Vírgen María de la Paz." Accessed July 29, 2016. http://renovacionfamiliarosj. blogspot.com/2011/11/historia-de-la-llegada-de-la-patrona-de.html.

Robeck, J.M. 2016. "Towards a Pentecostal Theology of Praxis: A Study of Three Pentecostal Churches with ENLACE in El Salvador." PhD thesis. Claremont, CA: University of Claremont.

Rubin, Jeffrey, David Smilde, and Benjamin Junge 2014. "Lived Religion and Lived Citizenship in Latin America's Zones of Crisis." *Latin American Research Review Special Issue* 49: 7–26.

Salas-Wright, Christopher P. Rene Olate, Michael Vaughan, and Thanh V. Tran. 2013. "Direct and Mediated Associations between Religious Coping, Spirituality, and Youth Violence in El Salvador." *Rev Panam Salud Publica* 34(3): 183–189.

Sawyer, Bradley and Cynthia Cox. 2017. "How Does Health Spending in the United States Compare to Other Countries?" *Kaiser Family Foundation*, May 22, 2017. Accessed October 18, 2022. https://healthcarereimagined.net/2018/01/09/how-does-health- spending-in-the-u-s-compare-to-other-countries-kaiser-family-foundation/.

Seccombe, Karen. 2012. *Families and Their Social Worlds*. New York. Pearson.

Seiff, Kevin. 2019. "It's so Dangerous to Police MS-13 in El Salvador that Officers Are Fleeing the Country." *The Washington Post*, March 3, 2019. Accessed April 23, 2021. https://www.washingtonpost.com/world/the_americas/its-so-dangerous-to-police-ms-13-in-el-salvador-that-officers-are-fleeing-the-country/2019/03/03/e897dbaa-2287-11e9-b5b4-1d18dfb7b084_story.html.

Silva Ávalos, Hector. 2014. "The Infiltrators: Corruption in El Salvador's Police." *InSight Crime*, February 21, 2014. Accessed September 18, 2017. http://www.insightcrime.org/investigations/the-infiltrators-a-chronicle-of-el-salvador-police-corruption.

Silva Ávalos, Hector. 2019. "Political Mafias Helped Empower Gangs, says El Salvador Security Expert." *InSight Crime*, January 24, 2019. Accessed February 19, 2019. https://www.insightcrime.org/news/analysis/el-salvador-political-mafias/.

Silva Ávalos, Héctor. 2016. "MS13 Members Imprisoned in El Salvador Can Direct the Gang in the US." *InSight Crime*. December 5, 2016. Accessed November 2, 2018. https://www.insightcrime.org/investigations/ms13-members-imprisoned-in-el-salvador-can-direct-the-gang-in-the-us/.

Silva Ávalos, Héctor and Bryan Avelar. 2016. "Case Against El Salvador's MS13 Reveals State Role in Gang's Growth." *InSight Crime*. August 3, 2016. Accessed August 6, 2021. https://insightcrime.org/news/analysis/case-against-el-salvador-s-ms13-reveals-state-role-in-gang-s-growth.

Smilde, David. 1998. "'Letting God Govern': Supernatural Agency in the Venezuelan Pentecostal Approach to Social Change." *Sociology of Religion* 59(3): 287–303.

Smilde, David 2007. *Reason to Believe: Cultural Agency in Latin American Evangelicalism*. Berkeley and Los Angeles: University of California Press.

Smith, Christian. 1998. *American Evangelicalism: Embattled and Thriving*. Chicago: University of Chicago Press.

Stanley, William. 1996. *The Protection Racket State: Elite Politics, Military Extortion, and Civil War in El Salvador*. Philadelphia: Temple University Press.

Steigenga, Timothy J. and David Smilde. 1999. "Wrapped in the Holy Shawl: The Strange Case of Conservative Christians and Gender Equality in Latin America." In *Latin American Religion in Motion*, edited by Christian Smith and Joshua Prokopy, pp. 168–181. New York: Routledge.

Stoll, David. 1990. *Is Latin America Turning Protestant? The Politics of Evangelical Growth*. Berkeley and Los Angeles: University of California Press.

Strazza, Kate. 2016. "Plata o Plomo: Recruitment and Ritual in Latin American Street Gangs." Master's Thesis. University of Pennsylvania.

The Economist. 2021. "The Influence of Central American Dynasties Is Ebbing." March 31, 2021. Accessed December 8, 2022. https://www.economist.com/the-americas/2021/03/31/the-influence-of-central-american-dynasties-is-ebbing.

Tilly, Charles. 1985. "War-making and State-making as Organized Crime." In *Bringing the State Back In*, edited by Peter Evans, Dietrich Rueschemeyer, and Theda Skocpol. pp. 169–191. Cambridge: Cambridge University Press.

Trading Economics. 2021. *El Salvador Employment Rate*. Accessed July 17, 2021. https://tradingeconomics.com/el-salvador/employment-rate.

Ullman, Heidi, Carlos Maldonado Velera, and Maria Nieves Rico. 2014. "Families in Latin America: Changes, Poverty, and Access to Social Protection." *International Journal of the Sociology of the Family* 40(2): 123–152.

UNESCO. 2009. *Overcoming Inequality: Why Governance Matters.* EFA Global Monitoring Report: Latin America and the Caribbean. Accessed April 9, 2019. https://en.unesco.org/gem-report/report/2009/overcoming-inequality-why-governance-matters.

U.S. Department of State. 2018. *El Salvador 2018 International Religious Freedom Report.* https://www.state.gov/wp-content/uploads/2019/05/EL-SALVADOR-2018-INTERN ATIONAL-RELIGIOUS-FREEDOM-REPORT.pdf.

Verza, Maria. 2018. "In El Salvador, Poverty and Gangs Drive Migration." *Washington Post,* October 24, 2018. Accessed November 2, 2018. https://www.washingtonp ost.com/world/the_americas/in-el-salvador-poverty-and-gangs-drive-migration/ 2018/10/24/cba5acdc-d7c5-11e8-8384-bcc5492fef49_story.html?utm_term=.96f19 43e1436.

Wadkins, Timothy. 2017. *The Rise of Pentecostalism in Modern El Salvador: From the Blood of the Martyrs to the Baptism of the Spirit.* Waco: Baylor University Press.

Walsh, Shannon Drysdale and Cecilia Menjívar. 2016. "Impunity and Multisided Violence in the Lives of Latin American Women: El Salvador in Comparative Perspective." *Current Sociology* 64(4): 586–602.

Ward, Thomas W. 2013. *Gangsters Without Borders: An Ethnography of a Salvadoran Street Gang.* New York: Oxford University Press.

Watkins, Ali and Meredith Kohut. 2018. "MS-13, Trump, and America's Interest in El Salvador's Gang War." *New York Times,* December 10, 2018. Accessed September 7, 2019. https://www.nytimes.com/2018/12/10/us/el-salvador-ms-13.html.

Weaver, James H., Michael T. Rock, and Kenneth Kusterer. 1997. *Achieving Broad-Based Sustainable Development: Governance, Environment, and Growth with Equity.* West Hartford, CT: Kumarian Press.

Weber, Max. 1946. *From Max Weber.* Translated and edited by H. H. Gerth and C. Wright Mills. New York: Free Press.

Willems, Emilio 1967. *Followers of the New Faith: Culture Change and the Rise of Protestantism in Brazil and Chile.* Nashville, TN: Vanderbilt University Press.

Williams, Philip J. 1997. "The Sound of Tambourines: The Politics of Pentecostal Growth in El Salvador." In *Power, Politics & Pentecostals in Latin America,* edited by Edward L. Cleary and Hannah W. Stewart Gambino, pp. 179–200. Boulder, CO: Westview Press.

Williams, Philip J. and Ana L. Peterson. 1996. "Evangelicals and Catholics in El Salvador: Evolving Religious Responses to Social Change." *Journal of Church and State* 38: 873–897.

Williams, Robert G. 1994. *States and Social Evolution: Coffee and the Rise of National Governments in Central America.* Chapel Hill: University of North Carolina Press.

Williamson, Chris. 2021. "MS-13: America's Most Notorious Gang—Steven Dudley | Modern Wisdom Podcast 316." YouTube video, May 3, 2021. Accessed September 9, 2021. https://www.youtube.com/watch?v=Q94Ng1m1mzI.

WOLA and IUDOP. 2020. *The National Civilian Police Force in El Salvador: Evaluating the Professionalization of the Civilian Police Force.* San Salvador: University Institute for Public Opinion, Jose Simeon Canas Central American University. https://www.wola. org/wp-content/uploads/2020/09/Police-SV-ENG-9.30.pdf.

Wolf, Sonja. 2017. *Mano Dura: The Politics of Gang Control in El Salvador.* Austin: University of Texas Press.

Wolseth, Jon. 2011. *Jesus and the Gang: Youth Violence and Christianity in Urban Honduras.* Tucson: University of Arizona Press.

Wood, Elisabeth Jean. 2000. *Forging Democracy from Below: Insurgent Transitions in South Africa and El Salvador*. Cambridge: Cambridge University Press.

Wood, Richard. 2014. "Advancing the Grounded Study of Religion and Society in Latin America: Concluding Comments." *Latin American Research Review* 49: 185–193.

World Bank Data. 2019. *Data for Latin America and the Caribbean*. Accessed April 9, 2019. https://data.worldbank.org/.

World Bank Data. 2021a. *Current Health Expenditure per Capita (Current US$)—United Kingdom*. Accessed July 18, 2021. https://data.worldbank.org/indicator/SH.XPD. CHEX.PC.CD?locations=GB.

World Bank Data. 2021b. *Net Official Development Assistance Received (Current US$)—El Salvador*. Accessed October 13, 2021. https://data.worldbank.org/indicator/DT.ODA. ODAT.CD?locations=SV.

World Bank Data. 2022a. *Current Health Expenditure per Capita*. Accessed August 18, 2022. Accessed January 30, 2022. https://data.worldbank.org/indicator/SH.XPD. CHEX.PC.CD?locations=SV.

World Bank Data. 2022b. Pupil-Teacher Ratio, primary—El Salvador." Accessed August 18, 2022. Data as of February 2020. https://data.worldbank.org/indicator/SE.PRM. ENRL.TC.ZS?locations=SV.

World Bank Data. 2022c. *Population, Total—El Salvador.* Accessed November 29, 2022. https://data.worldbank.org/indicator/SP.POP.TOTL?locations=SV.

World Health Organization. 2019. *El Salvador*. Accessed April 12, 2019. https://www. who.int/countries/slv/en/.

World Population Review. 2022. "El Salvador Population 2022 (Live)." Accessed November 29, 2022. https://worldpopulationreview.com/countries/el-salvador-pop ulation.

Wuthnow, Robert. 1994. *Producing the Sacred: An Essay on Public Religion*. Urbana-Champaign: University of Illinois Press.

Yagoub, Mimi. 2016. "480 Gang Members Infiltrated El Salvador Security Forces: Report." *InSight Crime*, February 22, 2016. Accessed July 8, 2019. https://www.insightcrime.org/ news/brief/did-480-gang-members-infiltrate-el-salvador-security-forces/.

Yelvington, Kevin. 2004. "Foreword." In *Salvadoran Migration to Southern California: Redefining El Hermano Lejano*, edited by Beth Baker-Cristales, pp. ix–xii. Gainesville: University of Florida.

Zovatto, Daniel. 2020. *The Rapidly Deteriorating Quality of Democracy in Latin America*. Brookings Institute, February 28, 2020. Accessed November 14, 2021. https://www. brookings.edu/blog/order-from-chaos/2020/02/28/the-rapidly-deteriorating-quality-of-democracy-in-latin-america/.

Index